SUCCESS AND BEYOND

Your Mantras for Peak Performance and Fulfillment

SUCCESS AND BEYOND

Your Mantras for Peak Performance and Fulfillment

Second Edition

R S Dabas

NEW AGE INTERNATIONAL (P) LIMITED, PUBLISHERS
New Delhi • Bangalore • Chennai • Cochin • Guwahati
Hyderabad • Kolkata • Lucknow • Mumbai
Visit us at **www.newagepublishers.com**

Published by New Age International (P) Ltd., Publishers
First Edition: 1986
Second Edition: 2014

BRANCHES

- **Bangalore** 37/10, 8th Cross (Near Hanuman Temple), Azad Nagar, Chamarajpet Bangalore-560 018, Tel.: (080) 26756823, Telefax: 26756820 **E-mail: bangalore@newagepublishers.com**
- **Chennai** 26, Damodaran Street, T. Nagar, Chennai-600 017, Tel.: (044) 24353401 Telefax: 24351463, **E-mail: chennai@newagepublishers.com**
- **Cochin** CC-39/1016, Carrier Station Road, Ernakulam South, Cochin-682 016 Tel.: (0484) 2377004, Telefax: 4051303 **E-mail: cochin@newagepublishers.com**
- **Guwahati** Hemsen Complex, Mohd. Shah Road, Paltan Bazar, Near Starline Hotel Guwahati-781 008, Tel.: (0361) 2513881, Telefax: 2543669 **E-mail: guwahati@newagepublishers.com**
- **Hyderabad** 105, 1st Floor, Madhiray Kaveri Tower, 3-2-19, Azam Jahi Road Nimboliadda, Hyderabad-500 027, Tel.: (040) 24652456 Telefax: 24652457, **E-mail: hyderabad@newagepublishers.com**
- **Kolkata** RDB Chambers (Formerly Lotus Cinema) 106A, 1st Floor S.N. Banerjee Road, Kolkata-700 014, Tel.: (033) 22273773 Telefax: 22275247, **E-mail: kolkata@newagepublishers.com**
- **Lucknow** 16-A, Jopling Road, Lucknow-226 001, Tel.: (0522) 2209578, 4045297 Telefax: 2204098, **E-mail: lucknow@newagepublishers.com**
- **Mumbai** 142C, Victor House, Ground Floor, N.M. Joshi Marg, Lower Parel Mumbai-400 013, Tel.: (022) 24927869, Telefax: 24915415 **E-mail: mumbai@newagepublishers.com**
- **New Delhi** 22, Golden House, Daryaganj, New Delhi-110 002 Tel.: (011) 23262368, 23262370, Telefax: 43551305 **E-mail: sales@newagepublishers.com**

ISBN: 978-81-224-3433-0

₹ 299.00

C-13-05-6929

Printed in India at Ajit Printers, Delhi.
Typeset at In-house.

PUBLISHING FOR ONE WORLD
NEW AGE INTERNATIONAL (P) LIMITED, PUBLISHERS
7/30 A, Daryaganj, New Delhi - 110002
Visit us at www.newagepublishers.com

Preface to the Second Edition

The book is about success, happiness and transformation through sharing a bit of my journey and the wisdom of others in the search of truth. As a seeker, public speaker, management consultant and as HR Professional my search included extensive reading and countless workshops and seminars as well as intensive training from renowned gurus on subjects like Empowerment, Ontology, Personality Profiling (MBTI), Mind Programming (NLP), Lateral Thinking, Emotional Intelligence, Vedanta, Yoga and Meditation. Along the way I encountered new age as well as ancient teachings on approaching life from a wide variety of spiritual paths. As a result of my exploration I have come to recognize and evolve a simple but effective way of self awareness and transformation which can help readers to realize their cherished dreams, remain happy and attain fulfillment.

Life has given me good amount of duality and contrasts to experience it from different perspectives. One set of challenges came into my life as a teenager, when before each sunrise, my day would begin by assisting my father in tilling the fields, walk 16 kilometers daily for schooling in the scorching heat/blistering cold and face the miseries of our farming family by witnessing our crops frequently getting washed away by floods or ruined by droughts. In contrast, a different set of challenges soon came to me when I was holding key management positions in blue chip companies in my thirties. While the challenge in the village was for survival and desire to come out of scarcity, the different challenge in the corporate world was to catalyze change and bring organizational transformations using Maverick approach and innovative solutions for achieving breakthrough results. I was fortunate to get personal training from Great Masters and the knowledge and wisdom gained helped me to meet the challenges of life or that of professional career with a joy and attain success in my various endeavors.

The challenging situations in the villages and the wisdom showered on me by parents, siblings and these Great Masters helped me develop a belief that the journey through life despite challenges is meant to be joyous, full of learning and serene and graced with a sense of self-empowerment. As corporate trainer I have conducted numerous training workshops and the participants found these techniques/approaches very useful and many of them urged me to write these in the shape of a book for larger benefit of readers. 'Success and Beyond' is an attempt in this endeavor and uses a blend of both Eastern and Western approaches to success, transformation and fulfillment.

All events in our life, whether we judge them as positive or negative, have purpose and exist in harmony with unfolding of life. It is the interpretations which we give that matters most. Each one of us is very special and unique and has own way of experiencing the world. 'Success and Beyond' is about self empowerment which is a power that uncovers and develops our innate abilities and strengths. This book can help you combine excellence and attain inner harmony and happiness by a new and higher self understanding. Such an understanding would reveal the beauty, grace, love, peace and powers that lie within you. This book is also intended for people who are working hard, may be even finding success in their life and work but are struggling to find a meaning or fulfillment in what they are doing. It is for those who are running the race of life either by ignorance or on a path that is not their choosing. It will help you challenge your assumptions, change your behavior and reshape your environment and circumstances.

Chapter 1 provides very inspiring examples of achievers, defines success, lists the qualities in these achievers and describes how they converted challenges into opportunities. It also explains the common causes of failures and usual mental traps and how to overcome them. Why we need to decide and set our goals and how to convert dreams into specific goals is featured in Chapter 2. It also includes the process of achievement. Chapter 3 deals with the subconscious mind and describes how it can be harnessed for our benefits. It also explains with examples the concept of self-image and mind patterns. Chapter 4 covering MBTI (Myers and Briggs Type Indicator) provides an explanation of various personality types to help you know your own type, its strengths, likely pitfalls of one particular type, understand deeply the other types of personalities and the nature of our difference from others. MBTI is one of the most widely used instruments in the world for self-development and interpersonal effectiveness. Knowing your type through introspection will help you greatly in your dealing with others, using diversity and solving problems more easily through team effectiveness. Attaining peak performance is one aspect but sustaining it is possible only by using natural laws to success. This requires a great deal of self-transformation which is explained in detail in Chapter 5. Chapter 6 features the art and science of emotional intelligence and highlights the ways in which you can develop this extremely important resource.

Once the awareness is developed of what needs to be changed, how to change it become the biggest challenge and requires mind-programming. NLP, considered as the science of excellence, is covered in Chapter 7 and will give you highly useful and proven techniques for effective change. It will provide practical applications so that you can be more effective and productive in all your endeavors. Chapter 8 explains stress and managing it effectively. At the end, Chapter 9 will take you beyond success to help you in achieving a blissful and fulfilling life.

The book is presented in a simple, comprehensive, interesting and ready to use manner with Indian context for the benefit of people from all walks of life. It will provide you a useful direction to realize your true potential and utilize it to attain better and astonishing results in your personal and professional life. I have shared some of my insights and learning with you. This book is a product of knowledge and experiences and can by no means be claimed as absolute truth. Neither the knowledge/contents are my monopoly as I have borrowed it from my experience and that of innumerable others and many sources which may have not been always noted. The book seeks to provide you the knowledge to make your life powerful but the knowledge needs to be transformed into meaningful actions using your wisdom. May your journey be enriching, joyous, meaningful and with amazing success.

R.S. Dabas

New Delhi

Acknowledgements

I would like to thank all those people who have helped me in my personal growth and journey to transformation and made it possible for me to write this book. My first and foremost thanks are to my parents: mother Hardevi and father Bhim Singh who never had been to any formal school but taught me the great values of humanity and life. Being the youngest among the siblings, I was fortunate to receive unconditional love and inspiring support from my brothers Jugjit, Chander, Prem, Gian, and sister Phoolvati who all guided me through their examples of self-sacrifice and caring. Without them, I would not have been the person I am today. My school teachers in the village, particularly Balbir Singh and Devanand were equally encouraging to me in the path of learning. Geetam and Uttra Khirwar, my parents-in-law, played a pivotal role in strengthening my spirit of explorations and excellence and always encouraged me. I am grateful indeed to all of them in shaping me.

I am also grateful to industry stalwarts and my employers particularly Sh. Satish Kaura, late Sh. Aditya Birla, Sh. Brij Mohan Munjal, Sh. Rajinder Gupta, Sh. SK Arya and Sh. Naveen Jindal who kept challenging me through their visionary approaches thus helping me to strive for excellence. The challenging roles provided by them encouraged me to experiment with transformational techniques at organizational levels and thus learn and grow in my professional career. I want to thank all my colleagues who worked with me in different organizations, clients, participants and thousands of HR professionals for supporting me in many of my endeavors including my role as President of National HRD Network-Delhi which provided a great platform for me for professional networking in India and beyond. The guidance and appreciations by Management & HRD Experts particularly Sharu S Rangnekar, Dr. MB Atheraya, Dr. Pritam Singh, Dr. PN Singh, Dr. Udai Pareekh, Dr. TV Rao, Mr. Tapan Mitra and Ms Anu Aga always encouraged me to preserve and emerge stronger in challenging situations. As a seeker I am also fortunate to be personally blessed by the Gurus, namely, Shri Shri Ravishankarji, Sh. SN Goenkaji, Sh. Dharmanandji, Swami Sukhobodhyanand and many others whose teaching guided me in defining a new meaning to life through meditation and spiritual bliss. I am equally fortunate to have been coached by Renowned Experts like Daniel Goleman, Marshal Goldsmith, Stephen Covey, Clauss Moller, Dr. Deepak Chopra, Paula Haron and Edward D Bano. I am indebted to all of them for significant contributions made to my own learning in the absence of which the writing of this book would not have been possible. I would also like to express my gratitude to numerous authors, scriptures, public speakers and seminar leaders and other learned persons who have contributed, even though anonymously, to my knowledge and helped accomplish this task.

This book could have never come into being without the support of my wife Neelam and our beloved sons Ateendra and Bharrat who have created an enriching environment on the path to fulfillment.

And last but not least, special thanks to my publisher 'M/s New Age International (P) Ltd. Publishers' and the editing team for making this possible.

Contents

Chapter 1

Pursuit of Success

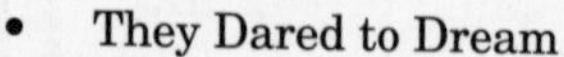

- They Dared to Dream
- Secret of their success
- Mental blocks to success (why people get struck or stopped?)
- What truly is the success?
- Success Mindset: Qualities that facilitate joyful success
- Problems are opportunities
- The brighter side of failure
- Behind great success there may lie a big failure
- Story of a man, who had a dream and perseverance. Honda
- Winners and losers
- Four steps to success
- Conclusion

Success is progressive realization of worthy goals.

- Earl Nightingale

Success is to be measured not so much by the position that one has reached in life as by the obstacles that one has overcome while trying to succeed.

- B.T.Washington

Champions are made from something they have deep inside them-a desire, a dream, a VISION. They have to have the skill, and the will. But the will must be stronger than the skill".

- Muhammad Ali

Success is a matter of luck. Ask any faiiure.

- Earl Wilson

If you think you can or think you can not, you are right.

- Henri Ford

Whatever the mind of a person can conceive and believe. He can achieve it.

- Napoleon Hill

Success has different meaning for different person. If we study the life history of successful people, we may find that successful people had their own unique journeys of achievements and failures but certain mix of qualities had led them to succeed in their chosen endeavors. We are listing here some of the interesting and inspiring examples of success so that we can learn from their journey of success.

They Dared to Dream

Dhirubhai Ambani, one of the most successful industrialist of India, who started with 150 Rupees, created Reliance Group, one of the largest business house of India. While receiving an international award, he was asked about his philosophy of success and he said—

"Our Dream has to be bigger.
Our Ambitions to be higher.
Our Commitment to be deeper.
And Our Efforts to be stronger."

M S Oberoi saw his mother struggling after his father's premature death. He started a career as a clerk in a hotel at Simla and worked hard to own that hotel and created later on 'Oberoi Chain of Hotels' which has more than **30 hotels in the World.** He had the dream and determination.

Bill Gate (Founder of The Microsoft and once rated among the richest persons in the World) began with a dream of supplying a program to IBM after seeing an advertisement in newspaper at a library. He might have been a college dropout but his determination to achieve his cherished dream made him one of the world's most successful business man.

Dr Abdul Kalam - Former President of India and earlier a well known scientist started his life from very humble upbringing. He used to sell newspapers in the morning to earn his school fees but never gave up his dreams. His dream for India 'Vision 2020' reflects his saying 'Dream is not what you see in sleep but what does not let you sleep'.

Narayan Moorthi worked as an employee of Computer Company and founded *Infosys*- India's great IT Company. He created many benchmarks in corporate governance and sharing wealth with his employees.

O P Jindal started from his native village Nalwa in Hissar District but had a passion for machines and despite the lack of professional education and beginning from a small tube factory, he created an industrial empire that now operates in more than 10 countries.

B M Munjal started by selling cycles and gradually created Hero Honda - World's largest two Wheeler Company.

Sunil Mittal promoter of Bharti Group opines 'You have to create circumstances to be lucky'. He believes that luck is an opportunity picked up by a prepared mind and rightly combined with desired efforts. He sensed a great opportunity in telecom revolution.

Rajinder Gupta 11th pass boy from Bhatinda worked hard to build a small factory in Barnala in 1985. Today ₹ 4000 Cr. Trident Group has emerged as one of the largest terry towel producer of the world and Trident Limited has been featured among "Great Place To Work". His philosophy is reflected in his company song 'nothing is impossible' (Kuchh be asambav nahi, sabhi kuchh sambav hai)'.

V Krishnamurthi who started as technician in BHEL at Truchi, then became Chairman of BHEL, SAIL, and Maruti is known for many turnarounds. Government of India also nominated him for many key positions due to his passion for excellence.

S Sridharan is known for his great achievements of Delhi Metro and Konkan Railways; has great passion for results and attained success, despite many bureaucratic hindrances. Even at the age of 75, his passion, commitment and energy are great traits of his leadership.

There are many examples of successful persons from ordinary and different walks of life, which are not only inspiring but also strengthen the belief that nothing is impossible. Napoleon Hill once said 'Whatever the mind of a man can conceive and believe, he can achieve it'.

While many achievers get the status of a celebrity or get acknowledged soon by public, but there are hundreds and millions of others as well whose success can also be iconic as they had their own unique journey of success but may not have been recognised.

Washington has said 'Success is measured not so much by the position one has reached in life but possibly by the obstacles that one has overcome while achieving those goals'.

Some of these interesting examples are listed here.

SECRET OF THEIR SUCCESS

Iswar Singh–From being a Driver to becoming an Entrepreneur of ₹ 700 Crore

Iswar Singh, an ex-serviceman, joined Maruti Udyog, the leading car manufacturer of India, as driver on trial basis in 1982. While many drivers kept themselves busy in either playing cards or gossiping during their idle time, Iswar Singh being different from others invested his time at the shop floor learning about car and its various components. In this process he never allowed his work to suffer and rather sought the consent of his superiors who were delighted to encourage such a hardworking and curious person. Within a short period of time, he not only acquired knowledge of various components but also had a good idea of its cost and the usual difficulties encountered by the vendor development department in locating rare suppliers. It was the period when Maruti was keen to develop local vendors for supply of various parts. Iswar Singh enrolled his superiors in his idea of making certain parts and Maruti was keen to help its employee in such endeavors.

By sheer hard work and perseverance, Iswar Singh is now a successful entrepreneur (Managing Director of Haryana Industries Ltd.) with a group, whose annual turnover is more than ₹ 700 Crore and provides employment to thousands of people. He has 5 plants at Gurgaon and other locations supplying sheet metal, plastic and rubber parts not only to his former employer Maruti Suzuki but also to other leading OEMs. His keenness and determination to pursue his dream helped him to sense and grab the opportunity.

Luck is an opportunity picked up by a prepared mind

Opportunity always knocks first at the door but only a person with enterprise and an open mind spots it. The one who puts in the right efforts reaps the benefits.

> *'Opportunities are like sunrises. If you wait too long, you miss them'*

Don't quit as you may be close to success- Story of Stephen King author of Carrie

He lived in a trailer and earned $ 60 per week from laundry job. He wanted to be a writer. Nights and days his trailer echoed with the noise of typewriter. Everyone rejected his manuscript. He doubted whether his papers were being read or not. One day he threw the manuscript into the garbage. His wife said, 'you should not quit when you are so close'. He started again by typing 1500 words per day and sent it to Bill Thompson. Later on Stephen King's classic '*Carrie*' published 5 million copies and produced a top ranked movie based on it in 1976.

He treated failure as an important part of success process: Walt Disney

You are never defeated until you accept defeat and decides to stop trying. As a young cartoonist, Walt Disney faced many rejections from newspaper editors, who said he had no talent. A church hired him to draw some cartoons. After watching a small mouse, he was inspired. That was the beginning of Mickey Mouse. Walt Disney was turned down for finance to build Disneyland by more than 300 banks, but he continued his efforts.

So what are the secrets of success of these and others achievers?

- They had dreams they believed in and remained committed to.
- They had perseverance and determination to bounce back.
- They learnt from their setbacks.

What is so common about these achievers and many more whose inspiring stories we listen or read in the news quite often? One common quality among all of them is that they all choose to succeed as success is a matter of choice. If we have strong will, there is nothing that we cannot achieve. Once we have ardent desire to do something, we will surely find the ways to do it. A mere wish would not make things happen. It is a burning desire, turned into an obsession that will generate the energy to bring you to achieve any goal that you may desire. This can be illustrated by the following story.

Burning desire is the true secret of success

There was once a young boy who wanted to seek the secret of success. One day he approached a wise man living up in the mountains. When he found the wise man at his hut, he asked, "Wise man, can you tell me the secret of becoming successful in life?" The wise man was silent for a while. After a moment of silence, the wise man led him to a nearby river. They kept walking into the river until the boy's head was fully submerged in the water. The boy struggled to keep his head above the water. To his astonishment, the wise man did not help him. Instead, the wise man held his head in the water. After a few minutes the wise man pulled him out of the water and they proceeded to walk back to the hut. At the hut the wise man asked to boy what he desired most when his head was submerged in water. To this he quickly responded, "Of course, I wanted to breathe, you old fool!" To which the wise man replied, "Son, if you desire success as much as you wanted to breathe, then you will find the true secret of success."

How can you say it is *Bad or Good* Luck– Hence why then count it?

The story is about an old man Shambhu who seemed to have everything. He had a beloved son, a prized horse, and many of the material things that most people want. But one day his most valuable possession, his horse, broke out of the corral and ran away into the nearby mountains. In one catastrophic moment, he lost this priceless asset.

On hearing of this calamity, his neighbors came to offer their sympathy. They all said to him, "your horse is gone, what a bad luck!" and they tried to console him. But he answered back, "How do you know it is a bad luck?"

Sure enough, a few days later, the horse returned home where he knew there would be ample food and water. Along with him, he brought back twelve beautiful wild stallions. When all the townsmen were saying, "What good luck, thirteen horses!" But wise Shambhu replied, "How do you know it is good luck?" They remembered his words the next day when his son, his only child Panku, tried to ride one of the wild stallions. He was thrown off, broke his leg, and was left with a permanent limp. When his neighbors heard about the accident, they came to him again and said, "Your son, forever a cripple. What a bad luck!" But the wise old Shambhu again asked, "How do you say it is bad luck?"

Sure enough, about a year later, a warlord came to town, saw every able-bodied young man, and took them off to battle. The battle was lost and all the warriors were killed. The only young Panku left in the village was the old man's crippled son, for he had not been conscripted due to his handicap.

Moral of the story

- You don't know what would be good luck or bad luck, so don't count on it. Go where you want to go and do everything in your power to achieve your goal.
- Luck is what you got and success is what you made. History does not remember lucky people but those who succeeded despite all odds are usually remembered.

Someone may put logic that successful persons usually express their gratitude to the Almighty on attainment of success and are thus, dependent on luck. Well expressing gratitude to all including the Almighty is a great quality that helps them in success and avoiding the trap of overconfidence. They believe in the efforts, keep improving the efforts but do not just depend on the luck and rather believe in creating circumstances to be lucky as explained by the philosophy of Sunil Mittal.

Opportunity knocks the door of many but only those who listen to it can grab it.

In 90s many NRIs while visiting their hometown in Punjab from Canada and America used to grumble over the lack of a convenient flight to Punjab or suitable transport system from IGI Airport at New Delhi. Timely reservation in the fast trains was also usually not available as e-ticketing was not yet started by Indian Railways till that time. With a state of helplessness, most of these NRI's, (Non Resident Indians) felt angry and frustrated . However one person saw it as a great opportunity and started a new air-conditioned bus service to the major districts of Punjab and established his 'Indo Canada Travel Service'. The buses had all the facilities and necessary comforts on the pattern, this promoter recognised in Canada and soon it became not only a very popular service at that time but helped in emergence of entirely a new market in the region. It truly reflects the saying 'in the midst of a problem there may be a great opportunity'. Do you cry over the problem or grab the opportunity?

So, the basic question is what makes some people grab the opportunity while others keep waiting or don't see it as opportunity? The answer can be related with the following.

What type of news attracts you more?

I frequently ask participants in my training workshops to share any thrilling news from the recent past. Surprisingly many of them start speaking of all negative stuffs or sad happenings reported in the newspaper or media and they immediately start criticizing what is missing in our system and simply become disappointed on sad news. I have to remind them a lot to help them recollect positive stuff or good happenings that can certainly leave us more happy and thrilled state. Well I am certainly not against their thinking and highly appreciate their concern for the society or need for improvements in our system but I would like to remind them that always being pessimistic may program our mind such that we may soon become deaf to all positive happenings and expectations. To experience the impact, I am sharing below an interesting newspaper story published.

Story of Fatima

Visakhapatnam- Sheik Salar, 26, a street hawker, used every rupee he earned to help his wife Fatima Bibi Sheik, 21, achieve her academic ambitions. And it was not in vain. Fatima completed her course at GVP College of Engineering with high marks and was given a plum posting by the software giant at a campus selection. Fatima and Salar stay in a slum at Rajendranagar. While Fatima went to college, Salar roamed around the city with a pushcart selling puffed rice, corn, 'chilli bhajjis' and 'pani puri', earning ₹ 150 per day. When she was married off to her distant relation Salar by her parents, Fatima was just 15 and felt that she would never achieve her dream of being a software engineer.

"I did not want to marry since I wanted to study further and achieve something," she said. She was crestfallen since Salar merely nodded when she told him about her dreams. But his nod meant a lot and he started saving money to help her study. By living frugally, Salar somehow got together ₹ 60,000 to pay Fatima's fee for the first and second year of her engineering course.

The Andhra Pradesh State Minorities Finance Corporation helped the couple pay the rest of the fee. "At the time of our marriage I was not sure how serious Fatima was about her studies," said Salar. "But when I realized that she got 536 marks in her SSC exams and stood first in her school, I decided to help her study." The 'pani puri' vendor was adamant that her future should not be spoilt because she married him. A junior college in the city provided her free intermediate education.

She secured a decent rank in the Eamcet exam and opted to join the electronics and electrical engineering branch. "We decided not to have kids till she got a good job," said Salar. "For this, I face much criticism from my parents." Fatima's eyes moisten when she talks about her husband. "You can't imagine the hardships he suffered to help me," she said. "In the last six years, he was my strength. He sacrificed all his joys for me."

"Fatima was always first in the class," said Asha Kanthi, her classmate. The wife of a poor pani puri vendor has become a software engineer in Infosys, thanks to her husband's support. In fact, she is the 1st student from college to get into Infosys. "We did not know her story then. Now she is our inspiration." Though happy at the turn of events, the couple is a bit sad when thinking about their being apart for three months, when Fatima would go to the Infosys campus in Mysore for training. Have they ever quarrelled? "When we have issues, we sit together and discuss and sort it out," said Fatima. She plans to take her husband along with her when she gets her posting.

What thoughts does this news bring to your mind? Many persons respond by saying 'Great and full of inspiration'. There are many such positive and inspiring news reported daily and you will start noticing such news if you start reading about them. In fact the newspaper reports both types of stories daily. If we start picking up only those stories which merely remind us of something negative or something missing, the mind will start getting conditioned accordingly. So be careful about what to read and what not to focus for your own benefit and for the sake of those who are associated with you including your children. More negative stuff we discuss at home, more pessimist we may make our children as well. Decide yourself what you want to nourish in your mind and to those in your surroundings. The principle of 'Garbage in Garbage out' and its relation with the development of our belief system can be understood by the following:

Production of your thought factory is in the hands of your two foremen

A- Mr. Triumph—In-charge of manufacturing positive (+) thoughts

B- Mr. Defeat—In-charge of manufacturing negative (–) thoughts

"A" says and produces reasons

Why! you can,

Why! you are qualified and capable,

Why! you will succeed,

"B" is expert in developing reasons

Why you can't?

Why you are weak?

Why you are inadequate?

Reminding you of how you could not do it last time.

- Both are intensely obedient. They snap to attention immediately. You have to give a signal.
- The more work you give either of these foremen, the stronger he becomes and takes charge of your Thought Manufacturing Division.

Can you use Mr. Triumph 100% of the time? Choice is truly yours.

Everyone has a lot of potential, it needs to be tapped

"Every individual has a lot of potential in his field of work. The potential however needs to be recognised and utilized," Given below is an interesting story, which drives home a very important message:

Ernst was having a small piece of land in a village at Texas in the U.S. He was working very hard in his field throughout the day but due to lack of knowledge and expertise, he could not make things happen. Moreover, the land was not much fertile and he did not have any other source of income, he and his family were going through a bad time. One day Ernst, completely demoralized and frustrated, decided to sell his farmland to settle somewhere else so that he could get some employment, and provide reasonable living to his family. When Ernst was about to sell his land, executives of oil

Exploration Company approached him. They offered him a proposal that he could give his land on lease to the company for oil exploration and if they struck oil; he would get royalty and become a rich person. If otherwise, he is not going to lose either as during the exploration period he would get some money good enough to support his family. The exploration work continued for few months and one day the oil got struck from the well. So, Ernst became millionaire overnight.

Ernst had not become millionaire overnight rather he was already millionaire because the oil was already there in his farmland, but he did not know it.

Chandro Devi - 62 year old grandmother from Johari village in Bagpat district of UP, discovered her true potential when her 12 years old grand daughter Priyanka persuaded her to learn shooting. Priyanka has found that her 'Dadi (Grandmother)' has a perfect aim in her 'Gulel' (a shooting device used in rural India to keep birds away from eating the crops). Chandro Devi was encouraged by all family members to learn Pistol Shooting from an expert of the village and was pampered to participate in different shooting events. And to the surprise of all, she became the highest scorer in her category in a national level event in Chandigarh. Later on Chandro Devi's achievement helped this village in getting a national level academy of shooting. Chandro Devi who has never been to school but is now instrumental in providing coaching in her village profoundly says 'there is good in everybody in terms of what one is capable of. ***If you recognize what you are capable of doing then you will do it. When you glimpse at your potential you create a passion for achieving that potential'.***

Similarly, each one of us is having a lot of potential, a lot of good qualities, a lot of enthusiasm and a lot of common sense. But who is going to exploit these qualities and potential? It is none but the self. Why people are not able to realize their true potential and become stopped in their path of success or get struck?

Mental Blocks to Success (Why People Get Struck or Stopped?)

When children are born, they are born to be successful by nature and are not programmed for failures. Somewhere in life many people start blocking their own success by putting powerful breaks which resist them to realize their dreams. Many of these breaks are used unknowingly and even if one becomes aware, one may find it difficult to change after sometime as one may not be aware of the trap and it becomes a mindset. If we release these breaks, we can achieve more from life and make it smoother and enjoyable. Like traveling down the road it is always good to be aware of roadblocks! The same is true in our journey towards success. We need to be aware of those things that will keep us away from our destination! The common causes that usually stop many people from achieving success can be classified in following manner:

1. No vision or lack of specific goal.
2. Limiting beliefs. (Living in one's own reality). Pessimism.
3. Reaching the comfort zones and lack of willingness to move to next level (Lethargy).
4. Illusion of success. (Complacency is different from fulfillment)
5. Carrying the burden of past upsets and not allowing space for future.
6. Not taking responsibility. Always blaming, rationalizing or justifying.
7. Fear of failure and hence not attempting. (Not trying the unknown)
8. Leave the efforts half-heartedly. Lack of perseverance.
9. Selective listening or non-listening or lack of understanding others' viewpoint.
10. Allowing energy sucking emotions to drain energy. (non forgiving attitude)
11. Adopting a short cut approach (immediate gratifications) or too long a road.
12. Choosing wrong goals and not being receptive to feedback.
13. Sycophancy due to lack of conviction and poor self-esteem (Syndrome of looking good in other's opinion rather than listening to self).
14. Picking the wrong people to hang out who keep you away from success.
15. Repeating mistakes and not learning from the mistakes.

We will discuss some of these factors in detail with examples in this chapter. However chapters no. 3, 5 and 7 of this book will help you to identify various mind patterns, blind spots and provide useful techniques to rectify these traps and transform into a new self.

Fear of failure and limiting beliefs, limit the success—Pankaj could not see an opportunity when it knocked at his door.

One day Pankaj came to my office and requested me to help him find a job since I was guiding people that time about career for a social cause during my free time. "What all have you done till now?" I asked him. "Sir, I have done a diploma in Electrical Engineering", he replied. "Good, and what steps have you taken to find a job for yourself?" I inquired. "I had applied in fifty odd companies. Out of these, five companies called me for interviews. But when I went there, the vacancies were filled by persons who had recommendations." I took his resume and told him that I would try my best.

I forwarded Pankaj's resume to few companies in my acquaintance, which were usually requiring fresh diploma holders. Few days later Pankaj got a call from a company asking him to come for an interview on 26th Feb. That particular day, I had gone out for a meeting and came back to the office in the evening. My secretary told me that a person called Pankaj wanted to speak to me about something very urgent. Next day when Pankaj walked into my office and I asked him 'how was your interview with that company?' His reply was "Sir, I didn't go for the interview". "But why?", I asked him in surprise, and why were you trying to contact me yesterday? I was shocked to hear his reply. "I wanted to find out from you whether you had already spoken to the concerned interviewer, as there was no point in attending the interview without proper recommendation."

It took me quite a while to convince him that he could get a job without a recommendation as well, since billions of persons in the world have done so, even if millions of others might have used recommendations in getting job. It was not the fault of Pankaj alone but his parents were more responsible for developing his attitude, since they influenced his thinking by always reflecting to Pankaj that it is only recommendation which will lend him a job. Pankaj merely learnt from the borrowed beliefs from his surroundings. It took me great deal of efforts to change his thinking as well as that of his parents and once convinced, he went alone to find a job and is placed well in a company at Gurgaon.

There is great saying "You always miss 100% of the shots you don't take". Pankaj is not alone, many of us have this fear of failure and we even do not try because of our limiting beliefs and thus miss many opportunities. The chapter on NLP will provide powerful techniques to remove various fears and phobias and to change the limiting beliefs.

Luck favour those who help themselves.

In a small town, there was a flood and everyone was leaving for safety except one man who was saying, "God will save me, I have faith." As the water level rose, a jeep came to rescue him, but the man refused saying, "God will save me, I have faith." As the water level rose further he went up to the second floor, and a boat came to help him. Again he refused to go, saying, "God will save me, I have faith." The water kept rising and the man climbed to the roof. A helicopter came to rescue him, but he said, "God will save me, I have faith." Well, he finally drowned. He questioned angrily to the God, "I had complete faith in you, so why did you ignore my prayers and let me drown?" God replied, "All help in the form of jeep, boat and helicopter were sent to you. If you don't take your step, who else can help you".

- Luck favour those who help themselves.
- Believe in the law of cause and effect rather than waiting for luck or wishing for something to happen without effort is worthless.

Beliefs and limitations of others if borrowed can impose limitations on us.

In a class of mathematics, thirty students were present listening carefully to the instructions of the teacher. Manish was sitting alone on the last bench enjoying a nap. At the end of the class when the bell rung, everybody left, then Manish got up in fright and noted down the two question numbers written on the blackboard.

That evening he worked till very late hours, trying to solve those two questions. After hectic efforts he managed to solve one of the two. Next day he went to school and showed his homework to his teacher expecting a great pat on his back. The teacher looked at his work and was surprised to find one of the most difficult sum being solved by Manish. He asked Manish "Whose help have you taken to complete this question?" "Nobody's sir, I did it on my own," he said. "Also tell me who gave you these sums to solve?" "Sir, its you who gave it, as you had written on the board yesterday these two question numbers so I assumed that it must simply be the homework." "No dear Manish these questions were the most difficult and unsolvable even by me. I had told the students not to attempt them and waste their time but complete the rest of the sums in that chapter," responded the teacher. Manish was plainly amazed and happy that he had achieved something great by not hearing the limitation imposed by his teacher. So, it is better to be ignorant to the limiting beliefs of others and try for the best. Otherwise the borrowed limitation can limit us as well.

- It is better not to have a belief about something rather than to have a limiting belief.
- You might have developed many such limiting beliefs. Discover and discard them.

Our real success or transformation can be possible only when we discard the limiting belief. You need to do it continuously. Henry Ford had said "If you think you can or think you can't, you're right".

Playing it safe is a trap

Many opportunities are lost because of playing safe approach. If it is taken after calculating pros and cons then it may be a conscious decision and we all need to be safe, but if we hesitate in taking even calculated risk then it may impact our success. Good advice is 'Take risks but don't gamble'. While the risk takers go with their eyes open, the gamblers shoot in the dark.

No risk, no gain

Go deep into the sea rather than just waiting for the fishes to come up to the shore. 'Many people who lag behind are like those fishermen who wait for the fishes to come up to the shore. They do at times, but not enough'. The statement by Lakshmi Mittal shows the difference in working between him who acquired Arcelor and became a steel tycoon and many others who just waited the things to happen.

Some people never try because they are afraid to lose. Ships that sail on water face risks of storms. But if they remain in the harbor, they would rust and that is not what they were built for. That is the difference between playing to win and playing not to lose. One cannot be committed to a goal or a cause and not take risks. Losers want security and winners want opportunity.

The most common fears among people are the fear of the unknown, fear of failing and fear of rejection. In a vicious cycle, the fear leads to anxiety and irrational thinking, magnifying the problem and blocking our success. Failure is not a worse thing as compared to failing without attempting.

Those who never strive and keep on waiting get only the scrap discarded by those who strive and move forward. Many persons lose opportunity because it was risky. Is walking on the road, not a risk or in that sense driving a car? Yes of course but still people walk or drive because they take calculated risk with eyes open and not gamble. Developing the courage to try something new requires knowledge, training, careful study and competency, which can be learnt through trial and experience sharing. Don't be afraid to lose. Take risk by keeping eyes open, but not like a gambler who shoots in dark always.

You always miss 100% of the shots you don't take.

A farmer was asked whether he had planted wheat for the season. He replied, "No, I was afraid it wouldn't rain." The man again asked, "Did you plant cotton?" The farmer said, "No, I was afraid of insects eating the cotton." Then the man asked once again, "What did you plant?" The pet reply came from the farmer, "Nothing, I played it very safe". Opportunity can therefore be related with the fact: "You always miss 100% of the shots you don't take".

Reality is what you see through your perceptual map

People always make their best choice out of alternatives known to them as per their perceptual map which is nothing but their filtered experience. The perceptual map is usually different from the true reality. We can be more effective when the gap between ultimate reality and personal reality is removed which is the beginning of self-transformation.

The frog in the well

There is a story of the frog that lived in a dark well all his life. One day a frog from the sea paid him a visit.

'Where do you come from?' asked the frog in the well.

'From the great ocean,' he replied.

'How big is your ocean?'

'It's gigantic.'

'You mean it's about a quarter of the size of my well here?' 'Bigger.'

'Bigger, you mean half as big?'

'No, even bigger.'

'Is it.... As big as this well?'

'There's no comparison of it.'

'That's impossible! I've got to see this for myself.'

They set off together. When the frog from the well saw the ocean, it was such a shock that his head just exploded into pieces.

Moral of the story

- You may not know what possibilities exist for you unless you have tried.
- People make their best choices as per their perceptual reality.

Are you focusing on long term goals or merely seeking instant gratification?

We live in an age of instant gratification. When people want to be instant millionaires, then they take shortcuts and compromise on their integrity. Remember that instant gratification allows us to focus on momentary pleasures rather than consequences.

Marshmallow experiment

The Stanford University conducted an experiment among four years old children.

The children were given a marshmallow each and told that either they could eat it immediately if they felt so or they could retain it. Also it was informed that if they keep marshmallow for 15 minutes, they will be rewarded with another marshmallow; the choice is theirs.

The observer then left and returned after 15 minutes and found there were two types of children-those who could not resist their temptation and ate the marshmallow immediately without thinking of the expected reward. The other group resisted the temptation and delayed their gratification.

Both groups were studied later on and it was found that the first group gave up in case of frustrations or obstacles very quickly; and became stubborn when they grew up in life as adults. The other group faced the challenge of life instead of giving up easily, did not shy away from social responsibilities and was generally more successful in achieving the goals.

> *Learning: Self-imposed delay of gratification and the ability to delay impulse in the service of a goal is the essence of self-regulation which is essential for any success.*

The moment you stay in your past, you are stealing it from your future. If you have lost one opportunity, do not carry the burden forever.

Suresh missed an opportunity a few years ago to purchase a piece of land which has appreciated now many folds. On seeing that land developed now as a commercial property he always repeats 'I was carrying that much of money in my pocket but my family did not permit me to buy that time which was offered to him by a friend almost at a throwaway price'. Since then the plot has escalated to more than 100 times. He simply is carrying a burden of guilt and rather than learning from the incident and becoming wiser, frequent repetition of his guilt is only fuelling to his position of being struck and stopping him avail any further possibility. More he carries the past upsets more he will be struck. The question is, 'what is the point in crying over split milk'. If you have lost one opportunity do not carry the burden of the past, be open for new possibilities and that would come when you forget it and come out of being struck.

Learning:

- Carrying the burden of past may stop you to attain present or future goals.
- Your reaction at the failure will determine how soon you will succeed again.
- If you have missed one opportunity, don't close your eyes for the next at least.

"People are not disturbed by the things that happened but by their perception of the things that happened".

There were two brothers in a small village. The twin brothers grew up knowing nothing else but poverty. Their father was an alcoholic and their mother a domestic worker. They grew up with very little. One day, their parents died on the spot in a bus accident. The brothers' condition became even worse. At the age of 17 they depart. Years later a family member decided to find them for a family reunion.

One of the brother was a wealthy engineer owning a construction company. He had a wife and two beautiful kids. The other was an alcoholic with no sense of direction for his life. The family member asked the engineer, "How did your life turn out like this?" "What did you expect with a childhood like mine?" he answered.

He moved on to the other brother with the same question. "What did you expect with a childhood like mine?" was his answer.

This tells us that, "People are not disturbed by the things that happened but by their perception of the things that happened".

Don't worry what others would say. Being nice and pleasing others can be a perilous trap. In trying to please other people, many times we find ourselves overreaching ourselves toward what lies outside our sphere of influence. In doing so we may lose our hold on our life's purpose. If you want to live a wise life, live it on your own terms and in your own eyes. Many persons suffer in their life because of the `looking good' syndrome. They are more worried about what others would say rather than listening to their own true feelings and finally end up not owning their decisions. Many others suffer because they have picked the wrong people to hang out with. They become products of their environment. It is essential to hangout with good quality people who will encourage you and strengthen your quest for success?

What Truly is the Success?

Striving to achieve

A. When a man sets a goal for himself and he is "working" to achieve that goal, he is on the path to success.

B. A man may set goals, but if he does not "work" towards them he is not on the path to success.

C. "Striving" involves and demands greater "utilization" of our vast, but hidden, potential.

Progressive

A. When a man reaches a goal, he must set other goals, higher goals. He is then on the path, on the journey to Success.

B. On reaching his goal, a man might have achieved success and a very big one at that point of time, but the moment he ceases to set other goals he ceases to be successful. Why? Because a man without a dream, without a goal does not live, he only exists. He stagnates. He decays.

Success is a journey, not a destination

Remember that your success begins when you decide what you want and you begin to work towards it.

- Success seldom comes by chance. It always comes by choice.
- Success is not measured in terms of what others have done.
- Success is related to, all those things you have yet to do.
- Success is measured in inches ....Not in miles.

Stephen Beck of American Foundation for Science of Creative Intelligence, in an article explains:

"We have technologies today for just about everything, for landing men on the moon, for putting micro-circuits, for agriculture and for a myriad of society's functions. What has been missing until now is a technology for developing the full potential of the human mind. It has been said that the greatest underdeveloped resource in the world today is human intelligence. More than 50 years ago, William James concluded that man is using about 5% of his total potential: the optimists among contemporary researches give figures that range up to 10%. So at best, 90% of human potential is underutilized".

A factory or other industrial enterprise functioning at only 10 per cent of its capacity would be considered very unproductive and action would be taken to change its operation. But when we are told that our personnel are performing with such limited use of resources, we don't know what to do."

"Goals are what keep us going. To be continually working is not enough. We must see clearly the next step. To keep moving after achieving one goal, we must set a new one."

Success is something beyond genes and is related to mental attitude: Why are some persons consistently more successful than others in their endeavors? Why is it that some people have better relationships, earn more money, have greater peace of mind, better health and seem to get all the joy and fulfillment in life while others do not? A common belief held by many of us is that success is the result of either good luck, heredity, our childhood environment, or some combination of all these factors which are beyond our control.

No one set of genes is common to all successful people. Successful people come in a wide variety of sizes, shapes, and colors, and with different physical and mental attributes. No two are exactly alike. There are examples of identical twins with exactly the same genetic code where one achieves great success and the other does not. Also, we all know that people who were not successful at one point in their lives and later went on to achieve great success, with their genetic code staying exactly the same in the process. Hence, there is something beyond the gene which result in success.

Impact of environment may work both ways (positive or negative): The second argument, that people are successful solely as a result of their environment or upbringing, has more validity. Particular environments tend to produce certain behavioral characteristics which are either positive or negative. Children raised in a ghetto environment have a higher incidence of failure in school and crime, than children raised in middle and upper-class neighborhoods. But it works both ways. Families raised in poverty have produced a good number of successful offspring; upper-class families have produced their fair share of failures as well. Success therefore cannot be guaranteed by environmental factors only.

However, there is clinching evidence to support the premise that success results more from certain mental traits and personality characteristics known as positive mental attitudes than from any other single factor. Certain set of qualities that can be developed facilitates success and are termed as success mindsets, are listed below.

Success Mindset: Qualities that facilitate joyful success

1. Power of visualization (seeing future) and ability to convert dreams into opportunities and goals.
2. Optimism and fire of enthusiasm about the goal.
3. Commitment to goal and perseverance of efforts. (Do not quit and be ready to travel an extra mile.)

4. Pleasure and pride in actions, liking the things that need to be done like a Karmayogi.
5. Proactive approach, accepting responsibility (enlarging the circle of influence, freedom to choose, reducing area of concern and assuming self responsibility).
6. Solution oriented, instead of being a problem (avoid grudging, fixing, and justifications).
7. Art of networking and seeking support from others (through credit sharing, complimenting others, maintaining give & take relationships, understanding & providing space to others and their view points, and enrolling others in one's ideas by offering what is for them as well).
8. Courage and not being afraid of falling (have faith in self, listening to heart and intuitions).
9. Curiosity to explore avenues and expand one's learning.
10. Learning from past mistakes.
11. Act with calmness of mind and going to the root cause of problems.
12. Ability to handle the negative (avoid criticizing, condemning, complaining, stay away from negative influences by not allowing other's negative impacts on you).
13. Maintaining values and practicing honesty, integrity, sincerity and humility.
14. Self renewal ability (self motivation, knowledge upgradation, self-esteem, good habit formation).
15. Win-Win approach and selfless attitude. (Swami Vivekanand has said that selflessness pays a lot-only problem is that, the people do not have the patience to practice it.)

Desire to achieve

Napoleon Hill has said, "Whatever the mind of a man can conceive and believe, he can achieve." A burning desire is the starting point of all accomplishment. A weak desire cannot produce great results. Success has to be striven for twice, first in the mind and then by physical efforts. The mind gives orders that determine the quality and quantity of our efforts. The stronger the orders, the stronger will be our action and the weaker the order, the weaker the effort. This strength or confidence comes from a prepared mind which is a product of planning and practice. Thus, mental rehearsal is vital for achievement and all winners know it very well. Do you dream to succeed/improve further or just keep doing the same things repeatedly blindfolded without knowing what results you are getting and why? The motivation to succeed comes from the burning desire to achieve a purpose.

Muhammad Ali had said "Champions aren't made in gyms. Champions are made from something they have deep inside them—a desire, a dream, a vision. They have to have the skill, and the will. But the will must be stronger than the skill".

Creative Imagination (the mental rehearsal of the goal)

A study was given some years ago in Reader's Digest in which a class of high school basketball players with similar skills was divided into three test groups to conduct an experiment. The class average for free throws was thirty-nine per cent.

Group I was told not to practice shooting free throws for one month.

Group II was told to practice shooting free throws for one month in the gym one hour every afternoon.

Group III was told to practice shooting free throws in their imagination for one month every afternoon for one hour.

The results indicated that

Group I's performance dropped from 39 to 37 % (minus 2). Group II's performance increased from 39 to 41 % (plus 2). Group III's performance increased from 39 to 42.5% (plus 3.5). Explanation: Group III imagined throwing free throws that scored every time! Group II knew their average was only thirty-nine, so they accepted failures in their drills. Group I neither practice in reality nor in imagination so they lag behind and proved to be the worst performers among the groups.

Mental rehearsal helps in setting the goal, creating energy, taking a mid review and course correction.

PROBLEMS ARE OPPORTUNITIES

Dhirubhai Ambani, the Chairman of Reliance group of companies, while receiving the honor of winner, he spoke about the importance of not giving up into adversities and accepting defeat as a great secret of success. His advice was:

> *"Let no one demoralize you. Pursue goals in the face of difficulty and convert those difficulties into opportunities."*

The founder of Kentucky Fried Chicken-Colonel Sanders had a small restaurant on a busy highway near Colby, Kentucky. A new highway was built-seven miles from his restaurant, because of which he put out of business. But he was not disappointed and said, "I've always thought that behind every problem there is an opportunity" That attitude led him to create a world-wide franchise organization which has turned into a great success.

Obstacles in our path are tests for success

A king had a boulder placed on a roadway. Then he hid himself and watched to see if anyone would remove the huge rock. Some of the king's wealthiest merchants and courtiers came by and simply walked around it. Many loudly blamed the king for not keeping the roads clear, but none did anything about getting the stone out of the way. Then a peasant came along carrying a load of vegetables. On approaching the boulder, the peasant laid down his burden and tried to move the stone to the side of the road. After much pushing and straining, he noticed a purse lying on the road besides that boulder. The purse contained many gold coins and a note from the king indicating that the gold was a reward for the person who removed the boulder from the roadway.

- Every obstacle presents an opportunity to improve one's condition.
- Remember that bigger an obstacle, the bigger can be the opportunity. Do you focus on obstacle or the opportunity?
- Honest work, without expectation of reward, usually leads to unexpected riches.

Achievers are part of solution

I was sitting in the room of a General Manager of my client company when someone knocked at the door. After seeing his face, the GM said a 'no' for the meeting with a dry face stating he was busy. After five minutes another person also knocked at the door of his room and after seeing who he was, the GM invited him inside with a warm welcome. I was keen to know why he had treated the two so differently. "The first one always comes to me with bundles of problems, reasons and justifications regarding why he could not do it," said the GM. "The second person also brings issues for discussion to find solutions but he gives a feeling that he is part of the solution. He is always keen to take responsibilities rather than justifications. Why should I not welcome him as he brings relief to me, while the first one may add up to my worries and create an ulcer."

Power of optimism

Optimist is a person, who expects the best in life and sees the good even in the bad, realizing that in adversity as well as opportunity there is something to be gained and that is the essence of success. Optimist believes that good luck is an opportunity meeting good preparedness and hence they keep their eyes constantly open, being ever prepared through their attitude of optimism. It's all in how you look at life. Optimists are simply people who have learned how to discipline their attitudes to their advantage. It is a mental skill and can be developed by anyone.

Pessimist on the other hand is a person, who expects the worst in life by focusing on what is missing and is wrong, forgetting to focus on what is available and what is right. Pessimists believe that regardless of the effort, whatever has to happen will happen and hence consider success a matter of pure luck.

We sent two sales person to Africa. One traveling down the west and the other towards the east. In those days, they had to walk down quite a lot.

After sometime one salesman sent a telegram: "All people bare-footed, no business possible-returning home."

The other also sent a telegram: "Huge potential exists. Send immediately 10 truck load of shoes."

- Thomas Bata

Pessimists: A behavioral profile

- Are unhappy when they have no troubles to speak of.
- Feel bad when they feel good, for fear they will feel worse when they feel better.
- Spend most of their lives at complaint counters.
- Always turn off the lights to see how dark it is.
- Stop sleeping on bed when they hear that more people die on bed than anywhere else.
- Cannot enjoy their health because they think they may be sick tomorrow.
- Not only expect the worst but also make the worst of whatever happens.
- Don't see the doughnut only the hole.
- Believe that the sun shines only to cast shadows.
- Forget their blessing and count their troubles.
- Know that hard work never hurts anyone but believe " why take a chance?"

An optimist says that he hasn't yet succeeded

One of the most universally acclaimed examples of this principle is Thomas Edison. Although Edison was thought of as an inventor, he didn't always enjoy the acclaim and respect in which he's held today. When Napoleon Hill interviewed Edison for the first time, he said, "Mr. Edison, what have you got to say about the fact that you've failed thousands of times in your attempts to create a light bulb?"

Edison replied, "I beg your pardon. I've never failed even once. I've had thousands of learning experiments that didn't work. I had to run through enough learning experiences to find a way that did work." In life also we all have had thousands of learning experiences; like learning to walk, we kept trying because we saw others succeed and based or this we also succeeded.

It's not that we are two-time, three-time, or hundred-time losers. For most of us, it's just that we haven't had enough learning experiences to get it right.

- For many persons, if just one experience doesn't turn out positively; they conclude that they're losers and give up trying. "I just can't do it," is the common conclusion. They stop trying.

The Brighter Side of Failure

Failure, when properly handled, can be a powerful experience for personal growth. It can pave the way to success. The following points are worth considering:

Never say 'No'. An attitude that says, "failure is an opportunity to begin more intelligently." In the face of failure giving up is not the answer.

Focus on the present and not the past. Being obsessed about yesterday's failure and punishing oneself for losses results in losing sight of other possibilities.

- *Rabbi Harold Kushner in his best-selling book When Bad Things Happen to Good People narrates the story of Martin Gray. Martin lost his family in a forest fire. Instead of demanding an inquiry into what caused the fire he chose to put his resources into a movement to protect nature from forest fire.*

Being challenged by failure. Being challenged by a failure can result in exemplary performance. One example is Roger Banister, who challenged by his failure to get a gold medal in Olympics, worked hard to break the Olympic record of a mile in 4 minutes.

Drop the "Failure" word. Big performers drop failure from their vocabulary. They refer to it as error of judgment or shortcoming or consider it as a starting point for course correction.

Learn from failure. Failure is like darkness but what one learns in the darkness is forever. Failure can provide a rich learning experience.

Failure is an important and necessary part of the success process.

When you start your journey to success, there will be setbacks and disappointments in the pursuit of any worthwhile goal. Most people do not understand a simple truth: it is almost impossible to succeed at anything significant the very first time. Failure is a vital and necessary part of the achievement process. No one learns to walk, ride a bicycle, or drive a car on the first attempt. The fear of failure is a major reason most people do not set meaningful, challenging goals at the first place. They do not have the self-image to accept and live with the possibility of failure and hence stop trying.

- But you are never defeated until you accept defeat as a reality, and decide to stop trying.
- Your attitude when you lose determines how long it will take you to win.

Behind Great Success There May Lie a Big Failure

- In 1913, Lee Dc Forest, inventor of the triode tube, was charged by the district attorney for using fraudulent means to mislead the public into buying stocks of his company by claiming that he could transmit the human voice across the Atlantic. He was publicly humiliated. Can you imagine where we would be without this invention?
- Walt Disney faced many failures when he started Disneyland. On the first day of its inauguration it was a big mess. The cement was still not settled causing constant difficulties in walking. The games did not work satisfactorily The press criticized him a lot. But he was still not disappointed and kept improving.

When a mistake is not a mistake

When you make a new mistake, it is not a mistake-it is actually a valuable lesson. But when you keep repeating the same mistake over and over again, it is a BIG mistake.

A mistake is something that brings misery to you in the long run, so why would someone knowingly commit a mistake? A "mistake" simply means you have "missed taking" a lesson that has come your way. Do not lament over your mistake. Just take the lesson from it. Do not justify yourself. Instead, feel the prick of the mistake. That prick enables you to take stock of the mistake.

When you point out a mistake to someone, do you see him as separate from yourself, or do you make him feel a part of you? Do your words make him more stressed or do they create more awareness in that person? Often you do not point out a mistake when it is required. This is also a mistake. Pointing out a mistake without consideration of time and place is also a mistake.

The fool keeps making the same mistakes again and again and never learns from them. Wise is the one who learns from his own mistakes. Wisest is the one who learns from other's mistakes.

Power of perseverance

Failing does not mean we have failed. Do we quit when we meet with an upset? Or bounce back with new vigor and improvement? Persistence is a commitment to finish what you started. When we are exhausted, quitting seems better. But winners continue unflagging in their quest. Excellence is not luck; it is the result of a lot of hard work and practice. Hard work and practice make a person better at whatever he is doing.

Creating joy in work and pride in action

Rajan completed his MBA from a state university and faced great difficulties in searching his first job. He felt ignored when most of the interviewers started advising him that it would have been better if he had done his MBA from any of the top class Business School or IIM. Rajan who was a farmer's son stayed in the village till his college days where there was no access to newspaper. As a result of which he was ignorant about the specified B-school at the time of MBA entrance test. Once got admission in MBA, he borrowed an education loan, as his peasant family was unable to afford the university fee. So he worked hard to get good scores aspiring for a good placement. But the real challenge started when he faced interviews for various jobs. Initially he had to face many rejections because he did his MBA from a state university, his lack of fluency in English and a rural upbringing also created hurdles for the sales job. One day Rajan saw an advertisement of a small anodizing company at Mayapuri, Delhi which supplied anodized name plates to major TV manufacturers. The eligibility criteria for the job seekers were B.Sc. graduates with 2 years experience in Sales. Rajan being a B.Sc. graduate with additional degree of MBA approached the company through a walk in interview. Rajan appealed to Mr. Khanna, the company owner that he may be given an opportunity based on his B.Sc. degree alone keeping aside his MBA degree, as the company was not looking for MBAs. Mr. Khanna was delighted to find an enthusiastic and a passionate young boy who was so eager to learn and contribute unlike many other MBAs who spoke of their entitlement as an MBA. Mr. Khanna offered him a salary of ₹ 400 per month and Rajan happily accepted it to begin his career with all zeal and expressed his gratitude to him. Although his MBA batch mates who had good schooling and were fluent in English had started their career at 3-4 times higher salary than him and few of them used to mock Rajan for bringing a shame to the batch by accepting such a low salary job and bringing down the prestige of his MBA fraternity.

Usually many MBA candidates were reluctant to do this type of job which is against their prestige. Rajan's job involved carrying 15-20 kilograms of anodized name plates/panels as a pillion rider on the motor cycle of his senior named Ravinder and supplying it to various TV manufacturers. Apart from it, the other responsibilities included, getting the quality and quantity checked by the store assistants at customer end, asking for payment and collection of cheques from accounts. It was a kind of dispatch boy cum loader job. This for a moment made Rajan also think about the 4 'Ps' read by him in Phillip Kotler's book on Marketing or the knowledge and case studies in the book written by Keith Davis on 'Human Behavior at Work' as these were hardly of any use to him in this particular job. So days went by and Rajan continued with his work to carry the finished goods material of 15-20 Kg by DTC buses.

On one such occasion, his old schoolmate Vijay, who was a conductor in DTC saw Rajan in a sweating condition carrying heavy load in both hands. He started taunting him for not following his advice of becoming conductor. Vijay also boasted his government job that was getting him double of Rajan's salary mentioning that Rajan education has gone in vain. Rajan was acquainted with the fact that even today he is a laughing stock in his village community by persons like Vijay. While traveling in bus and hearing such sarcastic remarks, Rajan felt demoralized but soon got determined to take up the challenge and prove his worth. He reached the Taxla TV factory at Okhla in Delhi to deliver the goods and collect cheques. His determination to overcome all odds and gain success became stronger when he met Mr. Raja Singh, the Promoter cum Owner of Taxla TV. Raja Singh's story was very inspiring as he had started as a vegetable vendor in Jangpura Delhi, was although an illiterate but a very successful person. Raja Singh took few minutes to complete his signature on the cheque stating proudly that he has learnt writing recently and not so proficient yet. Watching him to put signature on the cheque which took 5 minutes and listening to him was a great motivation to Rajan which fueled his determination to excel. After listening to Rajan's background, Raja Singh advised him with pearls of wisdom **'Either do the things you love to do or simply start loving what you are doing'.**

There was a sudden flow of thrill and new zeal in Rajan. Now he found a new joy in this simple act of payment collection which most of MBAs would found so boring. Now going to Daryaganj, Sadar Bazar or Anand Parvat in Delhi to carry the dispatch material had a different meaning for Rajan as he had started interacting and learning from different kinds of people. He learnt great lessons of perseverance in the simple act of payment collection and later on developed a fine art of enrolling others in ideas which became his unique skill as well. To grab a higher opportunity Rajan left this company. While leaving this company Mr. Khanna praised him for his efficiency that helped the company in timely collection of payment which really mattered a lot for such a sized company and offered his blessings. Rajan learnt many lessons of life from this job, like power of perseverance, seeking and creating a joy in work and more importantly the art of enrolling others. Today Rajan says that if he might had joined a bigger company or even MNC, he possibly would have missed these great lessons of career and life which he learnt from this small job of Rs. 400 per month. This 'JOY in WORK' helped Rajan to accelerate remarkably his career growth as he became General Manager in a large MNC within next 12 years and Vice President in a World Class Company in his 30s. Later on he led a prestigious professional association as its President and had addressed many of World Conferences in different countries as High Profile Speaker. While his earnings might have gone up many thousands times, it hardly matter that his batch mates used to ridicule him about starting his career at such a meager salary of Rs. 400 per month. Later on his same MBA colleagues elected him as the President of their MBA Alumni Association.

Now let us ponder upon some thoughts which truly reflect the above case.

- Success is not a one day lucky break but continuous effort towards your goal and development of your capabilities.
- You can always create a joy and challenge in what you are doing, discover that and you will have different meaning to your job.
- It does not matter from where you start from. What matters

is your own contributions and achievements. Life is not a one-day journey.

- Every work offers an opportunity to learn. It is you who have to be acquisitive enough to find that joy.
- If you missed one opportunity due to your ignorance or not being competent at that time or any other reasons, don't cry but keep your eyes open for future possibilities.
- Nothing comes by entitlement or merely by qualifications. You have to earn it by your effort, innovations and contribution.
- Success is not a comparison or defeating others but excelling in your deeds.

Story of a Man, who had a Dream and Perseverance. Honda

While he was still in school, Mr. Honda took everything he owned and invested it in a little workshop where he began to develop his concept of a piston ring. That was in 1938. He wanted to sell his work to Toyota Corporation, so he labored day and night, up to his elbows in grease, sleeping in the machine shop, always believing he could produce the result. He even pawned his wife's jewelry to stay in business. But when he finally completed the piston rings and presented them to Toyota, he was told they didn't meet Toyota's standards. He was sent back to school for two years, where he heard the derisive laughter of his instructors and fellow students as they talked about how absurd his designs were. Still he persevered and did not give up his dream.

Instead of focusing on the pain of the experience, he decided to continue his focus on goal. Finally, after two more years, Toyota gave Mr. Honda the contracts he'd dreamed of. His passion and belief paid off because he had known what he wanted, taken action, noticed what was working, and kept changing his approach until he got what he wanted. Then a new problem arose and there was a bigger challenge for him.

Japan was gearing up for war, and the government refused to give an entrepreneur the concrete that was necessary to build his factory. Did he quit there? No. Did he focus on how unfair this was? Did it mean to him that his dream had died? Absolutely not. Again, he decided to utilize the experience, and developed another strategy. He and his team invented a process for creating their own concrete and then built their factory. During the war, it was bombed twice, destroying major portions of the manufacturing facility. Honda's response? He immediately rallied his team and they picked up the extra gasoline cans that the U.S. fighters had discarded. He called them "gifts from President Truman" because they provided him with the raw materials he needed for his manufacturing process-materials that were unavailable at that time in Japan. Finally after suffering all of this, an earthquake levelled his factory. Honda decided to sell his piston operation to Toyota. His creative mind and the desire to succeed could find a new solution.

Honda made strong decisions to succeed. He had a passion for and belief in what he was doing. He had a great strategy. He took massive action. He kept changing his approach, but still he'd not produced the results that he was committed to. Yet he decided to persevere with his dream. A tremendous gasoline shortage hit Japan after the war, and Honda couldn't even drive his car to get food for his family. Finally, in desperation, he attached a small motor to his bicycle. The next thing, he knew, his neighbors were asking if he could make one of his "motorized bikes" for them. One after another, they jumped on the bandwagon until he ran out of motors. He decided to build a plant that would manufacture motors for his new invention, but he didn't have the capital needed for his new venture.

Then he made the decision to find a way no matter what! His solution was to appeal to the 18,000 bicycle shop owners in Japan by writing them each a personal letter. He told them how they could play a role in revitalizing Japan through the mobility that his invention could provide, and convinced 5,000 of them to advance the capital he needed. Still, his motorbike sold to only the most hard-core bicycle fans because it was too big and bulky So, he made one final adjustment, and created a much lighter, scaled-down version of his motorbike. He christened it "The Super Cub," and it became an overnight success, earning him the Emperor's award. Later, he began to export his motorbikes to Europe and the United States, following up in the seventies with the cars that have become so popular in the world.

Honda Corporation today employs over 100,000 people the world over and is considered one of the biggest car-making empires. It succeeded because one man understood the power of a truly committed decision that is acted upon, no matter what the conditions, on a continuous basis continuing his journey despite all odds.

Don't quit

When things go wrong
As they sometimes will,
When the road you're trodding
Seems all uphill;
When the funds are low
And the debts are high;
And you want to smile;
But you have to sigh;
When care is pressing you
Down a bit...
Rest if you must,
But you don't quit
Success is failure turned inside out, The silver tint
Of the clouds of doubt
And you never can tell
How close you are,
It may be near when it seems afar, so stick to the fight
When you're hardest hit...
It's when things go wrong,
That you must not quit.

Keep learning

Achievers keep learning, formally and informally, at work and in their personal activities, throughout their life. Learning helps achievers to choose wisely and courageously. In this information age today we need both knowledge and wisdom.

According to Chris Argyris of the Harvard Graduate School of business and education.

- Any company that aspires to succeed in the tougher business environment must first resolve a basic dilemma: success in the market place increasingly depends on learning, yet most people don't know how to learn. What's more, those members of the organization that many assume to be the best at learning are in fact, not very good at it. I am talking about the well-educated, high-powered, high-commitment professionals who occupy key leadership positions in modern corporations.

Story on give & take

Saurav and Gaurav were colleagues in office and knew each other since their childhood. After a hectic day at work they decided to stroll near the pool. While walking Saurav slipped and fell into the pool. Knowing that Saurav did not know how to swim, Gaurav immediately held out his hand and said, "Give me your hand". Saurav kept bobbing up and down in the pool, swallowing huge amounts of water but not heeding him. Gaurav tried again but with the same result. Gaurav paused to think for a little while knowing about Saurav's nature and realized his mistake. Gaurav then rephrased his sentence and said, "take my hand". Saurav only knew the language of taking rather than giving and he immediately grabbed his hand and was saved.

This story symbolizes what some of us do in our lives. If someone develops a habit of constant "taking" and not giving then he may not get the desired support that is needed as no one has succeeded without support of others. Taking support from others is an art we need to learn and giving to others is the beginning of developing this virtue.

If you want support from others, start giving first

Give to others what they need if you want their cooperation

A wise man once invited two warring groups to a feast. One group, made up of loving, giving, cooperative people, was seated at one table. The second group, an unloving, ungiving, un-cooperative bunch, was seated at another table. The meal was about to begin. The tables were laden with sumptuous food. The host announced:

"Have a good meal, but with only one condition: Eat all you wish, but without bending your elbows". The second group felt insulted by an orthodox instruction and staged a walkout even before the food was served.

The first group, the cooperative ones, struck upon a solution very easily: Without bending one elbow in the entire group, they stretched their arms across the table and fed each other!

Winners and Losers

- When a winner makes a mistake, he says, "I wasn't wrong".
- When a loser makes a mistake, he says, "It wasn't my fault".

- Winners see the gain.
- Losers see the pain.
- Winners see possibilities.
- Losers see problems.
- Winners believe in win-win.
- Losers believe that for them to win, someone has to lose.
- Winners see the potential.
- Losers see the past.
- Winners use hard arguments but soft words.
- Losers use soft arguments but hard words.

Four Steps to Success

Dreaming with belief is the 1st stage of success, effective and joyful action becomes the 2nd followed by feedback and improvisation.

Successful people adopt four steps

1. They start with a target or a goal (you can never hit one if you don't have one).
2. They take effective action (knowing is not enough).
3. They have the ability to read others and anticipate situations to know what response they are getting (feedback).
4. They keep adopting, keep adjusting, and keep changing their behavior until they find what works (continuous improvements).

Conclusion

Success is not a one-day affair, nor is being born with a silver spoon. It is a process and a journey, which requires a positive mental attitude, ability to persevere despite setbacks, continuous learning and improvements of our steps. It can be learnt and all great achievers had mastered it. You too can do it. Let us set our goals on the path to success and proceed towards chapter two.

Chapter
2
Deciding
and
Setting Your
Goals

- When the goal is clear our efforts become stronger
- The purpose of life came to them by the decisions they took
- Our decisions and purpose decide our life
- Difference between dreams and goals
- Art of setting goals
- Reason and art of writing your goals
- Using pleasure or pain motivation for success
- Making a change in your life
- The story of Helen Keller
- Power to beliefs
- Creative visualization
- Conclusion

A journey of thousand miles begins with the first step.

- Confucius

I am not discouraged because every wrong attempt discarded is another step forward.

- Thomas Edison

Imagination is more important than knowledge.

- Einstein

When we don't know our destination any road will take us there. Knowing the destination is very important. We never take a plane or train without knowing its destination. Yet many people go through life without setting their goal.

When the Goal is Clear our Efforts become Stronger

Florence Chadwick was on her way to becoming the first woman to swim *Catalina Channel* after conquering the *English Channel*. It was July 1952 when she was fighting dense fog, chilling cold and even sharks on her way. When she looked through her goggles she could not see the shore and gave up her quest. She was disappointed to find later on, that she was just half a mile away from the coast when she gave up. She gave up as she could not see her goal. She said in an interview, "If only had I seen the land I could have made it."

Later on Florence went back in Sept 1952 and crossed Catalina Channel despite bad weather. This time the goal was clear and efforts were stronger. She broke the men's record as well in her time period.

The Purpose of Life Came to them by the Decisions they Took

- Gandhi decided one day that enough is enough when he was thrown out from a train in South Africa for traveling in first class strictly allowed for whites only, and this decision changed the course of events in India and gave a momentum called 'Non Violence', to the world.
- Naveen Jindal who had returned from USA after MBA from University of Texas and was visiting his company's plant at Raigarh got shocked when he was asked by Govt. officials to explain why he has hoisted national flag on the administration block of his company Jindal Steel & Power Ltd. As a true patriot he had always cherished hoisting Indian Flag and now back in his own home country, he has been debarred to do so. He decided and got determined to challenge it and fight for the cause as to why the Indian Flag cannot be hoisted on buildings other than government as a fundamental right of every citizen. It took many years to fight in court for this genuine right of every Indian citizen to proudly hoist Indian Flag. He rightly demonstrated, 'a person with courage

becomes majority and a person with rightful goal is never alone'. Naveen Jindal apart from being a very successful Business Icon is now also known for his many path breaking initiatives related to environment, sustainable development, livelihood of masses, promotion of sports, population control, skill development and education etc. His pride for Indian Flag has now crossed national boundaries. He is creating many global benchmarks for his company by spreading operations across the world and bringing glory to his country. University of Texas, USA has recently named its school of Management as Naveen Jindal School of Management as respect to its alumnus. BT-INSEAD-HBR study has recently rated him as Best Performing CEO in India.

- A woman named Rosa Parks, one day boarded a bus in Montgomery, USA and refused vacate seat to a white person as she was legally required to do. This act of civil disobedience sparked a fire storm of controversy and became a symbol for future generations to follow. It was the beginning of the Civil Rights movement, a new awakening. Was Rosa Parks thinking of the future when she refused to vacate her seat in that bus? It was her decision to hold herself to a higher standard that compelled her to act. What a wide spread effect one woman's decision has had in USA!
- Consider the example of Ed Roberts. He was confined to a wheel chair. Ed has been paralyzed from tbe neck down since he was fourteen years old. He uses a breathing device and spends every night in an iron lung. Having fought a battle against polio, several times almost losing his life, he certainly could have decided to focus on his own pain, but instead chose to make a difference by helping other handicapped and underprivileged. Ed educated the public and initiated everything from wheelchair access ramps and special parking spaces. He became the first quadriplegic to graduate from the University of California, Berkeley, and later on held the position of Director of the California State Department of Rehabilitations.

Once you say you are going to settle for a second that is what happens to you in life.

Our Decisions and Purpose Decide Our Life

It's the decision made by us and the goals set in our life, not the conditions of our lives that determine our success and quality of life.

If you don't set a purpose, you'll find it easy to slip into a quality of life that's far below what you deserve. Whatever comes your way, you should be committed to that purpose and decision.

Unfortunately, most people never do this because they're too busy making excuses. The reason they haven't achieved their goals is because of the way their parents treated them, lack of opportunities, the right environment they missed the education they missed, they're too old, or too young. All of these excuses are nothing but belief systems created by them.

Taking your own decisions and setting a purpose gives you the power to get rid of any excuse to change any part of your life in an instant. If you often ask people who complain about their jobs, "Why did you go to work today?" Their answer usually is, "Because I have to" then 'have to do' becomes a burden. Choosing a decision makes it a 'want to do' activity and creates an element of joy in it.

If you really decide to do something nothing is impossible. So, if you don't like the current relationship you're in, make the decision now to change it. If you don't like your current job, change it.

It does not matter from where you begin but your decision about where you want to go matters the most.

Making a decision means committing yourself to achieve a result. Decision-making is a skill and like any other skill, it gets improved with practice. The more often you make decisions, the more responsible you become.

Important decisions that control your life should be focus upon, what things mean to you, and what has to be done to accomplish your desire.

Many of us don't make the majority of our decisions consciously, especially the crucial ones, in doing so we pay a major price.

- In fact, most people live like a river. Many people jump into the river of life without realizing its shore. So, in a short period of time, they get caught up in the present: current events, current fears, current challenges current jobs. Even in the river, they don't consciously decide where they want to go, or which is the right direction for them. They merely "go with the flow". They are directed by the environment rather than by their own values.

- As a result, they always feel out of control. They remain in this unconscious state until the sound of the raging water awakens them, and they discover that they're too deep inside the water in a boat with no oars. It is a crisis. At this point, they say, "Oh, God!" But by then it's too late. They're going to take a fall. Sometimes it's a financial fall, sometimes a fall of career or relationships. It's likely that the challenges confronting you in your life currently could have been avoided by some better decisions upstream.

Today's problems are our yesterday's compromises. Better planning could have avoided them.

- If we're caught up in the momentum of the raging river, how do we turn things around? Either we make a decision to put both oars in the water and start paddling like crazy in a new direction, or decide to plan ahead.
- In a similar way, set a goal for yourself where you really want to go, make a plan so that you can make quality decisions as and when needed.

We shouldn't allow our past to control our present and future.

One should not fear of wrong decision, as without doubt you will make many wrong decisions in your life. The only thing is to learn from them to make better decisions in the future. Remember: Success truly is the result of good judgment. Good judgment is the result of experience, and experience is often the result of bad judgment! We must learn from our mistakes.

If you're willing to learn from your experience, then even those times which you might think were difficult become great because they provide valuable insight that you will use to make better decisions in the future. Successful persons will tell you that the reason they're more successful is that they've made more poor decisions than you have.

Remember there is no failure in life, it is just a feedback. There's nothing you can't achieve if you follow the rule:

1. You clearly decide what to achieve and trust yourself.
2. Your willingness to take a strong and effective action.
3. Keep in mind what is working and what's not.

4. You continue to change your approach until you achieve what you want; using whatever life gives you in this journey.

Focus on long term

Sometimes when you make a decision and take action, in the short-term it may seem that it's not working. All great achievers certainly know this. In order to succeed, you must have a long-term focus. Most of the problems that we have in our personal lives and the situations when we give up our dreams arise from a short-term focus. It's lack of persistence. It's lack of continuous motivation and mental set up and emotional states. Success and failure are not overnight experience.

Conversely, success is the result of making small decisions as: deciding to hold yourself to a higher standard, deciding to contribute, deciding to feed your mind rather than allowing the environment to control you, these small decisions create the life experience called success. No individual or organization that has become successful has done so with short-term focus. You get whatever you expect to get.

- Mediocre thinking leads to mediocre results. Great thinking leads to great results.

  Dreams are the seeds of future

  Use your imagination, your ability to dream; for the highest achievement. Since history began, dreamers have been using their perspiration and aspiration to make their own unique contribution. Some examples are:

- Dhirubhai Ambani came to Mumbai with almost no money but he had a dream. M S Oberoi, even when he was a clerk in a small hotel in Shimla had the dream to own that hotel.
- Leonardo Da Vinci, aged 12 and illegitimate, vowed to become one of the greatest artists the world has ever known and one day to live with kings and princes.
- Napoleon, as a young boy, spent long hours conquering Europe in his mind and dreaming of how he would lead and mange his troops.
- Wright Brothers turned their dreams into airplanes. Henry Ford turned his dream of an affordable car into an assembly line manufacturing unit.

- Leander Paes had the dream of winning the Olympic medal in tennis when his father received an award at Kolkata.
- US President Kennedy during a visit to a school had asked the students what they would like to become and Bill Clinton had answered that he wanted to be a President like him; the rest is history.
- Abraham Lincoln, from a very poor family and despite many failures in his life, had a dream to bring harmony between black and whites in America and he was successful when he became America's First black President in 1860.
- Lara Dutta had a dream to become Miss India when she was just seven and later on she became Miss Universe 2000.

Everything starts as a dream. Stand by your dream. As the song's lyrics, "If you never have a dream, you'll never have a dream come true."

Difference between Dreams and Goals

Dream is something somewhere in the future you want to have or to achieve but is not necessarily measurable. Goals are different from dreams and wishes. Dreams and wishes are merely desires and remain weak unless supported by passion, dedication, and hardwork.

Goal is a specific event somewhere in the future you want to have or achieve and it is very distinctly measurable. Goals are dreams with deadlines and action plans.

Dreams vs.	Goals
I want to be healthy and fit.	I will exercise every morning for 30 minutes.
I want to be a trainer.	I will ensure that within next two years 10,000 individuals will participate and benefit by attending my workshops.
I want to have lots of money.	I will save 10% of my income every month.
I want to travel around the world.	I will visit U.S.A. and Europe by July.

Two Types of Goals

IMMEDIATE GOALS	An immediate goal is one that may be reached tomorrow, next week, next month or within a maximum period of six months.
FUTURISTIC GOALS	A futuristic goal is one which is beyond six months, a year, the next decade or thereafter.

Only a major challenging goal can provide meaning and purpose to your life. It gives you something to aim at, to work toward and to look forward to. Without a goal, you'll wander around like a crazy chicken, without any direction in your efforts. Since, you cannot measure any progress, you cannot feel any sense of accomplishment.

- Let us remember that "People who have no goals are doomed forever to work for people who do".

Seven facts about goals:

1. A person going nowhere might be sure of reaching his destination.
2. It is not enough to make progress; we must make it in the right direction.
3. You must have long term goals to keep you away from being frustrated by short term failures. – **Charles C Noble.**
4. Abraham Lincoln was great not because he once lived in a cabin, but because his goals takes him out of it.
5. To achieve happiness; we should be certain that we are never without an important goal.
6. You measure the size of the accomplishment by the obstacles you had to overcome to reach your goals.
7. An achieved goal is the starting point for future progress.

Importance of goal setting

Great reason for having goals: You gravitate toward what you think the most. If you have some definite goals in mind, your thoughts will help to take you there, as you will tend to be dwelling on your goals. If you have no goals, your thoughts will still take you towards what you think about the most. Your mind will take your dominant thoughts and propel you in that direction, assuming that your dominant thoughts are your goals. An empty mind is a devil's workshop.

Why goals are important?

'Goals are the vehicles by which we can become someone more than what we already are'.

"Life asks every individual for a contribution and it is up to that individual to discover what it should be."

'Goals are what keep us going'.

How often do we hear of someone retiring after forty years and dropping dead within a few short months? Once we lose our momentum, direction, we are in trouble!

Have you noticed that you have generally been happiest when you were in the middle of a project, and not at the end of it? Have you ever found that as soon as you finish a project, you look around for something else?

Let's understand two major points here.

It is human nature to have goals. We can't live without them or at least for very long. Therefore, if you don't have a list of your goals, you need one.

It does not matter how perfect or high your goal is at present, so long as you have one! Some people keep postponing their plans of life. Just because they are not sure whether it would be a perfect one or not, they prefer not to do anything.

- Take Karan who is planning to pursue MBA. He is just not quite sure whether it is good for his career. The trouble is, he has been making up his mind for the last ten years and he is now forty-seven!

If Karan goes back to his studies and finds it is not for him, then that is wonderful. Now, at last he knows. You see, people often say, "What a tragedy it will be if I choose the wrong direction!" What if I choose a goal and it turns out to be the wrong one, and it doesn't make me happy?" Actually, it is wonderful. He has now eliminated an additional possibility and knows more about what will make him happy and what will not.

- Successful people will see a wrong direction as a valuable learning experience while unsuccessful, unhappy people see a wrong direction as a failure.

The gains during the process of achieving may be more than what the outcome initially appears.

In addition to the actual goal itself, we may gain many things as additional bonus. Most important thing is not reaching to the goal but what we learn and how much we grow along the way in this process.

- Karan may say, on receiving his degree, "that he spent 3 years at the university just to get a bit of paper!" What he is failing to acknowledge is that he also met a lot of people, learned a lot about himself and had a lot of experience that he otherwise would not have had. It is not the bit of paper that is important but the journey he took. He has become a wiser person now.

While pursuing your goals, you may develop greater courage and determination, refine your powers of persuasion, learn about personal discipline, develop your stamina, achieve greater self confidence, and meet your life partner and much more. What you get in pursuit of your goal may be of less importance. The real question is, "What will you become?" out of this useful experience.

No goals are achieved without setbacks

- When a tree grows, it sheds leaves from time to time, and each time it grows a few extra to compensate for the losses. The net result is that the tree gets bigger but it does not do so without some loss and some struggle.

Unfortunately, some people think that their own personal progress should defy all the laws of the universe. Therefore Rashmi plan to lose weight, meanwhile not getting certain results, she finds it too hard rather impossible to do so and spent all her life in obesity.

> ***Dreaming with belief is the first stage of success; effective action becomes the second, followed by feedback and improvements.***

Successful people realize that they reach their goals only by continually correcting and redirecting their effort.

People are uncertain for their goals because:

If goals are so important then why many people still don't set their goals. Some reasons:

- Fear of failures/ rejections. If I don't make it, then I will fail. So why to set the goal.
- Lack of ambitions/ desires. It may be due to our upbringing, value systems, past conditioning, pessimistic attitudes or low self-esteem.
- Ignorance or lack of knowledge about goal setting. It is often found that with better knowledge, people start setting of goals and can be trained in this art.

Some people would rather look backward than forward because it is easier to remember where you have been than to figure out where you are going.

No risk, no gain

To achieve any goal, there is always some risk involved. To gain, we must risk. To make a rupee, we must risk losing it, and the people who make the most, risk the most. To have a chance of winning a game of Cards, we face the possibility of losing.

Winners take more risks than losers do. That is why they win so much. Necessarily then, winners lose also and many times more than the losers, but they play so often that their wins add up. We remember the winners for their victories, not failures. We remember Edison for his light bulb that worked, not for the truckload of bulbs that didn't. Gandhi is remembered for the success he got for India and not the long struggle he waged and was not successful every time.

We have a choice. It is the choice between really living, and merely existing. Getting a job is a risk. Crossing the road is a risk. Starting a business, a relationship or a family is a risk. Eating in a restaurant is a risk. Life is a risk. But let us take the advantage of risk.

Art of Setting Goals

While setting goals, take care that the goals must be:

1. Specific, as a vague goal is merely a dream or wish and will not lead us to focus.

2. Measurable, as it helps to monitor our progress.
3. Realistic, as otherwise it cannot be achieved in the appropriate time period and with the available resources. One cannot lose 20 kg of weight just in 2 days in a healthy way.
4. Achievable, as it should be challenging but not out of reach otherwise it may lead to demoralization.
5. Time bound, as the deadline will help you to plan the starting and finishing dates.

The other factors to be considered are that the goals must be challenging enough, worthy, stated positively, written down and personal to execute a plan one must not depend on others (action to be taken by self or along with others and not by wishing that others should do). In the later part of this chapter we will discuss the visualization process for goal setting.

First write all possible goals

Don't just write down one or two goals. Write down 10, or even 100 goals. It is advised to keep a diary in which you have the list of your goals!

Three good reasons to write down many goals:

1. Different goals have different gestation periods.
2. When we reach a goal, it loses its power and importance for us. You experience mild to severe depression once you achieve a goal, unless you've got another goal to achieve.
3. Do not limit yourself to just a few goals as the rule of universe is 'abundance'-there is no shortage.

If you have incredible goals, you'll get incredible results

It's not that people want too much. It's that they want too little. Be careful what you dream about, because you are going to get it! Our mind moves forward once it has something to aim at, but it doesn't cost any more to set great goals. If you have no goals, your first goal is to set goals. Write outstanding goals and you'll make outstanding efforts and create outstanding results.

Enroll others in your goals if their support is needed

If you're a beginner, it's best not to tell the world about your goals. If you do, others will shoot holes in them. In the beginning, it's preferable to share your dreams only with one or two others, who are like-minded and who will totally and unconditionally support you.

Once you achieve more and more of your goals and begin to build up a track record of success and achievements, then you can tell others about them. Sharing of your goals with those whom you will achieve them is enrollment and it is essential. Gandhi could enroll millions of Indians in the goal of making India free. After enrollment others will help you to realize your dreams.

Instead of making noise, let your actions speak. Once you start achieving your goals and people see what you're doing, they'll start calling you outstanding, extraordinary, unusual and different.

Deciding a purpose that is overriding

Goals are great, but by themselves they can be undirected unless linked with a great purpose. Leaves fallen from a tree lie in a scattered way on the ground. But leaves attached to a growing tree have the purpose of keeping that tree alive and healthy.

It's having an overriding purpose that makes the difference. A purpose that gives meaning to our goals. We may have hundreds of goals-some of which we are continually achieving-but we may have only a single purpose that we spend our life working for.

We all need a purpose, and we need to put it down in writing so that we're crystal-clear about it. If you don't have a purpose, your first purpose is to get a purpose.

- I had seen Sharu Rangnekar conducting training when I was just a student and he was in his Fifty's, and I have seen him recently doing it with same thrill and joy training corporate world even when he is in his Eighty's. When I asked him the secret of his passion and energy, he simply said he is just accomplishing his mission. The mission of motivational trainer is to empower, educate and enlighten as many people as possible and that is the fuel that keeps their spark alive. Find out what is your mission or create the one if not yet discovered.

Searching your purpose of life

To find your own purpose, our suggestion is that you go deep into yourself. Practice meditation if you can. Go into the secret compartment of your mind and ask yourself, "If I knew my life purpose, what would it be?"

The "Why" is our purpose? It determines the "What," which is our goal. And our goals determine the "How," which are the actions and strategies we undertake to achieve the results we want.

Once you have your statement of purpose, your life will become more meaningful. It could change your whole attitude.

- When you have a clear purpose, you won't have time for negativity distraction.

Reason and Art of Writing Your Goals

Goals are like magnets. They pull us towards them. They are a commitment to do. They set the subconscious mind to work.

But our subconscious can be devious. If we still harbor hidden fears and the subconscious realizes that its excuses aren't working anymore, it has another trick it can use. It can make us forget our goals. Today you decide that you are going to be a corporate President. But tomorrow, in the day-to-day rush of your life, the goal seems to fade from our consciousness, and the subconscious has a free ride again!

You may forget it.

Therefore, as soon as you set a goal, you need to write it down. Writing down a goal affirms that you have taken action and makes that action permanent. It is a concrete step. It makes it perfectly clear to the subconscious that you're not fooling around, and you really intend to achieve it.

Writing down the goals will not let you forget them

All motivational speakers have one thing in common. They all suggest, instruct and insist that we write down our goals. When you go for shopping, you make a list. You do it so that you don't miss anything. A list keeps you on track and reminds you.

Listing of goals is not the only thing we need to do, but it gives us a method and a structure in achieving what we want out of life. Still, most people spend more time planning birthday parties than for planning their lives. Lists work! They work for shopping and they work for life also.

How written goals work for you

1. ***Written goals develop belief:*** When you know precisely what you want and how you plan to get it, you develop belief in yourself.
2. ***Written goals save time***: They eliminate distractions and help you become occupied with the most important activities.
3. ***Written goals help you concentrate***: You begin to focus your mind on those things that you want in life. And when you focus your mind on anything, you get it.
4. ***Written goals help you make intelligent decisions***: They enable you to select and arrive at your priority of values.
5. ***Written goals increase self-respect***: When you strive to achieve what you want, you experience an intense feeling of satisfaction.
6. ***Written goals reduce conflict***: Because they can prevent you for taking on the spot decisions all the time and therefore reduce considerably the emotional stress.
7. ***Written goals keep your memory alive***: Because now they cannot 'escape' or 'get lost' in the new situations of your day-to-day life. By becoming your `prisoners' they serve you as repeated reminders and enable you to 'capture' what you want.
8. ***Written goals keep you accountable***: If for any reasons, you go off the track they give you a kick and get you back to the track of success. This is because you have nailed yourself down as you have committed yourself to perform.

Everything we do, we do 'Either to Gain or to avoid a Pain'

Everything we do, we do for a reason. There are two things that motivate people to success. We do the things either due to inspiration-our desire to gain pleasure (want to do) or out of desperation-our need to avoid pain (have to do).

- The little daughter of Dr. Edwin Land, inventor of instant photography and the founder of the Polaroid Corporation wanted to see her picture right away, and asked her father why it took so long to develop pictures. This inspired Land to put the development process right in the film and Polaroid was discovered.

- Founders of Microsoft Corporation Bill Gates and Paul Allen saw an advertisement for a personal computer kit in the magazine – Popular Mechanics and dreamt the future of computing. Bill Gates even called up his mother to tell her he might not call her for the next six months because he was writing a computer program for IBM. That is the way MS DOS was created and Microsoft founded.

Anthony Robbins is a great example of desperation as a motivator.

- A former vacuum cleaner salesman and health program seminar leader, Anthony was currently in a great financial mess, although he had tasted success earlier. He found that everything was slipping from his hand and his life was now reduced to a 400 squire foot apartment in California, washing his dishes in his bathtub. It wasn't the taste of success that pulled him forward, but the desperation caused by his current conditions that drove him to change them, that drove him further to take NLP training and turn his life around and become a great motivator.

Why do some people find it so difficult to motivate themselves? All high achievers say it takes motivation to reach their goals. Motivation isn't some secret formula sold only to star athletes and motivational speakers or great achievers.

At a specific time we may want to be motivated and there are times when we don't want to be motivated. There may be things that might not look great or very attractive but you are highly motivated towards them. There may also be things that we know are good and worthwhile but we hardly are motivated to take any action.

Therefore we need a motivation strategy when we don't feel like doing something, but we want it to be done. We want the results, but it's hard to get excited about the process. For example, when your boss wants a report on his desk by noon and the subject puts you to sleep because it's so dull. You don't feel the desire to do it but you want it to be done, as you know it is important for your job. Similarly we all know that we should exercise regularly, but doing it means sweat, pain and drudgery. We don't always want to be involved in the tough process of doing something but we want what we'll get when it's finished. That's when we need a motivation strategy, and that's what NLP can provide us.

How does motivation work?

Example of Desperate Motivation: You can find your own personal style of motivation in your daily wakeup routine.

- When the alarm buzz in the morning, do you mumble to yourself, "Oh no, let me sleep just a little more," and set the alarm again? When the alarm buzz again, your inner voice may say, "It's time to get up". Your brain might begin to show you picture of yourself rushing to the bathroom, hurrying up to get dressed up and missing your breakfast. But the bed is so warm and cozy, and you think, "No Problem; I can wear what I wore yesterday. Who needs break-fast?" So you again decides to sleep.
- Few minutes later the alarm buzz again. And this time your inner voice says, "You've got to get up or you're going to be late and it will be a great problem". This time, your brain starts showing you pictures of your angry boss, reminding you of his anger last time. The fear of losing good increment does not bother you at this moment as compared to the cozy sleep. You think you can drive a little faster to work. So again you go back to sleep.
- The alarm buzz again, and now the inner voice loudly says, "Hey it's time to get up. You must get up, otherwise!" Your brain now starts showing you the picture of your staff impatiently waiting for you, angry clients threatening to leave. In your mind, your boss is yelling and screaming at you, threatening to fire you from the job. Then as a consequence of it you relate the pain you will have in searching a new job. Your wife is threatening to leave you in front of your in-laws. The humiliation and fear has expanded to a great extent. And when this picture in your mind's eye has become big enough and bright enough and close enough and loud enough, then you say, "OK. OK. I'll get up." You're now finally motivated by conforming scenarios of what you want to avoid, that is, anticipated pain of the negative and undesired situations.

Examples of Inspiration Motivation: Let us now consider another type of motivation.

- Have you ever awakened at a beautiful rafting beach, fully aware of the fact that you are on vacation here? As you opened your eyes, you began to think of the various ways in which you could indulge yourself, the various things you could enjoy. What a great day it is going to be! The vivid scenes of the wonderful and delightful opportunities in your mind pulled you out of the bed like a magnetic attraction. The question was only "what shall I do and enjoy first?" The question of getting up or not at all entered your mind! You are fully enjoying your wake-up process.

- There have probably been times when you woke up in the morning for some important work, thinking about the things you are going to do that day, like making a presentation to the chairman about your achievements. You thought about how doing those things would take you towards what you really want with more enjoyment and feelings of accomplishment, competence, and confidence. You could see the glow on the face of your chairman after your presentation. You saw pictures of yourself doing things and moving towards the rewards for them. You saw how this day would connect to the next; leading toward the things you really wanted in life and making a great career.

Another example is that many executives change their job for the attraction of better challenges and bigger career rewards. On the other hand, there may be many others who postpone the change of job till the company is closed down or they are asked to quit.

Motivation works in both cases. It is the style that is different but both styles of motivation have advantages and disadvantages.

- The inspiration motivation may sometimes be so strong that the person may not even consider the problems that may come on the way. These persons are mostly visionaries.

On the other hand desperation motivation is more directed toward identifying and solving problems. But be aware of three things if you use desperation motivation (to avoid or away-from something).

1. First, when someone moves away from something, they're doing so because they're experiencing discomfort, fear or even pain. These may be strong incentives for them to take action. Farther they get from their problem or source of pain or discomfort, the less serious the action would be. As a result of this, people get away from motivation strategy will lose a lot of their motivation as the "threat" is experienced as farther and farther away - until the problem or threat arises again. Away-from motivation is often cyclical; it will tend to run hot and cold-from high motivation and then back again to normalcy.

2. Secondly, they don't pay much attention to where they're going to end up because people with this kind of motivation are moving away from distress, discomfort, or pain. Out of the frying pan and into the fire is what sometimes happens when too much attention is paid to problems only. They always focus on unnecessary requirement instead of focusing on the thing which they actually want. Or to put it another way, they won't see where they're going, because they keep looking backwards where they've been.
3. Thirdly, these persons need to pay attention to their level of anxiety or stress. People who use desperation motivation often experience a lot of pain and worry before they react; it could affect their health and well-being. In some businesses like the garment exporting companies it is considered a merit to work under pressure to avoid air shipment, yet the same decision could be made with a least stress. High blood pressure, tension and headaches are the results of storing up stress in the mind before finally taking action in case of desperation motivation.

Using Pleasure or Pain Motivation for Success

Like successful people, use pain and pleasure to motivate yourself and achieve your goals. "If you do that, you're in control of your life. If you don't, life controls you as" Anthony Robbins said.

Understanding and utilizing the forces of pain and pleasure will allow you to create lasting changes by going to the root cause of our behavior/nature.

- Let us discuss procrastination. Procrastination happens when you know you should do something, but you still don't do it. Why you are not doing it? The answer is simple: at some level you believe that taking action at this moment would be more painful than just putting it off. Yet, you may have had the experience of putting something off for so long that suddenly you felt the pressure to just do it, to get it done? What happened? You changed what you linked pain and pleasure to. Suddenly, not taking action became more painful than putting it off. This is a common occurrence that many of us face everyday.

If pain is the reason of change in life, then why is it that people can experience pain yet fail to change? They haven't experienced enough pain yet; they haven't hit the desired threshold of emotions.

- You're on your lunch break, and you're walking in a park where a music team is playing or a street show is going on. Will you stop and listen? It depends; first of all, on the meaning you associate to music or such an entertainment. May be the perceived pain of being late for office outweighs the pleasure one would get from listening the familiar melodies. Or may be one believes that enjoying music in the middle of the afternoon is waste of time and the pain of doing something frivolous and inappropriate is greater than the pleasure the music/entertainment could bring. Each day our lives are filled with these kinds of psychic negotiations. We are constantly weighing our own proposed actions and the impact they will have upon our life.

Life's most important lesson is that we learn what creates pain for us and what creates pleasure. This lesson is different for each of us and so are our behavioral responses.

- Many successful industrialists in interviews have revealed that their ultimate pain in life is being second-best at anything-they equate it with failure.
- Mother Teresa was a caring woman. Her care was so grave that she felt the agony of others. She felt so pleased to help the needy. She spent all her life in helping poor people who couldn't afford aid. The ultimate purpose of life was to improve the condition of the impoverished people, who so ever come across her way. She is still alive in the heart of Kolkata's people. She was so powerfully driven by the sensation that helping others out of misery alleviated all her troubles. The tranquillity she felt while helping others was incomparable to any of the ecstasy of her life. This spirit of angel is world famous as a great social reformer.

One decision that has made a tremendous difference in the quality of my life is that at an early age I began to link incredible pleasure to learning. I realized that discovering ideas and strategies that could help me shape human behaviour and emotion could provide virtually everything I wanted in my life. It could get me out of pain and into pleasure. Learning to unlock the secrets behind our actions could help me to connect more deeply with the people I cared about. It offered me a sense of joy and fulfilment. At the same time, I discovered an even more powerful form of pleasure, and that was achieved by sharing what I'd learnt in a passionate way. When I began to see that-what I share helps people to improve lifestyle, I felt ultimate pleasure! And my life's purpose began to evolve as a Motivational Trainer and HRD Expert.

- For a doctor, the decision to pursue a medical career so many years ago might have been motivated by a belief that becoming a physician would make him feel good? Many doctors I've talked to link massive pleasure to helping people: cease pain, cure illness, and saving lives. Often the pride of being a respected member of society was an additional motivator.
- Musicians have dedicated themselves to their art because few things can give them that same level of pleasure.
- A top-level corporate President of an MNC may have learnt to link pleasure by making powerful decisions that have a huge potential to build something unique and to contribute to people's lives in a lasting way.

If we link massive pain to any undesired behavior or emotional pattern, we will avoid indulging in it, at all costs. We may apply this approach to use pain and pleasure, so that in life. We can make vital changes, from the pattern of procastination to even drug abuse.

- Gandhi ji fought through non-violence and fasting which can be painful to others. Fasting for a cause, he survived for many days without food. The physical pain he experienced was considerable, but the pleasure and validation of drawing the world's attention to his cause had offset it.
- Great athletes by following intense physical exercise have converted the discomfort of discipline into the satisfaction of personal growth. This is why their behavior is consistent, and they get the results!

We can learn to condition our minds, bodies, and emotions to link pain or pleasure to whatever we choose. By choosing what we link pain and pleasure to, we can instantly change our behaviour.

- To get away from smoking, all you must do is to link enough pain to smoking and enough pleasure to quitting. You have the ability to do this right now, but if you are still not exercising this capability, it is because you've trained your body to link pleasure to smoking, or you fear that stopping would be too painful. Yet, if you meet anyone who quit smoking, you will find that this behavior changed in one day: the day he truly changed the belief of what smoking meant to him.

Using pain or pleasure to bring a change or set your goal

Write down certain actions that you need to take, which you've been postponed so far. Maybe you need to lose some weight; to stop smoking or it may be doing a new course like MBA in the evening. Now ask yourself the following questions:

- Why haven't I taken action so far?
- In the past, what pain have I linked to take this action?

It will help you understand that what has held you back. It may be that you've associated greater pain to do the action instead of not doing it. If you think you have no pain associated with it, think again. May be the pain is simple: maybe it's the pain of spare time out of your busy schedule.

Now again write down all the pleasure you've associated in the past with this negative pattern.

- For example, if you think you should lose some weight, why have you continued to eat chips, ice cream and drink Coca? You're really doing this because it makes you feel good. It gives you instant pleasure! No one wants to give up these feelings! In order to create a change that will last, you need to find a new way to get the same pleasure without any negative consequences. Identifying the pleasure you've been getting will help you know what your target should be.

In the next step write down what will cost you if you don't change now? What will happen?

1. If you don't stop eating so much sugar and fat?
2. If you don't stop smoking?
3. If you don't start consistently working for your MBA?

Be honest with yourself.

1. What's it going to cost you over the next coming years?
2. What's it going to cost you emotionally?
3. What's it going to cost you in terms of your self-image?
4. What will it cost you in your physical energy level?
5. What will it cost you in your feelings of self-esteem?
6. What will it cost you financially?
7. What will it cost you in your relationships with the people you care most?
8. How does that make you feel?

Don't just say, "I will be fat." That's not enough. Expand your pain fully with emotions. You've got to remember that what drive us are our emotions. So use pain as your friend, one that can drive you to a new level of success and motivation.

Now as a final step write down all the pleasure you'll receive by taking each of these actions right now. Make a huge list that will drive you emotionally, that will really get you excited:

- "I'll gain the feeling of really being in control of my life, of knowing that I'm in charge.
- I'll gain physical vitality and health.
- I'll develop more will power, which I could use in every other aspect of my life.
- My life will be better in all these ways, now and in future.
- By taking this action, I will live my dream."

Visualize all the positive impacts both in the present and future.

Making a Change in Your Life

Clearly define the person you want to be

What kind of person do you want to be? Who exactly do you want to be? What are your personal ideals? Whom do you admire? What are their special traits that you would like to make your own? If you wish to be an extraordinary person, if you wish to be wise, then you should explicitly identify the kind of person you aspire to become. If you have a diary, write down who you're trying to be, so that you can refer to this self definition. Precisely describe the qualities and the nature you want to adopt so that you may preserve it till you want.

How to make a change in your life?

Changing your own expectation.

List down the things you would no longer tolerate in your life and all the things that you aspired to becoming. Mahatma Gandhi, Dr. Abdul Kalam, Abraham Lincoln, Helen Keller, Martin Luther King are all inspiring examples who could raise your standards/expectations.

Find out and change your limiting beliefs

Your beliefs are like unquestioned commands, telling you how things are, what's possible and what's impossible, what you can and cannot do. They shape every action, every thought, and every feeling that you experience. As a result, changing our belief systems is central to making any real and lasting change in our lives. How much do you think Gandhi would have accomplished had he not believed totally in the power of nonviolent opposition towards the British Raj?

Choose a role model to change

Choose a role model, someone who is already getting the result you want and then tap into his/her knowledge. Learn what they're doing, what their core beliefs are, and how they think. And how they have achieved their success. Learn their strategy.

Many people know what to do but few people actually do what they know. Hence knowing is not enough! You must take action to change and achieve. There is an ancient Chinese proverb that says a walk of thousand miles must begin with a single step. And each step brings its own reward.

- First you should be committed to yourself. It seems hard but doing this process they become experienced, that they quickly reject new information that is inconstant with their firmly established beliefs.
- People remain convinced of their inadequacies mainly because they have experienced a good deal of mediocrity and failure in their lives, and it is only natural that they identify more with what they "know" and have experienced than with what they have not. Most people haven't experienced a great deal of success in their lives and if they have, they don't value it and go back to the old pattern.

Risk and change

All change involves an element of risk: risk of the unknown and risk of failure. But change, whether you like it or not, is inevitable. Hence you can choose by default or by design.

The Story of Helen Keller

- In a small town in Alabama, USA, on Jan 27, 1880, Helen Keller was born. When Helen was one-and-a-half years old she was struck with an unknown illness, experiencing a very high fever and severe pain. When she finally recovered, she was deaf and blind. When Helen was seven, her father arranged a tutor, Anne Sullivan to move in with the family. Anne eventually taught Helen how to communicate using finger movements, how to read by Braille, and eventually how to speak. Anne Sullivan was her constant companion throughout her journey of life.

- Despite her great handicaps, what did Helen Keller do with her life? She graduated from Radcliffe College with honors in 1904, alongside some of the most brilliant young women of her age. She became an accomplished public speaker and social critic, passionately dedicated to help disadvantaged groups such as the handicapped, the poor, and the oppressed. She wrote five books, and had as close friends many luminaries of the day including Alexander Graham Bell, Mark Twain, Albert Einstein, and Charlie Chaplin. She met with the kings and queens of Europe, and every U.S. President of her lifetime. At the age of seventy-five, she was the first woman to receive an honorary degree from Harvard University. Three films were also made about her life and achievements.
- She died on 1st June 1968, at the age of eighty-seven. She is an inspiring role model to millions of people across the world, for what she has accomplished in life regardless of what handicaps, real or imagined, may exist. It is a matter of application and dedication, having a cause you believe in and a strong determination. Helen Keller accomplished more than most other people. Essentially, she did not allow her limitations to hold her back and was determined to make a difference in her life.

Power of beliefs

"Faith is power to believe... and power to see".

You are a direct result of all your beliefs. The law of belief says that whatever you first come to accept and believe, it becomes your reality. Many people don't understand that we choose what we believe.

Beliefs send direct signals or commands to your brain that can help you recognise the hidden resources that lie deep within you.

Beliefs are the most powerful force for creating a positive change in your life. For even though you may hold beliefs that are based on insufficient, inaccurate, or invalid information, they have a direct effect on the way you think and the way you perform. The most damaging effect on you and your performance comes from false beliefs that you hold about yourself, for self-limiting beliefs only lead to self-defeating behavior. Self limiting beliefs, whether based on fact or fiction, become true for you to the extent you honestly believe in them. You then end up performing at a level not consistent with your true potential but consistent with your beliefs only.

> *As per your self-fulfilling prophecy, what you expect actually becomes your reality as you have yourself helped your mind to achieve it.*

- Volunteers were asked in one experiment, to solve ten identical puzzles. But the scores they were given were fictitious. Half of the subjects were told that they did well, seven out of ten correct, and the other half that they did poorly, seven out of ten, wrongs. On being given another set of puzzles to work on, the half who had been told they did well on the first batch actually did better on the other hand the half who had been told they did poorly did worse actually.

Faith and beliefs have strength to accomplish wonders

Read this incident which was narrated by a person:

- Many persons of my acquaintance have received various Common-wealth Fellowships, I also started believing that one day I will also receive such Commonwealth Fellowship. In Oct 1997, I received an invitation from IFTDO World Conference for participation. Knowing that my employer would not sponsor me as a company policy, I wrote to the IFTDO Conference Secretariat requesting a discount for a person like me who is keen to invest on his own to participate in IFTDO Conference for learning and promoting the cause of HRD Networking in India. I received a fax that I could participate on complimentary basis if the Commonwealth Secretariat in London approves my case as there is one such fellowship available to developing countries.

  But it needed to be forwarded through concerned Ministry and only 2 days were left for such approval. Although hardly anytime was left for such a long process, but my faith was so strong that this fellowship meant a lot to me and now was the time to avail it. So quickly I made a very urgent appeal for my case and applied through the nodal person in the ministry by enrolling him in my idea that how the IFTDO conference would be helpful to me in convening the upcoming 6th National HRD Conference back in India as I was the convener of the conference being the President of National HRD Network-Delhi. Surprisingly within one day, I received a telephone call from the concerned ministry that he had got my case specially approved from the London Commonwealth Secretariat on urgent basis and I could thus avail the opportunity.

Faith is essential to make an action effective and develop commitment. Our faith and expectations will determine the strength and creativity in our actions, which in turn helps in the end result.

Imagination

Imagination is very important to all learning and all problem-solving.

Hence CV Raman, JC Bose, Edison, Einstein or Bill Gates, all had excellent imagination. Whenever we record information in our memory banks, we use our imagination and our powers of visualization to create a picture. The effectiveness with which we create our picture determines how easily we recall the information. The more we develop our imagination the easier it will be to solve problems and remember facts.

Create an artificial experience of the success you desire

You can creatively imagine an event in your mind in every detail by conscious effort and it automatically becomes a part of your memory profile.

The brain cannot differentiate between an "actual" experience in real life and an "artificial" or simulated experience imagined clearly with precise detail. Either way, you are feeding new data into your memory. It's like running a dummy program and your computer accepts it as real data.

Studies show that there is a direct physiological relationship between simulated or artificial experiences and actual performance.

Your actual experiences during upbringing may not necessarily be the ideal. You might have experienced more failure than success in your life, and now these events might be holding you back. But none of this really matter if you are determined. With this tool of creative visualization, you can add new successes to your experience repertoire to fall back on and help to erase the effects of any negative programming of your past. Artificial experiencing puts you back in control. Hence when you are in charge of your thoughts, you are in control of your behavior. It helps to bridge the considerable gap between your actual potential and current performance.

Impact of mental images

The process of visual perception of an actual occurrence and the process of visualization, the forming of abstract mental pictures in your imagination are both identical events in our brain. Research shows that images produce the same emotional effects as sensory input. Imagining a sad or happy experience evokes the same emotional effects as sensory input during real life experience.

Mental rehearsal-An essential step for success

In any action you carry out, for example, while playing cricket and hitting the ball, your body is responding to programs, in your brain cells which, like a computer program, say "do this and do that". If you have a good program, you will hit very well. If you have an " I can't do it", then you just try to stay on the ground. Obviously as you practice on the ground, you gradually refine your automatic programs such that you hit better and better but your mental program matters a lot. You can ask Sachin Tendulkar.

- However many people believe that the only way to improve a skill say, cricket, is to physically practice it. Not so! Certainly you can re-pattern your brain cells through physically playing the game, but it is not the best way. The fastest way to improve at anything is to combine regular physical and mental practice.

The scientific discoveries prove that when you imagine yourself performing a task, your mental programs are altered the same way as when you actually perform it. Your brain undergoes electro-chemical changes within its cells which produce new behavior. To take a step further, it is fair to assume that we want these patterns on our brain cells to be as near to perfection as possible and the only place that you can perform perfectly is in your mind. We therefore need mental as well as physical practice for best results.

- Professional sports people, shooters, Olympic athletes intuitively visualize, and so it is common to see them in the field with their eyes closed, practicising their sport.

They are busy implanting patterns of brilliant performance' into their subconscious minds, which will ensure an improved game. This is not to negate the value of actual work and practice; it is to stress the fact that visualizing perfect end results will helps us to realize our potential with less effort and much sooner.

CREATIVE VISUALIZATION

This is what Leander Paes, the world famous tennis player from India, has to teach us about visualization.

- Leander had placed a photograph of his father in his study room. The photograph of his father was about receiving an award in hockey which Leander had witnessed himself. Based on this Leander used to visualize the scene in which he himself has been receiving the Olympic award in a large stadium. He imagined several thousand persons watching him on the occasion and applauding his great achievement. He has also imagined the reception he would get on his return at New Delhi airport and the great felicitation offered to him by the sports lovers at his home town Kolkata's best stadium. He even imagined his photograph on the front page of TOI holding the award. And finally he made it all possible and has received the award.

Focusing the energy really work. The technique is called visualization. First we visualize what we want, and then it helps us in putting all efforts in actually achieving it.

Our belief determines our action, and our action determines our results. Better feedback from the results generally improves our attitude and furnish new results. But the belief is the first step of all this.

Most of the people have succeeded in a goal by first visualizing their success.

- One of the best examples of visualization is Walt Disney Disney envisioned the movies he created before they were filmed. In fact, he was one of the developers of "storyboarding," the art of creating a complete story line on art boards before even beginning a movie. Walt "saw" before he started. He "saw" Disneyland in Anaheim was completed even before the land for it had been purchased. He "saw" Epcot Center in Florida,

Disneyland in Paris and Disneyland in Japan, and yet they weren't built years after he died. Walt visualized completely. He understood the power of visualization very clearly.

The process and steps of visualization

Creative visualization is the process of seeing the future outcome in your mind. It enables us to convert failure into success, sickness into health, fatness into slimness, losers into winners and much more. This process is not only painless but joyful also. You can use it to open up your life to widening horizons, to purposes the possibilities that will enable you to serve yourself and your colleagues in many beneficial ways. It even works to help the CEO to uphold his company at the peak of success.

We may be using visualization in the form of bad mental habits as well, like worrying, for example. When we're not focused on some specific task or chain of thoughts, we tend to fall into a state of nonproductive and negative thoughts.

Our mind can only hold one dominant thought at a time. Think optimistically; creatively, imaginatively and constructively.

If you want to replace any bad habit like worry, you need to replace it with a good habit like visualizing yourself as calm, cool, poised and centered, in every situation. Since you own your imagination, you can discipline it positively and correctly for your own betterment. Any good visualization requires the following steps.

Step 1: Reaching the alpha stage with relaxed awareness

Sit in a comfortable position, perhaps sitting on your favorite chair. The best position, if you can master it, is the Indian lotus position, cross-legged on the floor with the palms of your hands upward, your ankles on your thighs. This posture, once mastered and made comfortable, affords the body the best circulation and most concentrated use of the mind. If it's too difficult for you, you may sit in a chair or lie on your back as per your choice.

If you choose to recline in your bed, you can do so and once you're finished creatively visualizing you can also sleep if you desire. When you're positioned comfortably, take a deep breath that relax you totally and absolutely. Inhale through your nose (take in this breath slowly which concentrating on the experience of inhalation itself).

When you're inhaling, notice the life-force energy of the air you're breathing. It will energize you once your recognize it. Fill your lungs, and hold it for thirty second, silently affirming to yourself, "I am relaxed". Then exhale through your mouth. Then take another breath and with each inhalation, take the breath deep into your body. Most people breathe in a very shallow way. Really fill your lungs with air.

Feel your breath till every atom of your being and then slowly let it out. Slowly you will be in a calm state fully relaxed. You can also use any of your own method for such relaxation.

Step 2: Creating a stage for your imagination

Now, imagine yourself on the stage of a theater in a favorable photograph of yours that you can glance at just before you close your eyes. Your self imagination is center stage while you sit watching.

Act now on this stage by creating whatever you want. Perhaps you'd like to have a new car or would like to make a great presentation to a large audience at Taj Palace. Allow your inner eyes to imagine a car on stage. See the colors, run your hand over the polished surface. You see your self on stage sitting in a new car and smell that "*new car's odor*". You turn on the engine and the stereo, feel the steering wheel, and you go away as you press the accelerator of your new car. You can do it similarly with your dream of making great presentation at Taj Palace. Use all your preferred senses to see what you want to see, feel what you want to feel and hear what you want to hear.

After gaining expertise with this stage technique, you can graduate to picturing yourself in the movies or on video! Now the limitations of a stage setting disappear. You can use your imagination and be out driving that car and through green fields and a highway. In case of a presentation hear the loud applause of your audience has given to you after such an inspiring speech.

One variation can be to imagine walking down to a stage or into a movie and becoming one with the self you were previously observing. Psychologists call this "associated" visualizing, which is more powerful than "disassociated" observing. Once again make sure you include sounds, feelings, sensations and smells. Include all of your five senses to the extent possible.

Step 3: Using and changing the past experience to create a future outcome

After you have advanced to the point where you can visualize the future you desire, you can move on to the next stage, which allows you to call on past experiences to help you actualize that future. Your mind is like a videotape library containing a complete record of all your experiences. This fact kept Captain Gerald Coffee alive in a POW concentration camp in Vietnam for seven years. Captain Coffee began by visualizing repeatedly what it would be like when he was free again.

He then recalled old "videotape" images from his past, when he was free. Finally he superimposed one on the other. The resulting visualization, which he did day and night, was so total that he was able to stay alive and sane until he was finally got freed.

We can use our minds to play back experiences and impressions that we've recorded since our childhood. We can then use these recordings to embellish, solidify and give power to the goal we're visualizing. The mind acts like a gigantic filter. It goes back through our past experiences and brings to the surface memories that might be useful in the future in achieving our outcome.

If you don't like the video being played across your mind, you can change it! It's never too late to have a happy childhood, or a happy life experience.

You can reproduce, rewrite, review and re-script what happened in the past and make it the way you want it to be.

Ankit used the visualization techniques described here to focus on his past in order to remove his water phobia and Parul did it to use the elevators by removing the lift phobia she developed five years back when she was stuck in the lift for half an hour. That experience in the subconscious of Ankush was keeping his fear level high and preventing him from becoming a swimmer.

Rejuvensting is an extreme example of rewriting the script. You can find the negative video in your library and give it a new script. More details on this are presented in the NLP techniques/exercises discussed in subsequent chapters.

Step 4: Use your preferred senses

In making or remaking the videotape of the imagination, employ all five senses: taste, touch, smell, vision and hearing. It will increase the impact of the process.

Make sure you use all of your senses precisely. For vision, make your imagined screen as big as the best movie theatre you've ever seen. Make it alive with the 3D technology. Add the equivalent of the best sound system so that you can hear everything perfectly. Allow aromas to suffuse your olfactory senses. Touch it. Feel the texture, the grain, the warmth (or coldness) of it. If it's edible, taste it. Put it to your tongue and imagine its taste. Now combine the senses in one glorious sensual experience of what you're imagining.

For beginners it is suggested to first determine which of your inner senses is more sensitive and then start with that. For example, if touch is the easiest for you to imagine, begin by feeling the sun kissing your face as you hold a photo or some other representation of your goal. For those with touch sensation as the preferred sensation patting on the back can be more effective. Similarly for visual sensation, making a scene or using pictures can be more appropriate. Those with kinesthetic sensation can hear the sound of a new experience. The objective is to use those senses in which you are more comfortable.

Step 5: Work on the process of achieving by starting with the end result

By using your inner vision, work on the result you want to achieve and then expand into all the small steps before and afterward upto the reward stages or further.

- Mary Lou Retton's goal was to win a gold medal at the Olympics. She wanted it dearly and "saw" it completely. She worked out the writing of her visualization with her colleague and friend Dr. Denis Waitley. She is said to have repeated the visualization ten thousand times. She saw herself relaxed. She told herself, "I have the right to be here." She saw herself go through every motion letter-perfectly. "I see myself coming off the high bars with poised elegance. I see myself throw my arms victoriously into the air. I see mom with tears of joy streaming down her face. I see the digital scoreboard reading out a perfect ten. I see the audience giving a contract from Wheaties for three million dollars." The center of her focus was getting over the bars. But she extended her imagination in both directions until she saw the entire process as clearly as if it were actually happening right before her. Actually doing it was simply repeating something she had already done ten thousand times in her mind.

Visualization should be closed with a ritual, if it is to be productive. Use the same closing each time regardless of what you have visualized. The closing should be both relaxing and inspiring.

Conclusion

Many people have a good aim in life, but for some reason they never pull the trigger. Goals are important and vital and your belief in their achievement is the first part of success. But achieving them requires us to take strong and effective action. To make our action stronger and effective, let us now go to chapter 3 to understand the great powers of our sub-conscious and utilizing the dormant powers lying within all of us.

Chapter

3

Subconscious Mind—Your Reservoir of Power

Conscious Mind 10%

Subconscious Mind 90%

- Inner and the outer world
- Law of cause and effect
- Power of thoughts
- Levels of mind
- Self image
- You are the product of your thinking
- Life patterns and dramas
- Principle of concentration and attraction
- The power of words
- Power of affirmations
- Suggestions have both powers
- Left and right brain-the two hemispheres
- Creativity
- Reprogramming your mind for Success

He who knows much about others may be learned.
But he who understands himself is more intelligent.
He who controls others may be powerful.
But he who has mastered himself is mightier still.

- Lao Tze

Solutions begin with self.

- Carl Jung

We know what we are but know not what we may be.

- William Shakespeare

A mind, which is not open, is not mind at all. It is only a machine.

- Dr. Ken Keyes

'Inspiration is what gets a person started, motivation is what keeps him on track and habit is what makes it automatic'.

One cannot change the outer world if one does not change one's inner world. Man is what he believes. All success in life is the product of mind. Our conscious mind has the power to think. It can accept or reject. But the subconscious mind always accepts. It makes no distinction regarding input. The REAL you, me and everyone else live at the level of the subconscious mind. The subconscious mind is extremely powerful. It can transform you into anything you would like to be. Rich and famous, thin, happy or sad, it is the real us. It is very much like a computer and it operates just like a computer. Let us understand in this chapter how the subconscious mind works, how our habits are formed and in what way we can utilize our inner powers.

- If you always do what you have done earlier, you will get what you always got.

INNER AND THE OUTER WORLD

Success is a product of our mind. It is the psychological make-up of the human being that determines how much success each one can have and achieve in life. We can change everything outside but nothing tangible will happen till we change what is going on in the mind.

Even if we have the best education, all the advantages in the world like position and power, but deep inside our mind we may have subconscious fears that can hold us back. If we have fear of failure, fear of rejection, feeling of guilt, resentment, uncontrollable anger or other negative emotions, they will hold us back year after year because they drain our energy both physically and mentally.

What happens in our outer world is essentially a reflection of what is going on in our inner world. Everything in our life moves from the inner to the outer world. In one's life one cannot change the outer world if one does not change the inner world. We find that most people however think that the best way to solve their problem is by changing their external factors, ignoring their intuitions.

Every man and woman who have achieved or accomplished great things in life has indeed changed his or her internal outlook first, i.e. changed what goes on in their thoughts, and as their thinking changes, their world outside also changes to reflect it. We can always judge a person from his outlook, that what is going on in his mind. If the inner world is rich and harmonious, focused and clear, the outer world is prosperous, peaceful and stable.

Your fundamental beliefs about yourself and your world are the principal determinants of your success in life. In fact, it is through your beliefs that you create the very world you live in.

Law of Cause and Effect

Always there is a cause for an effect and an effect for a cause. It is as natural as the law of gravity. It operates equally at the physical as well as at the mental levels of a person. The coconut seed has always produced a coconut tree and coconut trees subsequently produce coconut seeds. For instance, when a person falls ill, there must be a cause for it. The cause of illness may be bacteria or virus. Nothing happens in the universe without a cause. There is a prior cause for every effect in your life. Your thoughts are the cause and your circumstances are the effect. If you want your life to change in the future, you have to change your thinking in the present.

- What we sow is what we reap. First deserve and then desire. If we fail to achieve our objective, remember that we do not deserve it. Something has gone wrong with our efforts, look into it and correct it.

The rewards you receive in life come as a result of your performance, not your potential.

The great teaching from the farmer

The farmer truly knows the law of cause and effect and first sows before he reaps. What can he teach us?

1. We must have the desire to sow. Desire is the starting point.
2. As we sow, so shall we reap! If we sow corn then we will only reap corns, and not tomatoes.
3. We must sow before we reap. We must give before we get. We cannot expect the fireplace to give us heat before we put in the fuel. Some people are constantly looking to get before they give. It does not work this way.
4. When we sow a seed, we do not reap a fruit alone as our harvest is manifold. If we sow a positive seed our harvest will

be manifold in the positive, and if we sow a negative one the harvest shall be manifold in the negative. It is not uncommon to see people going against nature's law.

5. A farmer knows that he cannot sow and reap during the same day. There is always a period of gestation depending on the crop. The wheat takes about 5 months and the sugarcane about 8 months.

We are not only the product of our past but determiner of the future as well. One's present difficulties are the result of one's past unintelligent actions and one's good future is possible by one's intelligent actions.

Thought > feelings > actions > habit > character > behavior

Behavior is a function of character. To change behavior one needs to go to the source which is thought.

Your fundamental beliefs about yourself and your world are the principal determinants of your success in life. In fact, it is through your beliefs that you create the very world you live in.

The practical application of this concept works in this way:

- The beliefs you hold are the direct result of all the thinking you have, or have not, engaged in. Beliefs are latent but powerful forces buried deep in the conscience of your mind.
- Your beliefs, in turn, create your expectations about results and future outcomes. Expectations are active forces at work in your mind.
- Your expectation in turn determines your attitude. Your attitude, once expressed, determines your behavior.

Consider the following cause-and-effect relationship to see how personal beliefs represent the very foundation of your life.

When you change your thinking,
you change your beliefs,
When you change your beliefs,
you change your expectations,
When you change your expectations,
you change your attitude.
When you change your attitude,
you change your behavior.
When you change your behavior,
you change your performance.
When you change your performance,
you change your life!

You cannot change your life by trying to change your life alone. You cannot change your performance by trying to change your performance alone. You cannot change your behavior by trying to change your attitude alone. You cannot change your attitude by trying to change your attitude alone. You cannot change expectations by trying to change your expectations alone. You cannot change your beliefs by trying to change your beliefs alone. But you can change the imagination internal representations you hold in your mind that represent your deep-rooted thinking. This way you can bring about change in all the other aspects of your life that are important to you.

Your beliefs are the conscious decisions you have made in the past about yourself and what you expect or do not expect to accomplish. Just think some of the successful people you have met, the great thinkers, business executives, and community leaders you have admired. What is unique about them? Aren't they all generally very confident, enthusiastic and optimistic? If they have become successful by being this way, then you can as well. You need to look at the world and the circumstances as they looked at them, and in this way allow yourself to excel as they excelled.

Real breakthrough comes when you realize that the belief system you are holding now is limiting or unreliable, since it is based on information that may be inaccurate, insufficient, or irrational or based on the past. Few of us really know that our own inherent talents and abilities have rarely been fully and properly tested and utilized.

We acquire our beliefs from our prior experiences-or more correctly, from our interpretation of these prior experiences. Therefore, most of the beliefs you now hold are more in the nature of a subjective opinion than objective facts. Only by a critical reassessment of longstanding beliefs can you change them and move ahead with your life. This necessarily involves doing some deep introspection.

• Your success therefore lies in your own thoughts.

POWER OF THOUGHTS

Our thoughts have energy and affect us at the physical, as well as at the mental levels.

Examples:

(i) The thought of forgiving someone or of a serene seaside can bring inner peace.

(ii) The thought of eating a mango can water our mouth.

Everything is created twice, first in the mind of the person, and then subsequently physical creation takes place. For any physical creation there must be a corresponding mental creation. Belief is an important ingredient for the actual creation.

We know that as you sow, so shall you reap. The thoughts are seeds, which will produce their own fruits, depending on the type of thought. Our desire, feelings, wants and ideas are all thoughts. Our attitudes, relationships and our plans are nothing but thoughts. We relate to everything and everyone in this world through the mechanism of thought. We are thus a product of our thoughts.

Thus thoughts are forces and they are just as important as our actions. The erroneous thinking is just as powerful as correct thinking. What we are madeup of is what we think. Our thinking influences the world around us.

Think big

- You are as big as you think you can.
- You should always use cheerful and positive words to describe yourself and others.
- Build castles and do not dig graves.
- See what can be possible and not just what is present now.
- It does not matter what you are, the thing which matters is what you plan and achieve.
- Why should you think small?
- Think always that your job/ goal are important and serve a purpose in the link.
- First be committed to yourself.
- How you think determines how you act.
- How you act in turn determines how others react to you.

Levels of Mind

The mind basically operates at two levels:

1. The Conscious Level (Conscious Mind)
2. The Subconscious Level (Subconscious Mind)
3. The Conscious Mind, the logic-bound mind, holding only 7% of our brain capacity, consists of four parts.
   a. Analytical Part-it looks at problems, analyses them and figures a way to solve them.
   b. The Rational Part - this gives us a reason why we behave in any particular fashion, which comes from our past conditioning or experience.
   c. Will Power -this part does not last very long for "the harder you try, the more you fail." Will power loses out to imagination.
   d. Temporary Working Memory -the memory we need just to get us through an average day.

This is the part of our mind which thinks, reasons and which is where our free will lies (choice). The conscious mind can accept or reject any idea or thought that we choose to entertain or not to. The 'thoughts' we choose eventually determine the kind of results that we attain in our life.

The conscious mind has two functions:

1. Sensing and becoming aware through the 5 senses: eyes, ears, nose, tongue and skin.
2. Making choice.

Thus at this conscious level one is free to choose.

The Subconscious Mind, is which has powerful mind intelligence, where 93% of our intellectual capacity lies. It consists of five parts:

1. Lazy—non—judgmental and non—analytical.
2. Emotional—the feeling mind, love, caring, hate, anger, guilt.
3. Habits—bad habits, good habits and utilitarian habits.
4. Permanent Memory—like a video camera, it records everything that has happened from the day we born.
5. Self—preservation/the Protective Mind—protects us against danger, real or imagined.

To understand how the subconscious mind works, you need to understand how a computer operates. A computer can only operate based on the programming that is installed in it. The programming enables it to function in various pre-determined ways. You know that if you change the programming in a computer that you buy at a store, it no longer can operate on installed. It must operate on it must operate on the new programming, information that has been installed in it. Well, this is the way our subconscious mind works. It is a computer.

We program our computer everyday of our lives through our experiences. When we are born, our computers are basically non-programmed; there is a little bit of programming in it, but not much. Every day we add programming to our internal computer. The type of person we are is based on all the programming that has been placed into it and will continue to be placed into it until we die. On the personality front, we are the sum total of our life's experiences.

The subconscious mind is also known as the feeling mind. It is the power center in us. It functions in every cell of our body. Every thought that the conscious mind chooses to accept, the subconscious mind will accept that thought. It has no ability to reject. It expresses itself through feelings and actions. Any thought we consciously choose to impress upon the subconscious mind over and over again becomes fixed there. It will continue to express itself. These fixed ideas are referred to as habits or patterns.

At the conscious level one can reject an idea, but if it is impressed in the subconscious mind, then it has to be expressed. (If one is feeling angry inside or having any resentment, it will get reflected automatically in one's actions, behavior, or facial expression or communication whether verbal or non verbal).

Subconscious thinking takes place without your full knowledge, although you are often aware of how your body is reacting to it. Thus you are a product of your thinking in all you say and do.

Our subconscious mind has two functions:

1. To store past experiences for reference.
2. To program for automatic or impulsive actions.

- If I ask you to imagine cutting a juicy lemon, the chances are that you will almost experience the juice on your fingers and even experience the sour taste in your mouth. Now if I ask you to imagine Lumbamba (a fruit found in Africa), you will not get any feeling in the mind as you may not have experienced it earlier in your life. When you asked your conscious mind to locate the past experience so as to relate with Lumbamba, you got a blank response. This is because the subconscious mind, which is the store house of all past experiences, has no such experience in the store. Since, you may have not tasted Lumbamba.

The subconscious mind behaves like a machine. This is the part where the programming is done, whether positive or negative. By changing the negative programming, one can become more effective and capable.

Conscious thinking is carried out more or less with your full knowledge of the process taking place. You are aware of the act and it often involves your inner voice talking to yourself. On the other hand, subconscious thinking takes place without your full knowledge, although you are often aware of how your body is reacting to it.

SELF IMAGE

We all carry with us a mental picture, or model or blueprint of ourselves. We may not be able to recognize it consciously. However, it is always there with minute details and defining characteristics. It is formed from the belief we hold about ourselves. This is formed from our past experiences, failures, successes or humiliations. The way other people have reacted to us particularly in childhood has a tremendous impact. From all these we construct unconsciously a "Self image". Once we have this picture it becomes "true" as far as we are concerned. We do not even question anymore its validity but proceed to act upon it.

Self-image (patterns) has a servo-mechanism and acts like an autopilot. If we try to go against our goal, our self-image corrects us and brings us back on the original thought path and the person is again on the same track. Unless the self-image inside is properly placed or programmed, no change can become permanent.

There are two important factors:

1. All our actions, feelings, behavior, even our abilities are always consistent with this self-image. In short, we will "act like" the type of person we conceive ourselves to be. Not only that, but we literally cannot act otherwise, in spite of conscious efforts or will power.

   For example, "Failure type person"-will find some way to fail, in spite of his good intentions or will power. Even if there is opportunity of success he will fail to utilize it.

   Similarly, a person who conceives himself a victim of injustice, "meant to suffer" type of person, will invariably find circumstances to justify his belief.

   The self-image initially rejects any radically new view of itself. If a new idea seems consistent with the ideas already present in the system, and particularly with the individual's opinion of him, it is accepted and assimilated easily.

Since your behavior is consistent with your self-image, other people see you according to your own perceptions of yourself. Infact, what you see in yourself is what you get from others. A person's self-image must be realistic as well as appropriate to make him effective in life. You must be proud of it and feel comfortable living and expressing it. It should also allow you to function at your best.

People around you react to you everyday as you act out your self-image. You will be getting either positive or negative feedback in direct proportion to how well you are satisfying the needs of other people. Have you ever noticed that when you are feeling nice about yourself, other people become very nice? Isn't it funny how they change! The world is a reflection of self. When we hate ourselves, we hate everybody else. When we love being that we are, the rest of the world also looks to us wonderful and great.

The self-image is the blueprint which determines exactly how we will behave, who we will mix with, what we try to do and what we will avoid; our every thought and every action stems from the way we see ourselves. Believing this image to be a reality, we proceed to live absolutely within the periphery of this picture created by the self.

Therefore, our self image determines:

- How much we like the world and how much we like living in it.
- Exactly how much we will accomplish in life.

If you see yourself as poor at mathematics, you will mostly have difficulty with figures. Perhaps sparked by some bad early experiences, you would have developed an attitude that says, "No matter what, I can't do math'." Therefore, you don't try. Generally, you will fall further and further behind. Even if you do succeed sometimes, you may say, "It's a fluke." When you don't succeed, you say, "There! That proves what I have been saying all along about my utter inability to deal with math!" Chances are that you are going to prove to everyone that you are a hopeless case; the more you believe it, more deeply embedded that self-image becomes. If your self-image says you are always a failure, then you will succeed in being exactly that.

2. Self image can be changed. Why the efforts towards change in the past failed, because the attention was directed externally. Permanent change is possible only if the self image in the subconscious mind is changed. One cannot think positively about a situation as long as one holds a negative concept of self. The inner self must be changed.

- Self-image is an important and integral part of your personality. It is your own idea of who and what you think you are. It is the personal opinion you hold of yourself in the light of your past successes and failures. Your self-image sets up psychological barriers in your mind that determine what you expect or except to accomplish in your life. When you expand your self-image, you also expand the areas of new possibilities for yourself. A properly defined new self-image can discover the strongest force within you-the creative powers of your subconscious mind.

The world around us might have programmed us to think small, and we think and do the things we are programmed to do. So through new software, we change the computer program in our electronic brain in the form of new mental images.

- In his book *Psycho 91 Cybernetics* Maxwell Maltz describes self-image as our "conception of the sort of person we are". All your actions and emotions are consistent with your self-image, and it is the vehicle to bring about meaningful change in your life. You cannot alter your self-image by wishful thinking or will power alone. You can do it by conscious rational thought using creative imagining techniques.

First and foremost important step towards a vast improvement in our results would be to change the way we think and talk about ourselves. A non-assertive person can begin to become assertive as soon as he changes his ideas about himself.

Let us learn from this example narrated by a friend of mine about self image.

- "I used to get phone calls for voluntary help/counseling which I have been initially enjoying. Later on, it became such a trap that I used to get calls even at late night and although it was not the appropriate time to entertain such requests, but due to my own self image inside - 'a great helping person', I was unable to say a straight NO. And I was not truly enjoying this late hour counseling but was unable to say no fearing what others would think of me. I was getting trapped due to this 'looking good' self-image. After attending a workshop and getting an insight, I decided one day to break my self-image. Initially it was a bit painful what others would think of me? But with a little practice and a strong determination I could transform myself. My philosophy now regarding help is a bit different. Let me continue helping people as it gives me satisfaction, but it has to be at my convenience first. No mcre looking good."

If you see yourself as someone who is always broke, you will remain broke. If you see yourself as financially well off you will be prosperous. We continue to perform within the prescribed range of our self-image.

- Suppose Amit expects to be happy about fifty per cent of the time. Therefore, whenever things are going extra well for Amit, he'll think, "Wait! Things aren't meant to be this good! Something is bound to go wrong any minute." When it does, Amit takes a deep breath and says, "I knew it couldn't last." In reality there are people in the world who remain unhappy all the time, and still there are many others who are happy nearly all the time.

We create our own quality of life, based on our own self-image regarding happiness.

So we decide our own worth and how much happiness to expect.

You are the Product of your Thinking

Your self-image is a very important component of "who do you think you are". It is also the only component over which you can exercise any control. Your feelings are just automatic; they are direct result of the picture you hold of yourself in your mind.

The self-image sets the boundaries of your achievements. It defines what you can and cannot be. The development of an adequate, realistic self-image will help you to develop new capabilities, new talents, and turn failure into success. Another facet of self-image is the consideration of the "ideal-self".

The primary role models in our life have shaped us to a great extent. We were shaped by how our parents, other family members, teachers, relatives and friends behaved and responded to.

If you don't know your destination, where you want to go in life, how can you expect to be there? Do you ever start a car without knowing where you want to go? Of course not. You always have a destination in mind and you always get there. Where you want to go, you need to make a conscious decision. You have to program your subconscious mind in an appropriate way in order to get there.

Aristotle has said, "Men acquire a particular quality by consistently acting in a particular way". Program your mind by acting out the role of the kind of person you want to be, assuming you already have the particular characteristic or ability you desire. You have to visualize it daily and make it a part of your routine.

A useful technique for this is self motivation. It involves repeating positive declarations and assertions to yourself about things that you want to change. This has to be accompanied with a sincere conviction in your imagination and a faith in the process. We will discuss this later on.

The Eagle

Once upon a time, while walking through the forest, a certain farmer found a young eagle. He took it home and put in his barnyard along with chickens. After sometime it start having, whatever chickens eat/feeds on and also behave like them. Once a passer by asked the farmer, that why he let eagle (the king of all birds) to live with chickens in the same barnyard?

"Since I have given it chicken food and trained it to be a chicken, it has never learned to fly", replied the owner. "It behaves as chicken behaves, so it is no longer an eagle." `Still', insisted the villager. "it has the heart of an eagle and surely can be taught to fly".

After a long discussion, the two men agreed to find out whether this was possible. Gently the villager took the eagle in his arms and said, "You belong to the sky and not to the earth. Stretch your wings forth and fly." The eagle, however, got confused; he did not know who he was and seeing the chickens eating their food, he jumped down to join them again.

Undeterred, the villager took the eagle on the following day to the roof of the house, and urged him again saying, "you are an eagle, stretch forth your wings and fly". But the eagle was ignored of his identity and world, thus jumped down once again for the chicken food.

On the third day, the villager rose early and took the eagle out of the barnyard to a high mountain. There, he held eagle (the king of birds) high above him and encouraged him again, saying, "You are an eagle. You belong to the sky as well as to the earth. Stretch forth your wings now and fly" The eagle looked around backwards towards the barnyard and up to the sky. Still he did not fly. Then the villager lifted him straight towards the sun and it happened that the eagle noticed other eagles soaring in the sky. He began to tremble and slowly he stretched his wings. At last with a triumphant cry, he soared away into the heavens.

It may be that the eagle still remembers the chickens with nostalgia; it may even be that he visits them occasionally in the barnyard. But as far as anyone knows, he never returned to lead the life of a chicken again. He was an eagle though he had been kept and tamed as a chicken.

- All changes in our life begin with a change in our self-image.

- To what extent will your potential be utilized depends on your self-image. It sets the boundary of your achievements.

Accept full responsibility for your self-image

Those persons who genuinely like and accept themselves as valuable human beings are also able to broaden their horizons and accept new challenges as a normal process of growth. They can perform at higher levels of effectiveness at everything they attempt and are generally happier as well. People with a positive self-image always manifest their high self-esteem in optimistic and constructive interactions with other people. Their zest for life simply gets reflected to others in a natural way.

Alternately, people with low self-esteem always attempt to compensate for their sense of inadequacy with actions stemming from either superiority or inferiority complex.

Our interpersonal relationships also get affected by our self-esteem and self-image factors. The way you relate to others is directly affected by how you feel about yourself. The measure of your self-esteem is the degree to which you like yourself which in turn determines both the quality and extent of all your relationships with others. Those who do not accept themselves as valuable and worthwhile human beings hold a low opinion of themselves and they always manifest their frustrations and insecurities in their interactions with other people.

Let us consider a case based on the natural cause-and-effect relationship that occurs in this way:

- Event, (which is out of your direct control), leads to
- Perception, (which is within your control), leads to
- Self-talk, (which is within your control), leads to
- Feelings, (which are out of your direct control), lead to
- Behavior, (which is out of your direct control),

Situation: You have not received your promotion once again and somebody junior to you has got it. Although you have more seniority and a better education, a younger person is selected for promotion.

Your perception: 'He is luckier than me'. The appraisal system gives preference to younger people.

Your self-talk: "I am not deserving, considering my age; I am not a productive employee; I am not as good a performer as the one selected for promotion."

Your feelings: Rejection, insecurity, unhappiness, frustration, anger, depression, and resentment.

Your behavior: Loss of zeal, less interest, less enthusiasm, and less effort in your present job, all leading again to a lower performance.

The result: You are out to prove that your own interpretation is correct; as evidenced by your perceptions and self-talk! In the process, you are creating a problem in your mind that does not exist in reality. Note that if you simply changed your perception of the event and your own self-talk, you would totally change your feelings and behavior.

If you only remove the single word "not" from your inner communications, your self-talk becomes: "I deserve; I am a productive employee; my experience is a great asset to the organization, I am as good as the one selected for promotion. I may not have got promotion as it is beyond my control or I still need improvements in working to desired level." In this way you will adopt an optimistic attitude which not only helps your self-image but would also enable you to perform better and these create the conditions for future promotion.

You are what you think

Most of the time you are simply exercising the mental faculty known as recall, by which you replay your past experiences, much like music on a tape, in the form of mental pictures or images that have been previously recorded in your subconscious mind. You revert to previous programming, your internal memory files, if you wish and the result is habitual behavior. Previous programming is your only basis for comparison and you necessarily act in a preconceived way or expect a similar outcome to repeat itself. In such a case, the law of beliefs applies.

All that you accomplish or fail to accomplish in life is a direct result of the images you hold in your mind.

Did you know that you actually think in images and not in words?

An image has a much greater impact on your brain than words, reflecting the fact that the nerves from the eye to the brain are twenty five times larger than the nerves from the ear to the brain. You often remember a person's face but not his or her name, for example. The old saying, "A picture is worth a thousand words," is true.

Consider the word Beach as an example

- Someone may think of a seaside *Beach* where one relaxes after a strenuous swim in the waters. It could be the warmth of the sun on your body or the feel of the soft sand between your toes. Others may imagine an isolated beach stretching off in the distance for several kilometers without a person in sight. If you were knocked unconsciously by a massive tidal wave as a child, for example, your feelings about a beach may well be radically different. It probably is a place you prefer to avoid.

Be aware of what you are telling to your mind?

People have in their lives today exactly what they keep telling their minds they want.

Each of us have the choice to think and act either optimistically or pessimistically, constructively or destructively. Why on earth would people then choose the negative? The point is that no one consciously makes such a choice each time he or she thinks. You simply have allowed yourself to become conditioned to think in what has become a habitual way, and it just repeats itself. Almost all of your thinking as an adult is done habitually at the subconscious mind.

- The chains of habit are generally too small to be felt until they are too strong to be broken.

Habits are a significant influence in your life. They can be the best of servants, and help you reach new heights; equally they can be the worst of enemies to bring you down. Habit is simply the result of thinking in a habitual way. Almost all of your thoughts are echoes of your past perceptions and programming.

Let us now examine how our mental patterns are formed and what impact they have on our habits/performance in life.

Life Patterns and Dramas

Our subconscious mind is responsible for most of the results that we get in our life. When we find the same type of behavior repeating itself in our lives, it is the subconscious part of our mind that is responsible. Many of us have recurring patterns-the same old experience or behavior keeps on cropping up. Do you know somebody who is always late?

In an office Mr. Saurabh an employee used to reach late regularly at 9.15 a.m. instead of the prescribed time of 9.00 a.m. with the plea that the charter bus from his locality starts late. When the office timings has changed to 9.30 a.m. he again got late. When questioned he made the excuse that the next available charter bus from his locality is also 30 minutes later than the first trip. The question is, cannot he take the first charter and be 15 minutes before the time instead of 15 minutes late.

He has not been trying to be late consciously, but in his subconscious he has a program that said, "you have always been late and it is Ok to be late"... and that program is running his life. If he has accidentally got up early and found himself on target to arrive on time, his inner voice would have helped him to sort out the problem without any delay. He simply has a pattern of coming late and unless it is broken through self programming, it will keep on repeating. Of course, situational threat can many times work better in such cases when the person is forced to change himself as we have discussed, pain and pleasure are two different forms of motivation.

Many persons in corporate houses have programmed their mind for late sitting in the office and cannot reach home on time even if the job allows them to do so on certain days. They would simply expand their activities which necessitates their sitting late in office.

Drama patterns

You can always find people who have drama patterns. Their lives are long dramas. You meet them on the way and make the fatal mistake of asking, "How are you?" You find out that the dog has just died, there was a fire in the neighbor's house and a relative has just been diagnosed from a very serious disease that you had never heard of. Whenever their life threatens to go smoothly, or an opportunity comes in their way, a little subconscious voice says, "Hay, this can't be right!" and very soon another drama emerges. They will create problems out of opportunities and never lose any opportunity for a problem!

We will discuss later on what we can do about these patterns, but for the moment, let us identify some more patterns in life.

Accident patterns

Some people have a talent for having accidents. They spend their lives falling off ladders, bicycles, out of trees, getting electric shock and having car accidents.

Sickness patterns

You can also find many persons with a sickness pattern. Some people get cold twice a month. Some people get sick every time a big opportunity comes along. Some people get sick every Monday morning! And they are happy on Friday evening with a saying Thank God it is Friday (or a Saturday in many other cases).

Mess patterns

Some people are great in making a mess. They don't consciously try and do it, but their pattern is so strong! Their desk is a mess, their files are a mess, and their hair are a mess. Everything is a mess. You can come along and straighten every thing out for them and within twenty minutes, their office, their bedroom, their car, their lunchbox, papers and all look like they have been through a hurricane. Everything is again a mess.

Broke patterns

Have you met someone who is always broke-without money? People with a `broke pattern' work on an automatic program. Whenever they get any spare cash, they go looking for somewhere to get rid of it or spend it. If you even double their earnings, they would still be broke! In fact, the reason why most people who win lotteries lose the lot, is that their inner voice is saying, "All this money doesn't feel right. It doesn't belong to me. You'd better do something about this." The credit card has further helped them in spending without capacity and later on asking for money.

Indispensable patterns

If you have the indispensable pattern, you absolutely know that within three minutes of your going on holidays, the office will be hit by an emergency. Whenever we leave, all hell breaks lose. So such a person can never take leave or go for holidays. How can he? The office runs because of him. "How would office run without me"?

- A dog was walking under a bullock cart thinking he is the one who run the show. After some time the dog stopped, thinking the bullock cart will also stop. But it continued.

Job change patterns

- An ex-colleague of mine, who was thinking to change his job, came me recently. He said, "My company is down, our products are inferior, competitors have come in big way, I can't make any progress here, XYZ company is so great" (XYZ is where he wants to apply and surprisingly two years back he found the same attraction in his present company also).

  I asked him, "How long have you been in this job?"

  He said two years.

  I said, "What about the job you had before that?"

  He said, "That one I had for about two years."

  "And the one before that?"

  "Less than two years." "And before that?" "About the same!"

  I said, "Where is the problem-with you or the company?"

  He said, "With me!"

  I said if you are the problem then why do you change companies?

Opposite to this is a pattern of sticking to a company even if the company is on the verge of sickness or is desiring him to quit. Many people have damaged their career because they could not think of a change when it was highly desirable and would think of changing the job only when they are asked to leave.

I always miss out pattern

It manifests in our buying a wrong property, going on vacation either too early or too late, being born not with a silver spoon, and starting schooling in a not so famous school! Always being in the right place at the wrong time! Also, we may have the right talents but the wrong teachers or the right teachers but the wrong talent.

Meant to suffer pattern

There are people who always feel they are born to suffer and are suffering because of their destiny. They keep on collecting grievances like a ticket collector and justify their stand. Even if they get the best of conditions in their professional and personal lives, still they will find fault in something and start suffering. In their opinion they were born to suffer and have to undergo suffering.

Blame other pattern

If anything goes wrong or is not as per their expectations they start blaming others. Their story/tape starts automatically.

- In a company a new manager on joining invites blunder on asking for pen, stationery, table chair, computer and such other items needed as per his entitlement. The concerned dealing person immediately started playing his pre-recorded tape. "You don't know this company. Our store is in mess; our purchase persons can never be trusted. Finance section always feels that they are spending money from their own pocket and always delay the payment of suppliers. The finance section is afraid of audit and vigilance. Our suppliers never keep their word. The transporters are always late in delivery as there is usually some problem on the road. Have you seen the conditions of our roads and that of national highways? The whole country is in big mess. And even see this government. He eventually ends up meaning 'Unless you change this Prime minister and the Govt., how can I give you a pen just now"? His tape started from pen and ended finally with Prime Minister! You start feeling why you triggered him?

Some persons find it easy to rationalize by blaming others so that they can avoid taking responsibility.

Some more patterns or those with different names are the following:

People are nasty;
Life is horrible;

Why is the world doing it to me?

Failure pattern;

Last minute pattern.

Apart from these negative patterns there are, however, some very positive patterns, which you can relate to.

The "I'm always healthy" pattern

Our state of health is determined by the programs we have between our ears which determine who we are and what happens to us. This person will program his habits and routines to remain healthy.

Do you know somebody who is "ALWAYS IN THE RIGHT PLACE AT THE RIGHT TIME?" They go into business just as the boom starts, they sell their house just before the price falls, and buy a house just before the cost goes up. How do they do it? It is something beyond luck also! Being in the right place at the right time is a pattern.

What about the "WHATEVER I DO, I ALWAYS END UP MAKING MONEY" pattern? Some people have it! Or the "WHATEVER I BUY, I ALWAYS GET A GOOD DEAL" pattern? Someone will say he is always lucky.

Other patterns include the "I TRUST PEOPLE AND THEY ALWAYS TREAT ME WELL" program and the "WHATEVER I DO IS ALWAYS FUN AND EASY" pattern.

You may want to retain the good patterns. What about the patterns you don't want? Thus we ask ourselves, "These rotten patterns I have-when will they change? When will they stop?" The answer is "life changes when we change!"

Remember. If you always do what you have been always doing, then you will always get what you always got. So do it differently if you want a different result and do it now.

How are the patterns formed in our life?

Right from birth we begin to form behavioral patterns. Thus, they are persistent and tenacious. Certain incidents affect us deeply specially those related to;

(a) Something may have gone wrong at a young age which we are not able to understand as a child and then try to rectify the situation or fix it as per our limited interpretation.

(b) Incidents of approval sought or denied with a feeling that I am not accepted here or by this group and what should I do to win this recognition/ approval.

(c) Getting a feeling when you consciously start thinking of success and start drawing conclusion that success can be achieved in such manner and thus gradually develop your own winning formulas in life.

Many of our other current characteristics result from early childhood experiences. In early years we are open-minded and empty-headed: we absorb information like a sponge. Since our first relationship is with our parents, their influence on our later lives and our later relationships is huge. Partly consciously and mainly subconsciously, we create patterns in our lives, based on the experience we had with our parents.

The quality of our relationships with our parents also creates its pattern. If, as children, we had experienced guilt or disapproval then we will continue to attract and associate with people who treat us as "bad" people. Similarly, if we experienced love and approval as children, then as adults, we will gravitate towards people who treat us with respect. In short, we attract to what we expect and the world treats us as we believe we deserve to be treated.

We have just got an idea of the pattern formation relating to our childhood. However, realizing that a problem recognized is a problem half solved, it is valuable to be aware of your patterns and have some idea of how they came about.

Reflections of poor self-image in daily behavior

We must work continually on maintaining our positive and healthy self-image. The following behavior traits are some of the examples indicating that there is considerable scope for improvement in our self image.

- Criticism of others
- Jealousy
- Pessimistic inner voice
- Experiencing guilt
- Failure to give compliments
- Non-acceptance of compliments
- Not asserting what we want (frustration of undelivered communication)

- Inability to receive and enjoy affection
- Constant poor health
- Failure to give affection and love

Self-image can certainly be changed. It can sometimes be a painful process in the beginning but would become enjoyable later on when positive results start coming.

Some tips for boosting self-esteem

Always speak well of yourself

If you have nothing good to say about yourself, keep your mouth shut!

Accept compliments

Always say 'thank you' or words to that effect.

Give compliments

One of the easiest ways to feel good about ourselves is to recognize the beauty and worth in others.

Praise yourself

When you do something right, give yourself a pat on the back. Acknowledge your value.

Separate your behavior from yourself

Your behavior is not connected to your self-worth. If you do something silly, like smash into another person's car, it doesn't make you a bad person. You simply made a mistake and learn out of it.

Treat your body well

Exercise and nourish it well. Your body is the only one you have got.

Let people know how you expect to be treated.

In particular, set an example by the way you treat yourself and them. Nobody should accept abuse from anybody!

Work at having pleasure in work and do not carry any guilt

Read good books, which give you ideas and inspiration. Stagnation comes when ideas blocked.

Always imagine in your mind how you want to be, not how you are-use affirmations.

Create your own merit for positive self-esteem

Never depend on the admiration of others. There is no strength in it. Personal merit cannot be derived from an external source. It is not to be found in your personal associations, nor can it be found in regard of other people. Who cares what other people think about you! You have been given your own work to do or you have taken it up yourself. Get to it right now, do your best at it, and don't be concerned about who is watching you.

Relationship between self-image and the subconscious

Our subconscious behavior and our subconscious programs are linked with our self-concept. For example, when we are feeling badly about ourselves, we tend to blame ourselves. This may in turn take the form of junk foods, accidents, illnesses, over indulgence in alcohol or drugs and so on. It is not necessarily a conscious act. It is simply that our treatment of ourselves will automatically reflect how much we like ourselves.

Evidence is available to suggest that people who have accidents are often feeling bad about themselves at the time, and that the accident become a part of subconscious punishment. Therefore it is very important that we do all in our power to be optimistic. This will ensure that we can stay happy.

A poor self-concept says. "I don't deserve anything." This leads to a person subconsciously sabotaging his/her own happiness. Whenever exciting opportunities come along, a chance to take a holiday arises or a chance to learn a new skill presents itself, that person will either consciously or subconsciously find reasons why it can't be done.

Power of mind

In his book, Man's Search for Meaning, Viktor Frankl describes the brutal experience of being confined to a war time concentration camp.

- He observed that he lived because he wanted to live while most of the prisoners died, because they wanted to die. They lost their will to live because their minds became consumed by the tormenting misery of their existence. He, on the other hand, singled out any small incident of optimism and let his mind dwell on that. An extra crust of bread or a shoelace would bring joy and significance to his day. His frightful experience in captivity revealed to him that electric fences, chains, locks and cells do not deprive an individual freedom if he has opted to do so.

"One's ultimate freedom is the ability to choose one's attitude in any given set of circumstances," Viktor Frankl discovered. The true test of a person is if he can maintain a positive attitude even in the face of adversity.

Effect of thought on health and body. Your body is the servant of your mind. It obeys the operations of the mind, whether they are deliberately chosen or automatically expressed. At the bidding of negative and depressing thoughts the body sinks rapidly into disease and decay; at the command of glad and beautiful thoughts it becomes clothed with youthfulness and beauty as it obeys our mind fully.

People who live in fear of disease are the people who get it. Anxiety quickly demoralizes the whole body, and lays it open to the entrance of disease; while impure thoughts, even if not physically indulged, will soon shatter the nervous system and later on the body. The person, who says, `I don't want to be sick' has an uphill battle to become well.

Happy thoughts build up the body in vigor and grace. The body is a delicate instrument, which responds readily to the thoughts by which it is impressed, and these thoughts will produce their own effects, good or bad, upon it.

Your mind affects your well being and life

Your mind affects your life. We always gravitate towards what we think of the most. Quite often we find that when somebody says I don't want it to happen, it really happens. The principle is "think of something and you move towards it". If I say to you "don't think of a black elephant wearing shades" what will fill your mind? An elephant. Hence never say to the mind "I must not forget that book" as you might forget it. Rather say in the mind "I want to remember that the book has to be carried" and more chances are, you will remember it.

This is because your mind works on pictures. Your mind simply does not, cannot and will not work on the reverse of an idea. Therefore when a football coach screams out to his player `don't miss it' he is asking for trouble. When you ask your children `don't break the antique or don't fall while carrying the glass of water' you are surely inviting trouble.

Many parents can better coach their children by using positive language, which paints the picture of a desired result in their children's mind. Like, you cannot pass without good marks, verses "saying I am sure your excellent scoring will help you get admission in that prestigious college". The tennis player who wins always says "this point is mine". The fellow, who misses, is the one who say "I had better not blow this shot". Those who fill their minds with thoughts like 'I don't want to be lonely', I don't want to be broke' continually find themselves in the very situation they didn't want.

Optimism works because optimistic people dwell on what they want to achieve. They then necessarily gravitate toward their goal. Always think about 'what you want?'

Utilizing the unlimited powers of your subconscious

- The mind is like an iceberg while you are more aware of your outer or conscious mind, the part with the greater impact is hidden. All of your conscious thoughts contribute to the building of your subconscious mind. When you learn to drive a car it takes a lot of conscious thought and effort. Over time your mastery in driving a car became a part of your subconscious program such that now you would rarely miss the brake! Your bodily functions, your attitudes and all of your learned skills are keyed into the subconscious.

Conscious mind is the source of your thought, and the subconscious is the source of your power. Your subconscious mind contains your programs for walking, talking, solving problems, when you are asleep, healing your body, saving your body from danger and much more. Your subconscious programs are responsible for your successes and failures. Furthermore, it does not matter whether, what your subconscious takes to be true is actually true? You will reap results consistent with what your inner voice say should happen. For example, if you consistently walk, talk and think 'success', then you will inevitably develop a subconscious expectancy of success. You will attract success, and you will demonstrate success.

Our subconscious mind has an almost miraculous ability to solve problems. You may have experienced going to bed and ardent to find solution to a problem. Finally, you decided to stop worrying and go to sleep. Next morning you awoke to find that your subconscious had found your answer and presented it to your conscious mind.

Daily, you create programs in your subconscious by your thoughts, so watch what you think. Use your mind as all successful and happy people have used theirs. Implant your goals into your subconscious as if they have already been achieved. For example, if you want to be a confident person, continue to see yourself, brimming with confidence in your creative imagination. See the goal already achieved with your inner mind.

- To become healthy or wealthy, you can use the same principle by continuing the picture of ideal end result. Tell yourself that you are already enjoying the fruits of good health and the prosperity you desire and your inner mind will go to work for you. The principle works consistently and infallibly. Some people spend their time demanding logical explanations and trying to figure out how it all works while their neighbors are using these laws of the mind to get healthy, wealthy and rich. If it gets results, do not think of the logic. You can find it out later on.

We get what we expect

We tend to attract what we expect in life. Many mothers in India offer curd to their children when they go for any important occasion like an interview or an examination. She declares that you will succeed. It is not the curd but an imagination passed on the child and it matters many times more than the bowl of curd. It is not the curd that has all the power; it is the mind of the child who feels blessed and great.

- If Deepti says, "People only come to visit when my house is in a mess," she will find that pattern repeating. If Ranjan says that he gets a cold every year, you can bet he will. If one says, "Whenever I put some spare cash together, I always get an unexpected expense that wipes me out, "He will keep getting wiped out.

Doctors find that their patients tend to heal in accordance with their expectations. It is well established that their own expectations matter a lot in the recovery of cancer patients. One person says, "People always ignore me, treat me badly, rip me off," and he finds, that is how life will continues to deal with him. Another person says, "People always treat me well," and he is treated well. We get what we expect to get.

Your reality is what you perceive and select

- You only select the information that you need or which your mind feels the need of.

In view of our past conditioning and faulty perception, it is possible to end up with a lot of garbage stored in your memory files. You then keep on repeating it as a recycle process.

Consider the case of selective perception. It allows certain information to enter your consciousness and be recorded, while allowing other information to be completely ignored.

- If you have owned your wristwatch for at least a year you might have looked at your watch more than 3650 times. That is a lot of looking at a display face which is quite small.
- Here is a test that shows how selective perception works. Please DO NOT look at your watch as you start answering the following questions. Assuming your watch is not a digital one.
- Does it have normal or Roman numerals, dots or slashes to indicate hours?
- Is the display the same for all twelve numerals or are there any different symbols to denote 3, 6, 9, and 12 o'clock?
- What is the color of the background of the display face of your watch?

Now take a few minutes to decide your answers and check your watch very carefully to see how many questions you have correctly answered.

Most of the persons fail to answer all these questions correctly. Isn't it amazing how you concentrate on narrow information "bytes" and in doing so, eliminate up to 90 per cent of all the available information?

Your reply may be that you only need the byte information. Yes that is the point we select that, information which the mind decides should be selected and it works on past conditioning. We are always perceptive.

Principle of Concentration and Attraction

As we know `what you focus on will expand'. The law of concentration says that whatever you first concentrate on and dwell upon grows in your experience. Most of the people are unaware of their hidden potentials, and they recognize it when they concentrate on a particular area of their life. You can control what you concentrate on. You can develop a success consciousness by concentrating on successful outcomes; equally, you can develop a failure consciousness by concentrating on unsuccessful outcomes. The conscious mind can hold only one thought at a time, either positive or negative; it can never hold two thoughts simultaneously. Let us consider some examples:

1. Don't (One attracts to what one doesn't want if one focuses on it). In New Delhi the earlier traffic signals were 'don't jump the red light'. Later on it was replaced by the symbol 'Relax-Life is fast-Relax'. The traffic police in a survey found that the people have started responding to it with better results.
2. Hate (One becomes what one hates in others). One subordinate used to hate his boss saying everything would be OK when this person retires. After the retirement of that boss when he took over him, the reporting staff found that he too has become the true copy of his earlier boss. He simply copied the bad part of his boss and became like him.

One reason so few of us achieve what we truly want is that we never direct our focus; we never concentrate.

You attract what you hold in your mind

The study of various religions and literature confirms "you attract what you hold in your mind. Your mind is a magnet".

In his classic best selling book, Think and Grow Rich, Napoleon Hill wrote,

- "Our brain become magnetized with the dominating thoughts which we hold in our minds and, by means with which no man is familiar, these "magnets" attract to us the forces, the people, the circumstances of life which harmonize with the nature of our dominating thoughts."

Shakti Gawain, author of Creative Visualization says,

- "Thought and feelings have their own magnetic energy which attracts energy of a similar nature.... This is the principle that whatever you put out into the universe will be reflected back to you. What does this means from a practical standpoint is that we always attract into our lives whatever we think about most, believe in most passionately, expect on the deepest levels, and/or imagine most vividly".

Principle of attraction

The principle of attraction says that whatever first grows in your consciousness, you attract that into your life. You will always attract the people and circumstances that harmonize with your current dominant thoughts. If you go about your day expecting good things to happen, you will literally radiate self-confidence, enthusiasm, and a sense of purpose. You will attract people who are like mind and repel those who are of a different kind.

You may be surprised to find how many good things and circumstances you'll instinctively attract to yourself if you are positive, feel good about yourself and life. But it work both ways. You'll also surprised to know that many negative things get magnetize to worsen your life even more. Then you'll become pessimist.

When people nurture a particular thought for a very long time and progressively allow it to nourish the image attached to it, they get the result they expected and focused on.

One attracts the weaknesses in others if one focuses on it

> The Director of a company used to focus on what is missing in a proposal or an improvement plan and the staff used to get so discouraged that slowly the improvements or new proposals stopped coming to him. The new Director always appreciated first the good points in any plan and focused on the positive side of it and the people were always keen to tell him their ideas.

We attract what we fear

The things that we love most and fear most will tend to occupy our thoughts most of the time and so will we tend to attract those very things. When we want to say in the mind `I don't want A to happen' we will gravitate towards A only. Successful people move toward success. Failures try to run away from failures. If there is one mental principle that can transform losers into achievers, it is the "focus on what you want" principle. Many persons in life focus on what they do not want rather than spelling out and working towards what they want. We must focus on what we want.

Focus on what you want. Dwelling on your fears will bring them upon you. Fearing loss is not living in the present. Fearing loss is living in the future.

Confront your fears and they will disappear

Another fascinating principle is that often, when we finally develop the courage to meet a problem, the problem disappears and we don't have to face it. Also, we often find that once we decide to face a fear, the fear evaporates. When you jumped into a difficult task, it wasn't half as bad as you anticipated.

Story of two frogs

A group of frogs were traveling through the woods, and two of them fell into a deep pit. All the other frogs gathered around the pit. When they saw how deep the pit was, they told the two frogs that they were as good as dead.

The two frogs ignored the comments and tried to jump up out of the pit with all of their strength. The other frogs kept telling them to stop, that they were as good as dead. Finally, one of the trapped frogs took heed to what the other frogs were saying and gave up. He fell down and died.

The other frog continued to jump as hard as he could. Once again, the crowd of frogs yelled at him to stop enduring and better die. He jumped even harder and finally made it out.

When he got out, the other frogs said, "Did not you listen us?" The frog explained to them that he was deaf. He thought they were encouraging him the entire time.

This story made us think about

1. An encouraging word to someone who is down, can encourage them to achieve their goal.
2. A destructive word to someone who is down, can have negative effects. Be careful of what you say.

The Power of Words

Our thoughts affect our circumstances and so do the words we utter. Our words build our attitude and they determine what we will attract and experience.

- A person came to me recently and said, "I am tired of being a burden on my family. I want to be happy! How do I do it?" I said, "The first thing you can do is to open your mouth only when you have something positive and constructive to say. Not to talk all the time negative about yourself. You will appreciate the change and so will your family". I saw him a week later and he was still griping. He said to me, "I want to be happy and I am not. How can I do it?" I said, "I gave you my best advice last week!" He said, "I am still not happy". I replied, "I know that is because you are not serious enough about it. Yet! When you are really serious, you will be happy".
- He needs to recognize that he is the only person running his mouth. At some stage he will need to take responsibility for his own thoughts. He will need to get serious about what thoughts he has in his head and the need to change his attitudes and the words he is using.

Similarly patients go to the doctors and get well soon. Now do they need to blame-their 'condition'. The issue remains, what makes that person happy and healthy tomorrow? Words affect our personal power. Be aware of it.

Our subconscious mind always filters the word we use and they become a part of our character. They tell others how serious and how committed we are to get results. There are some words that will generally undermine our progress. Every time we use the word ' try', we indicate that we are not in control. If you are going to `try' and do a good job, `try' and arrive on time, 'try' and be happy, you are suggesting that you may do it or may not. Substituting a word like 'will' for `try' is challenging and confronting and will get us much better results. When you are using I can't, it is undermining your personal power. Saying, "won't" instead of "can't" will usually be closer to the truth of reflecting your control on the situation and is more empowering. So use always powerful words if you want powerful results.

Power of Affirmations

A positive thought that you repeat to yourself is called affirmation. Using affirmations allows you to select quality thoughts and implant them into your subconscious so that you can feel better, perform better and achieve better. No simple slogan is going to transform your personality overnight. You cannot hope to change everything all at once. But you can become more patient, more empathetic, and more confident if you concentrate on one behavioral trait at a time using positive affirmation through visualization. You can develop a new habit pattern of thought in five to seven days if you practice in your imagination and do it regularly.

When you imagine yourself achieving a goal or doing it in a particular manner, your brain accepts the experience as real, so real in fact that you will feel the same emotions and sensations as those that would take place in real achievement.

- Suppose you are driving out on a highway and you have a serious headache. Here is your opportunity to combine the power of words with the power of thoughts. You begin to repeat to yourself, "My head feels wcnderful!" Or "my head is relaxed and at ease." As you begin to tell yourself this, no doubt a little voice in the background will be saying, "You are lying. You have a headache!"

Despite this, if you continue with the positive affirmations, the thought you are feeling well will take root in your subconscious. You will indeed start to feel better, half an hour later, chances are the thought will cross your mind, "I had a headache, a while back. It has gone now".

You can repeat these sentences to yourself daily.

"Every day in my life and in every way I am getting better, better and better."

Affirmation does not mean that you never have to put in any effort. It means that you have a shortcut to conditioning your mind for whatever you want. If you choose to make them a regular part of your life, you will find that they are very simple and powerful tools.

There are some rules to keep in mind when using affirmations. Firstly, as we discussed earlier, your mind will always move towards what you most think about. Therefore if you design an affirmation like, "I won't argue with my wife," or "I am not sick," you won't be thrilled with the results! Your mind will keep forcing you towards what you say you don't want. If you think about it, you may know of people who spend all their time talking about what they don't want, and wondering why they always get it.

- If you recall few teachers in your school might have made your classmates and you write lines like, "I won't talk in class" or "I would not tell a lie" and "I won't be late," and "I won't throw things at others". Little did they realize that, structured in those negative instructions, they were actually promoting misbehavior? The right affirmation would have been "I will always speak the truth" and so on.

The second principle to keep in mind with affirmations is that they are much more effective when you say them out loud with force/ emotions or write them down. Saying or writing them keeps your mind on track. You also involve more of your physical senses when you speak or write, and hence the effect is more powerful. Many persons use the bathroom mirror for their affirmations.

Third thing to bear in mind with affirmations is that constant repetition is important. Usually you forget over 90 per cent of everything you hear once in a day. But if you hear the same thing repeated over a period of time, you might remember it. This type of learning experience is called "spaced repetition." If you want to restructure a belief system that you have had for twenty years, it will require some persistence and regular practice.

Suggestions have Both Powers

Everything that you see, hear and read, along with everything that you experience has influence on you. We are literally surrounded by a suggestive environment - friends, family, the home, the workplace, peer circle, TV radio, newspapers and magazines-that significantly affects how we think and feel about ourselves.

You are constantly receiving suggestions from your external environment, and in most instances, you accept these self-instructions as valid. Unfortunately, no one has the time or ability to test everything he or she encounters or experiences in life by critical assessment and in-depth analysis.

Suggestions can work both ways. They can help us and damage us also unless we have the maturity to dissociate ourselves from negative suggestions.

Self-suggestions have a profound impact on our attitudes, and in turn a dramatic effect on individual behavior and performance.

Left and Right Brain-The Two Hemispheres

Let's study the conscious and subconscious parts as they relate to the brain's two hemispheres.

Our left hemisphere of the brain is usually, the analytical and logical part that controls language skills such as reading, writing and memorizing names, dates, and various facts. It evaluates information/situation in a rational, logical way, performs literal interpretations of words, concepts, understands time, and controls the movements on the right side of our body.

Our right hemisphere is usually the creative, intuitive and artistic part where dreams and imagery originate and fantasies are born. It is dominant in thinking about problems holistically, that is, as an integrated whole. It deals in images and concepts and can process several pieces of information simultaneously and perceive spatial relationships. It is responsible for artistic, musical, and imaginative creations and controls the movements on the left side of our body.

Conscious, left-brain thinking usually predominates in our society, is more valued, and receives the most attention particularly due to the present trend of our schooling. The student, who adds and subtracts correctly, remembers names, and works in a logical, organized manner, gets the most recognition. The person who daydreams in class and fantasies a great deal is considered less productive, and is usually awarded lower grades. Not surprisingly, most children grow up believing that memory retention skills and conformity are more valuable than artistic or creative abilities. The memory can also be increased by a balanced use of both sides of the brain.

If the two hemispheres are used properly, they work in complete harmony together and fully complement one another. They support each other in a way they contributes what it does best to the thinking process.

Stephen Covey, the author of *Seven Habits of Highly Effective People* says that we should manage from left and lead from right.

A mechanical engineer will use the right brain to conceive the spatial relationship and intricate design of a large bridge, but the left hemisphere must perform all the mathematical calculations regarding weights, dimensions, and stresses.

Since the conscious, directive part of the mind controls analytical, logical thinking it draws specific conclusions from various inputs, resulting in decisions such as good-bad, right-wrong, yes-no, and so on. Conscious rational thought operates in real time and can concentrate effectively on only one thing at a time. It carries out the process of "experiences". It selects information, compares it with past experiences, evaluates, and decides. It also selects goals and assigns problems for resolution to the subconscious.

Creativity

- Stagnation comes in life when ideas get stopped.

You must think creatively if you want to succeed.

An excellent definition of creativity is involving the use of skill and the imagination to produce something new or a work of art. The subconscious is a vast storehouse. It contains the wisdom of the past, the understanding of the present, and the vision of the future. By tapping into its vast reserves, you can create new thoughts about anything that you choose to think about. You may wish to develop artistic, scholastic, or professional talents, reach specific goals that are meaningful and important to you.

There is a direct link between creativity and optimism. Optimistic people are those who habitually consider a wide range of possibilities, the various options that are available to achieve a particular goal. An optimist can find value in any idea and the reasons why it will work. Alternatively, a pessimist focuses primarily on reasons why an idea will not work.

Functions of our subconscious and the process of creativity

- The subconscious takes charge of the total management of your immensely complex physical machinery. Breathing, blood circulation, and food digestion are prime examples of essential life supporting activities that your subconscious carries out. You can affect each of these up to a certain point by conscious effort.

For example in every twenty-four hours, without any conscious effort, your subconscious controls:

- your breathing 23000 times.
- your heart to beat 100,000 times.
- The other major subconscious thought activity is the storage and retrieval of all information related to experience at the

conscious level, whether the experience is real or imagined. They are noted, accumulated, and stored to form the basis for your personal belief system. This, in turn, affects your day-to-day thinking and behavior. It is this activity that supports your built-in success system or goal striving mechanism that transforms the mental images you conceive into their physical counterpart. Each mental image you focus on leaves a photographic imprint or footprint in memory, and you proceed to retrace those steps again, when you think in similar terms at any point of time.

- Problem-solving or conflict resolution is the other important subconscious activity. If you are consciously trying to solve a personal or business problem, or to create something new or original, your subconscious processes will help you to resolve the problem. A search will be done in your memory files first to find a possible answer from the existing ones. If a suitable one is not available, the mind will transcend your own accumulated knowledge and seek out sources for inspirational concepts or ideas.

Let us now consider the concept of "sixth" sense. You probably have had experiences in your own life when, after failing to find the missing link to a particular problem you are facing since long. The answer simply "propped" into your head out of nowhere when you were relaxed. This often occurs at a time when you least expect it and are involved in a completely unrelated activity. Many find this happening early morning. The answer knocks at the door of your mind as if it were looking for a home. How it found your address, nobody knows! This ability to access information from a source beyond your conscious self is a real wonder to your mind. You may have heard the story of Archimedes who discovered the Principle Of Buoyancy when he was taking a bath in the tub.

So allow your mind to let go for creative thoughts. The logical explanation to this process may be that new patterns are formed internally by the overlapping of two more mental images already stored in memory to form a third, new picture. The key to stimulating creative thought is to learn how to allow your mind to let go, thus permitting creative ideas and concepts to bubble the conscious level. That is why the mind needs rest for creativity to emerge.

An inhibiting factor is that our school system indeed, based on Western culture, has allowed conscious thought to dominate most of our mental activity. Conscious thought is language-oriented and logical only. Intuitive solutions come from the subconscious.

Intuitive powers can be developed with silence and in a chapter 5 we have discussed the Power of Silence.

Before the subconscious can respond in a creative way, it must be challenged by the conscious part of the brain. When you begin to consider some of your possibilities and potential for high achievement, for example, you will start to get some answers. Actively pondering your possibilities by conscious thought somehow triggers the subconscious into considering a variety of solutions. Our mind, like all things in nature, has a natural tendency to maintain the status quo. When finally challenged by a goal or aspiration, it will respond in such a way as to satisfy the demand and continue to work on the solution before returning to the neutral state.

Your conscious and subconscious are always seeking out an internal equilibrium. Your conscious mind determines the level and the subconscious automatically follows its lead.

To purposely activate the creative powers of the subconscious mind is a great ability and is available to anyone who chooses to use it. But it takes a great deal of desire, wanting to get ahead, and an element of trust and faith.

Divergent thinking and convergent thinking

There are two entirely different thought processes involved in creative problem solving.

The first thought process is known as divergent thinking and it consists of expanding all aspects of the problem itself. The other manner of thinking is known as convergent thinking and it proceeds in exactly the opposite direction. It involves reducing the problem into smaller, more manageable parts. It zeros in, on key factors, for implementation, for in-depth analysis, discards unworthy options, and selects others for implementation. Convergent thinking is reductive.

Typically a converger is prone to premature action, not having adequately studied the totality of the problem. A converger tends to make snap decisions based on insufficient information and inadequate exploration of all possible options. Some of the most typically rigid thinkers are the people who cannot innovate well or accept others.'

Creativity is a thinking exercise. It is a developed mental skill aimed at generating new ideas that may be more useful than the old ones. A new idea is usually only a combination of old ideas recast in a different light. The only real wealth in the world is a new idea and someone willing to act on it.

Our success system

One cannot force a successful outcome by sheer will power alone. You cannot consciously go for a task hoping to succeed, simultaneously imagining and working on the fear that things will go wrong. Nor can the mind concentrate on the reverse idea. If a cricket player wants to catch the ball but fears inside "I don't want to drop the ball". Then the mind will focus only on the "drop the ball" aspect of the concept. The thought must be positive and expecting success, for example: "I see myself catching the ball, I have done this successfully many times before, and I know I can do it again. "If this is what you want the result to be".

Your success system will work as per your mental orders

The success system in you is designed to bring into reality whatever image you accept and project into your mental screen. While the role of the conscious mind is always to produce the picture, the role of the subconscious is always to ensure that all of your actions, feelings, and behavior are consistent with this picture.

Therefore the subconscious is always the obedient servant to the conscious perception process and is activated by mental pictures or suggestions. But once it has received its instructions from conscious mind, it becomes the most powerful influence in your life. It accepts all your instructions without question, records them in every detail, and refers back to them on appropriate occasions.

Hence you are destined to repeat as habit all learned behavioral patterns over and over again until you make a conscious decision to change the image. In other words, you have to provide your subconscious with a new set of goal-images if you want to bring about a change; otherwise, it will automatically refer back to previous programming for its instruction. You always dance to the tune recorded on your mental tape. You always act the part, unconsciously, of the person you see yourself to be.

Your subconscious can do no wrong. It works perfectly. It has no equal, works night and day-never complaining and never failing to deliver precisely what you keep telling your mind.

Reprogramming Your Mind for Success

As an analogy just imagine your subconscious mind as a large room with only one door at the front. A security guard that represents your conscious mind protects this front entrance. His primary job is to limit entry into the room according to certain specific criteria laid down by you.

When you were born this whole room was empty and the guard was permitting everyone to enter. As you grew older and experienced various new events and happenings, your room began to fill up with a variety of beliefs and opinions about yourself and your world. These beliefs and opinions joined together to form a kind of exclusive club, eventually determining your personality and becoming somewhat assertive about it. This club became so assertive and exclusive at some point that it began to tell the guard just who he could let in to join the group and who he could not. In other words, when the subconscious mind didn't feel comfortable with the qualifications of a particular applicant (a new belief or opinion), he was refused access. The club was exercising its right to allow, only those new members who were compatible with the long term residents. The most powerful occupant in your room is your self-image "clique," which together forms a consensus about who you are and what you are capable of achieving and what type of person are allowed to enter.

Garbage in, garbage out is also the rule of this mind, which is stored in memory. The most prominent feature of all garbage is its smell. If garbage has been stored in your mind, and there is a lot of it, then the unfortunate guard at the front door acquires the same characteristic. He begins to smell as well. He can't help but smell because he guards the only door the stench can exit from. Then our facial and non verbal reactions also speak the language of our garbage inside.

How have you been programmed?

All of us entered the world as a blank slate, with little basis for thinking or acting in any particular way. Every detail of all your experiences after birth is stored in memory for future reference.

During your upbringing you have been conditioned to perceive and believe in a manner consistent with the experiences you have had and the people you have associated with. You then ended up adopting the opinions and beliefs your primary reference groups imposed on you. Now, as an adult, most of your programming is based on our intuitions. Instead of listening to outside suggestions, you tend to rely on self-suggestions to decide on, who you are and what you can do.

As an example if you were told and believed that the Sun rotates around the Earth, then this is what you'll remember, even though it is not the correct answer. You have developed conditioned responses to a wide variety of external stimuli and acquired a pattern of repetition over and over again before getting fully imprinted in the mind. These can be changed only by the same process called reprogramming. What you then start believing about yourself determines what you say to yourself.

Can you recall ever saying to yourself any of the following?

"I would like to do it, but I don't have the family background or education".

"I would like to do it, but you know that my experience is not in related line."

"I would like to do it, but I don't know the right people/ connections."

This is big but very dangerous as it depart you from your achievement. You get stopped by yourself when you continually tell yourself you cannot succeed. It is a process of justification you have discovered.

If the negative and destructive beliefs have already entered into your subconscious mind and you want to change yourself; it is not enough to realize that you have a lot of talent, ability, and intelligence to work with. Positive thinking by itself is not the answer. Logic and reason alone will not bring about the changes you need in order to move ahead, since they are external to your subconscious self. If change could be effected from outside your subconscious memory bank, how different your life would be! You could eliminate unwanted habits such as drinking, smoking, and overeating simply by thinking about them at the conscious level and saying, "I am going to stop."

Sheer will power and determination are not enough. It is not enough to keep telling yourself, "I am capable, an optimist, I can do anything," because, deep inside, your subconscious does not believe you on the bases of your self-doubts and past experience.

Neuro-Linguistic Programming (NLP)

For effecting a change inside, there is a tried and tested method that works. This technique involves positive affirmations and creative visualization at the alpha level of mind when we are ready to approach our subconscious in a state of silence inside.

The only way to reprogram your mind for success is to change what has been entered into your subconscious. NLP is a very effective technique for it. In the relaxed alpha state, you have improved access to your subconscious mind, the power base representing your true potential. The way is not blocked by the conscious mind, which is always making judgments and editing out any thoughts deemed inconsistent with your current beliefs. All of the usual concerns, problems, and preoccupations of everyday life represented by the beta brain wave state are not present to complicate your thinking. The power of silence is available to help you.

If your existing internal maps aren't getting you the results you want in any field, then you need to look for more effective models or mental maps. NLP allows you to acquire these by discovering what has made other people successful in various fields, and using their models as your own. If you were not programmed for the desired level of your success through your upbringing, don't worry, you can still do it using NLP.

We shall discuss in detail the techniques of NLP in chapter 7.

Chapter

Knowing Self and Others Using MBTI

- What is MBTI?
- Application areas of MBTI
- Knowing your own personality type
- How various types of persons behave in daily situations/work settings
- Extroversion and Introversion
- Sensing and intuiting
- Thinking and feeling
- Judging and perceiving
- Art of getting along
- How to relate with others using MBTI
- Effect of MBTI on work setting
- Dealing with various types of personalities
- Importance of various types and their roles
- Constructive use of personality differences
- Use of MBTI in choosing career
- Typical type biases
- Different drums and different drummers
- Story of Lili

WHAT IS MBTI?

MBTI, Myers-Briggs Type Indicator, is registered trademark trusted in the United States. This explanation is not a substitute for promoting an MBTI ®. It is simply an introduction to personality type or psychological type. We hope it satiate your appetite for learning more about the Myers and Briggs model of personality development and its message of developing human understanding.

Background of the MBTI ®

After many years of research and development, various instruments have been developed by Myres and Brigg for understanding normal personality differences. Since its inception in 1943, the MBTI or Myers-Briggs Type Indicator® has evolved and been perfected through continual test research and development of ever more accurate questions. Millions of people have taken the tests that have evolved from time to time. Real understanding and effective use of MBTI can be made by person-to-person follow-up verification by a qualified practitioner, further explanation will give only approximations of the type.

APPLICATION AREAS OF MBTI ®

Since MBTI explains the basic patterns in human functioning, it is used for a variety of purposes, like the following

- Understanding the self for enhancing personal effectiveness.
- Academic counseling, selecting suitable career options and career development.
- Improving team effectiveness.
- Management and leadership training.
- Problem solving and leveraging diversity.
- Counseling in relationship.
- Education development.
- Reducing conflict in multicultural training.

KNOWING YOUR OWN PERSONALITY TYPE

The best way to understand your personality or psychological type is to take an official MBTI® (Myers-Briggs Type Indicator) instrument from a professional who has met the standards necessary to be "qualified" to administer the test. An excellent resource for "qualified" persons is the Association for Psychological Type. You can know and understand your personality type reading the descriptions of the four "dimensions" or aspects of Type, and choose which characteristics in each pair describe you the best (for example, Extrovert or Introvert, Sensing or Intuitive etc). Your personality type is made up of your natural "preference" for each of these four dimensions. It is simply a question of degree of preference or reflecting your natural styles/ true nature in your working.

1. Where is your energy directed? Or which is your most natural energy orientation?

Extroverts get their energy by interaction with others and are usually spontaneous in communication. Their energy is directed, primarily outward, towards people and things around them. Introverts' energy is primarily directed internally, towards their own thoughts, perceptions, and reactions. They first reflect on thoughts before speaking and are energized by inner reflections.

Extroverts therefore tend to be more naturally active, expressive, social, and interested in many things, whereas Introverts tend to be more reserved, private, cautious, and interested in fewer interactions, but with greater depth and focus. In parties, extroverts take initiative to interact and mix with more persons as compared to introverts' who prefer to meet only selected few and reserve their energy.

Every person has two faces. One is directed towards the outer world of activities, excitements, people, and things. The other is directed inward to the inner world of thoughts, interests, ideas, and imagination.

While these are two different but complementary sides of our nature, most people have an innate preference towards energy from either the OUTER or the INNER world. Thus one of their faces, either the Extroverted (E) or Introverted (I), takes the lead in their personality development and plays a more dominant role in their behavior.

Extroverts often	*Introverts often*
• talk a lot	• talk less
• have a high energy	• have quiet less energy
• think out loud	• think before they act
• like to enjoy others company	• are comfortable spending time alone
• are easily distracted	• have good concentration
• like variety and action	• like a quiet environment for concentration
• develop their ideas through discussion	• enjoy focusing on a project or task
• learn new tasks by talking and doing	• develop their ideas internally
• enjoy interacting with people	• learn new tasks by read & reflect
• are interested in how other people do their work	• are enjoy working alone with no interruptions

Are you Extrovert (E) or Introvert (I)? It can be decided by the matching of more description of your nature under the E or I category.

2. What kind of information do you naturally notice and remember? Or which way of understanding is most natural?

Sensors have good observation ability and notice the facts, details, and current realities of the world around them whereas Intuitive persons are more interested in interconnections, implications, patterns, future trends and relationships between facts. The Sensing (S) side of our brain notices the sights, sounds, smells and all the sensory details of the present. It categorizes, organizes, records and stores the specifics from here and now. It is reality based, dealing with "what is." It also provides the specific details of memory & recollections from past events. Therefore Sensors tend to be practical and literal people, who trust past experience often have good common sense.

On the other hand Intuitive persons tend to be imaginative, conceptual people who trust their hunches and pride themselves on their creativity and gut feelings.

The Intuitive (N) side of our brain seeks to understand, interpret, form overall patterns of all the information that is collected then record these patterns and relationships. It speculates on possibilities, including looking into and forecasting the future. It is imaginative and conceptual.

While both kinds of perceiving are necessary and used by all people, each of us instinctively tends to favor one over the other. Are you Sensor (S) or Intuitive (N)?

Sensor often	*Intuitive often*
• focus on the facts and specifics	• focus on ideas and big picture
• admire practicality	• admire creativity
• have straightforward speech	• have roundabout thoughts
• are more realistic	• are more imaginative- see more possibilities
• are more present oriented	• are more future oriented
• focus on immediate issues	• follow their inspirations
• provide a realistic and practical perspective	• provide connections and meanings
• improve the perfect standard ways of doing things by fine tuning	• like solving new and complex problems
• build conclusions by collecting facts drawn on their and other's experience	• start with big picture and then fill facts/ details • prefer change and new ways of doing things

3. How do you decide or make choices?

Thinkers make decisions based primarily on objective and impersonal criteria-what makes the most sense and what is logically right. Feelers make decisions based primarily on their personal values, how they feel about the choices and what is being liked by others.

Therefore Thinkers tend to be analytical, and are convinced by logical reasoning. In contrast Feelers tend to be sensitive, empathetic, and are compelled by extenuating circumstances and a constant search for harmony. Thinkers are good implementers of rules whereas Feelers are good motivators.

The Thinking (T) side of our brain analyzes information in a detached, objective fashion. It is our logical nature. The Feeling (F) side of our brain forms conclusions in an attached manner, based on likes/dislikes, impact on others, humane and aesthetic values. It is our subjective nature.

While everyone uses both means of forming conclusions, each person has a natural bias towards one over the other so that when they give us conflicting directions - one side is the natural trump card or tiebreaker.

Thinkers often	*Feelers often*
• are objective	• are subjective
• are comparatively cool and reserved	• are usually warm and friendly
• are honest and direct	• are sensitive and diplomatic
• are naturally critical in order to be good problem solvers	• try mostly to please others and appreciate them
• are motivated by achievement	• are motivated by being appreciated
• focus on the tasks	• focus on people's interactions
• use logical analysis to understand and decide	• use values to understand and decide
• want mutual respect and fairness among colleagues	• want harmony and support among colleagues
• are firm-minded, can give and take criticism when appropriate	• are empathetic, prefer to accommodate
• apply principles consistently	• apply values consistently

4. What kind of environment makes you more comfortable?

Judgers prefer a structured, ordered, and fairly predictable environment, where they can make quick decisions and have things settled so that after finishing a project they are free to do other things.

Perceivers prefer to experience as much of the world as possible, keep on probing further for betterment and perfection, they like to keep their options open and are most comfortable adapting to new requirements.

Therefore Judgers tend to be organized and productive while Perceivers tend to be flexible, curious and perfectionists. They may appear non-conforming to others and would prefer to use resourcefulness.

A Judger approaches the outside world with a plan and is oriented towards organizing one's surroundings, being prepared, making decisions, reaching closure and completion.

A Perceiver takes the outside world as it comes; adopting, flexible, open-ended, receptive to new opportunities and changing game plans.

Judgers often	***Perceivers often***
• are punctual	• are not punctual
• may appear serious & more formal	• are playful and casual
• like to make plans and stick to them	• like to wait-and-see
• work first, play later	• play first, work later
• keep limited options	• explore more and more options
• like to finish projects best	• like to start projects best
• want to plan their work and follow the plan	• want to have flexibility in their work
• like to get things settled and finished	• like to be spontaneous
• feel supported by structure and schedule	• feel restricted by structure and schedule
• reach closure by deciding quickly	• leave things open as long as possible
• focus on timely completion of a project	• focus on enjoying the process

Are you Judger (J) or Perceiver (P)?

Assumptions underlying the theory of personality types

- These preferences are inborn.
- Our environment can enhance or impede the expression of type.
- Sometime people use all four processes (Sensing, Intuition, Thinking, and Feeling) in both extroverted and introverted attitudes.

- Type is dynamic, not static.
- All the types are equally valuable in our life and working
- All types are randomly divided in the population.

Some Key Words describing various types	
Extroverted (E)	***Introverted (I)***
Active	Reflective
Outward	Inward
Social	Reserved
People	Privacy
Expressive	Quiet
Breadth	Depth
Sensing (S)	***Intuitive (N)***
Specifics	Patterns
Present	Future
Practical	Imaginative
Facts	Associations
Literal	Thematic
Experience	Variety
Thinking (T)	***Feeling (F)***
Logical	Compassionate
Analytical	Personal
Justice	Kindness
Fairness	Harmony
Critique	Appreciate
Analyze	Empathize
Principles	Values
Judging (J)	***Perceiving (P)***
Organized	Flexible
Structure	Flow
Manage	Experience
Decisive	Curious, Deliberate / Spontaneous
Closure	Openness
Plan	Emerge
Productive	Receptive

Our orientation to outer world and the way other see us

EXTROVERSION (E)	***INTROVERSION (I)***
• Focus is on outer world of people and activities. Direct their energy and attention outward. Feel deprived when cutoff interaction from the outside world.	• Focus is on inner world of ideas and experiences. Direct their energy and attention inward. Regularly require an amount of "private time" to recharge batteries.
• Receive energy from interacting with people and taking actions. Usually open to and motivated by outside world of people and things.	• Receive energy from reflecting on thoughts, memories and feelings. Motivated internally, mind is sometimes so active it is "closed" to outside world.
• Good at greeting people. Communicate with energy & enthusiasm.	• May appear not so warm in greeting. Keep energy and enthusiasm inside.
• Like variety and action. Impatient with long and slow jobs.	• Can work on one project for long time. Dislike distractions.
• Act first, think/reflect later. Often act quickly without thinking.	• Think/reflect first, and then act. Think before he acts. Interested in idea behind the job.
• Prefers to communicate by talking.	• Prefers communication in writing.
• Active energetic time with people. • Accessible. Being center of attraction. Enjoy wide variety and change in people relationships	• Quite and thoughtful time alone. Impenetrable & subtle. Being reserved. Has to be drawn out. Prefer one-to-one communication and relationships.
• Talk first and think later on. • High disclosure.	• Think first and then talk. • Cautious disclosure.
• Express feelings and emotions freely.	• Express little inner feelings and emotions.
• Meeting new people. Seek opportunities to communicate.	• Being alone or with one whom he knows well. Think issues in mind & share the result with selected few.
• Readily takes initiative in work and relationships.	• Take initiative when the situation or issue is very important to them.

The way we gather information categorize it and understanding things

INTUITION	*SENSING*
• Focus on how things could be improved. Like solving new, complex problems.	• Focus on immediate issues and what works now.
• Mentally live in the Future. Oriented to future possibilities, imaginations, patterns, implications provide connections and meanings.	• Mentally live in present capture available opportunities. Oriented to present realities. Provide a realistic and practical perspective drawn on experience.
• Using imagination and creating/ inventing new possibilities is automatic-instinctual.	• Using common sense and creating practical solutions is automatic-instinctual.
• Dislikes doing things repeatedly. Prefer change, new ways of doing things.	• Likes an established way of doing things. Can perfect standard ways by fine tuning.
• Enjoys learning new skills. Preoccupied with unknown & new. Memory recall emphasizes patterns, contexts, and connections.	• Enjoys applying what is already learnt. Preoccupied with known experience. Memory recall is rich in detail of facts and past event.
• May reach to conclusion quickly using 6th sense, get sudden ideas. Follow hunches.	• Usually reach to conclusions in step by step logically and carefully with thoroughness.
• Uncomfortable with details and lengthy fact. Want whole picture.	• Need facts, figures, evidences, & details. Concerned with parts.
• Dislike taking time for precision.	• May be good at precise work. Patient with routine.
• Rely on imagination or insights. Wants possible future challenge to be discussed.	• Trial and error learn and rely on direct experience. Living life as it is.
• Like nobel and unusual suggestions. Try new things/ Ideas. Comfortable with ambiguous, fuzzy data and with guessing its meaning.	• Like tested & tried methods, specific examples and straight-forward suggestions. Like clear and concrete information; dislike guessing when facts are fuzzy.
• Start with big picture and then fill the facts. Can omit details if not needed.	• Build to conclusions by collecting facts. Can't be comfortable without details.
• Think of possibilities even non-existent. Best improvise from theoretical understanding. Agenda a starting point.	• Deal with actualities. Best improvise from past experience. Inclined to follow the agenda in meetings .
• Design plans but not necessarily carrying it out.	• Carry out carefully laid down detailed plans with precision.

Which is most natural when you decide? The process of coming to conclusion

THINKING TYPE (T)	*FEELING TYPE (F)*
• Get energy in identifying, what is wrong in something so they can solve the problem.	• Get energy by appreciating and supporting others and look for qualities to praise.
• Use logical analysis to understand and decide. Are good in putting things with logical orders. Anticipate or predict the logical outcome of choices.	• Use values to understand and decide. Like harmony and will work to make it happen. Good at examining the effects of choices on people.
• Instinctively search for facts and logic in a decision situation. Naturally notices tasks and work to be accomplished.	• Instinctively employ personal feelings and impact on people in decision situations. Naturally sensitive to people needs and reactions.
• Focus on the tasks. Logic based on causes and effect. Easily able to provide an objective and critical analysis.	• Focus on people's interactions. Logic based on values, likes & dislikes. Naturally seek consensus and popular opinions
• Accept conflict as a natural, normal part of relationships with people.	• Unsettled by conflict; have almost a toxic reaction to disharmony.
• They mentally want to escape themselves from the situation to examine pros and cons objectively.	• Mentally place them in the situation to identify with others and take decision based on their values about people.
• Reach conclusions using established principles, systems, rules and regulations consistently.	• Reach conclusions using values, humanity, ideals, mercy sentiments and uniqueness of situation.
• Are firm-minded, can give criticism when appropriate. Are able to fire people when necessary.	• Are empathetic. Prefer to accommodate and reach consensus. Dislikes talking unpleasant things.
• May hurt people unintentionally. Excess criticism may demotivate others.	• Enjoy in pleasing people. Warm. Inability to reprimand can lead to country club culture.
• A good decision is which is fair. His strength lies in organizing facts into logical sequence .	• A good decision is which makes other happy. His strength lies in bonding, winning commitments.
• More important is to be right than liked. Want fairness.	• Taking others' emotions into account is important. Want harmony.
• Maximize implementation. Can analyze situation and make system, strategy, plans better.	• Maximize acceptance. Can generate passion and evolve the spirit.

Attitude to structure and time-orientation to environment

JUDGING (J)	*PERCIEVING (P)*
• Like to live in planned, orderly and organized way. Sticking to plans and schedules is very important to them. Draft many details in advance before moving into action.	• Like to live in a flexible, spontaneous way and prefer to stay open to new information, gather more data and last minute options. Comfortable moving into action without a plan; plan on the spot.
• Feel supported by structure and schedules. Set schedule and stick to it (time punctuality). Dead lines are very important. Advance planning.	• Feel restricted by structure, schedules and deadlines. Detailed plans and final decision may be seen as too confining. Wants flexibility.
• Focus on task-related action; complete meaningful segments before moving on. Work best and avoid stress when keep ahead of deadlines.	• Like to multitask, have variety, mix work and play. Naturally tolerant of time pressure, work best close to the deadlines.
• They are energized to get things settled and finished. Reach closure by deciding quickly and then start new. Focus on timely completion of a project.	• They are energized by their resourcefulness in adapting to new demands of the moment. Poor in closing. Prefer to leave things open, wait & see, use creativity and change the course. Focus on enjoying the process.
• May dislike the interruption in the work/project they are doing even if a priority comes.	• May start too many projects/ tasks and have difficulty in finishing them.
• Get the needed information and then take a quick decision.	• Consider all possible angles for a long time before any decision.
• You can know his stand in advance and predict him. Naturally use targets, dates and standard routines to manage life.	• You can not predict him (options open). Instinctively avoid commitments which interfere with flexibility, freedom and variety.
• Keep appointment dairies /notes about commitments.	• Keep appointment dairies to minimize the task.
• Well prepared for actions.	• On the spot decision making and instant actions.
• Start meetings at a pre- arranged time.	• Start meetings when all are comfortable.

Case study on art of getting along

Deepak came out of his boss Rajeev's office feeling that he had failed again. His boss Rajeev has just dismissed his progress report on a project with no justification. Deepak had carefully structured report describing in great detail. Deepak was hoping that his boss Rajeev would be impressed.

Deepak came back to his seat and started reflecting what had happened in boss's office and why did he made his boss repeatedly angry. Today's incidence was one of the many during the last 3 months. Deepak started reviewing today's scene in his boss's office. When he presented the report, his boss Rajeev said "Damn Deepak, get to the big picture I don't want all this detailed report. I can't waste my time reading about every detail of the project. I need a summary of the major problems. That is why I gave you this job. But cannot you talk about major problems unless you know the details, cannot you get to step 'c' by skipping over steps a and b, Deepak had argued 'In this project you can" his boss Rajeev had said.

' But you asked for a detailed report.

' It certainly looks that way" said the boss?

And that was it. Meeting adjourned. Deepak's hard work was not mentioned.

Deepak recalled back that how his previous boss Jagdish used to appreciate his detailed reports and even recommended his promotion as Rajeev's Asst. Manager. And beside Jagdish, his previous bosses always appreciated him.

Deepak was totally frustrated and angry with his boss. Ordinarily, he stayed late at work, but today he was in no mood to provide company an extra minute of overtime. He got up and left the office.

On the way home, he was thinking about his boss only. How much he wanted to work with Rajeev. He was also achievement oriented as his boss. He wished he never had a promotion.

Deepak has an idea of talking about today's incidence with one of his colleague, Ashok, who was also reporting to his present boss and they both had been getting along very well for the last five years. In fact Ashok got along well with his boss, colleagues and subordinates. Deepak thought perhaps Ashok could give him some tips.

Deepak also wondered how his colleague Ashok attended the meetings, with brief summaries of progress reports and answered his boss Rajeev's question. Yet with shallow and brief reports he earned the respect and confidence of his boss.

Next day when Deepak met his friend Ashok, he told him what had happened yesterday with his boss.

Ashok listened to him attentively and talked about value of building networks in the dept. and got to know what each person ticks. He also talked about looking at a global concepts and broad possibilities instead of focussing only on details. He said "details slow you down, Deepak. It is boring, surely the facts are important but then they are not everything. Your boss has no patience with details".

"If my boss hates details he should have at least appreciated my work" argued Deepak at the end of the lunch. Deepak felt that his friend Ashok was only criticizing him. They both left the place.

That afternoon Deepak was more certain than ever that his approach to the project report was correct. He wrote a memo to his boss that progress report should be the standard for reporting to the superiors and he even argued the Govt. regulations demanded such details.

The next meeting between Deepak and his boss was disaster. The following week Deepak was fired from his job.

Now comment briefly on the following questions

1. Who was right? Deepak or his boss and why?
2. Was the punishment given by the boss (firing Deepak from the job) fair & justified?
3. What was the source of conflict between Deepak and his boss?
4. Was Deepak too stubborn?

5. Why did Ashok & (boss) Rajeev get along well while Deepak did not?
6. Why was Deepak getting along well with his previous bosses?
7. How could this situation could have been prevented?

Let us now view this case after getting the knowledge of MBTI

- Source of conflict is the preferred style

Boss – Rajeev's Type is –INTJ

I: He expects his subordinates to understand without communicating.

I: Never gives clear ideas / indications nor gives positive feedback.

N: Intuitive – wants big picture not details - Main idea.

T: Critical thinkers. Harsh, short tempered (lack of empathy).

N: His least choice was S. Could not deal with details and lengthy information.

J: Boss was judging which did not allow him to change his position.

Had Deepak known the style of boss, the situation would have possibly been different?

Subordinate Deepak's type is –ISTJ and hence

S: is dominant which is opposite to boss.

I: uncomfortable in communicating, did not ask questions, and clarifications (worked on assumption).

J: Deepak's J did not allow him to change his report once written, despite Ashok suggestion.

Deepak's previous bosses were ESTJ and were comfortable with details (S), while Rajeev was not (N). Each pushed his strength on each other's weakness.

His friend Ashok had ENTP Type

N with E of Ashok fits his boss INTJ

Ashok was always to the point (N), omitting details that turned his boss off.

He used to ask questions from his boss to fill up the gap with just the necessary amount of details.

- Most of us impose our dominant styles on each other. If we know the personality type of the other person with whom we are interacting, we can deal with him better by understanding him deeply.

How to relate with others using MBTI

If other person is Extrovert Type then – E

- Listen, be active responder.
- Be energetic, enthusiastic.
- Support his need for communication.
- Recognize his need for social interaction.

If other person is Introversion Type then -I

- Relate one to one (He wants privacy).
- Value his need for privacy.
- Give him time to change, focus, respond (let him take his own time).
- Also ask questions to draw him out and seek clarification.
- Do not expect from him an instant response.

If other person is Sensing Type then – S

- Give him details. Further if he is introvert also, give details in writing.
- Be orderly and organized.
- Use fact with evidence (and written reports for introvert).

- Be direct and avoid ambiguity.
- Use reports with break ups (verbal for E and written for I).

If other person is Intuitive Type then – N

- Give him an overview first.
- Discuss opportunities for future and important issues.
- He can live with ambiguity.
- Ask what if, let him imagine.
- Help him to draw a vision, ideas.
- Give him time to reflect, or seek clarification and grasp your ideas.

If other person is Thinking Type then – T

- Be logical and objective. Use verifiable data.
- Avoid personal opinion and value impositions.
- He expects quality, so don't compromise. Do your home work thoroughly.
- Since T types are not tactful, do not allow your feelings to be hurt, if you are not given feedback or appreciation.

If other person is Feeling Type then – F

- Be honest and sincere.
- Friendly and personal. Show your feelings.
- Avoid blaming the person.

If other person is Judging Type then – J

- Do not disturb his order/schedules.
- Value his time because he values.
- Take his deadlines seriously.

If other person is Percieving then – P

- Be open to options and change (flexible).
- Let him set his own deadlines.

Other key points in relating with others

1. Find out the dominant style of your boss/top managers.
2. First generation entrepreneurs persons are usually N (intuitive) but not necessary.
3. We have a tendency to change / adjust as per need.
4. With experience one can adjust himself to meet other's need by being aware of types and becoming careful.
5. It takes time to build relations but a minute to spoil.

How can he appreciate?

A person in my acquaintance is a typical `Thinking' type by nature. He is an excellent troubleshooter, problem solver and can always find what still needs to be improved. However, he can hardly appreciate people. I frequently go to him to take his opinion about my brochures or any other proposals but only after I have spent considerable time in perfecting it. Without uttering a single word of appreciation for the efforts made by me, he would simply jump to a critical evaluation and point out what needs to be improved. My wife was once accompanying me to such a meeting and was shocked to observe his behavior. She said. "This person has no heart. He is jealous of you and can only criticize". Since I have my knowledge of MBTI, I was fully aware that he could never appreciate any work because he is a typical `thinking type'. He is an excellent problem solver and would always think objectively directly coming to the point but without appreciating the efforts made. If I had to get a good evaluation of my proposal, he is possibly the right person to do so. Expecting appreciation from him would be foolish on my part. Hence, I never take his evaluation as criticism. After attending my MBTI program my wife has stopped feeling bad about the fault finding nature of this person as she now understands the strengths and pitfalls of a typical 'Thinking' type.

Effects of personality types on work situations

EXTROVERSION	*INTROVERSION*
• Like variety and action • Enjoy interacting with people • Develop their ideas through discussion • Learn new tasks by talking and doing • Interested in how other people do their work	• Like silence for concentration • Enjoy focusing on a project or task • Develop their ideas internally • Learn new tasks by reading and reflecting • Enjoy working alone with no interruptions
SENSING	*INTUITION*
• Focus on immediate issues • Provide a realistic and practical perspective • Like to perfect standard ways to do things by fine tuning • Build to conclusions by collecting facts • Draw on their own and others' experience	• Follow their inspirations • Provide connections and meanings • Like solving new, complex problems • Start with the big picture, fill in the facts • Prefer change, innovative approach
THINKING	*FEELING*
• Focus on the tasks • Use logical analysis to under-stand and decide • Want mutual respect and fairness among colleagues • Are firm-minded, can give criticism when appropriate • Apply principles consistently	• Focus on people's interactions • Use values to understand and decide • Want harmony and support among colleagues • Are empathetic, prefer to accommodate and reach consensus • Apply values consistently
JUDGING	*PERCEIVING*
• Want to plan their work and follow the plan • Like to get things settled and finished • Feel supported by structure and schedules • Reach closure by deciding quickly • Focus on timely completion of a project	• Want to have flexibility in their work • Like to be spontaneous • Feel restricted by structure and schedules • Leave things open as long as possible • Focus on enjoying the process

Dealing with Extroversion is different from Introversion

As a consultant I have been working with two different plant heads of the same group requiring different ways of handling. If a long distance call comes in the morning, my guess that it is possibly Raman on the line proves mostly true. Raman as a typical 'Extroversion Type' was always keen to share with me the plant achievements, direct me for the next course of action and decide my next visit without allowing me to even utter a single word so far. He was enthusiastic in his discussion and spontaneous in his response. On the other hand, Satish the other plant head who was an `Introversion Type', never used to call me. Rather I had to take my own initiative in proposing the next plan of our interventions and he would ask me to submit it in written through email and allow him 2-4 days to study it. And I knew that once he was committed after detailed study; he would not change it whereas Raman might redirect me the same evening to change my plan. My knowledge of MBTI helped me to understand that dealing with Raman had to be different from enrolling Satish. I was rather enjoying dealing with both without getting upset.

Importance of various roles and tasks in management

In an organization or a work situation usually all roles and tasks are needed to a lesser or greater extent depending on its uniqueness.

Intuitive Roles-N

Plan, Visualize, Forecast, Anticipate, Envision, Create, Innovate, Take risk, New approaches, Inter-connect.

Sensing Role-S

Facts, Details, Specificity, Data-Borne, Documentation, Present-Focus, Step-by-Step, Pragmatic, Brief.

Extroversion Role-E

Knowledge of Environment, Harnessing it, Relating to it, Dealing with it, Impact on/of Environment, Build links.

Introversion Role-I

Working with own ideas/concepts, Standing up, Reflect, Concentrate, Learning from own mistakes, In-depth.

Thinking Role – T

Objectivity, Rule-bound, Non-personal, Firmness, Analysis, Discipline, Direct and Control, Task oriented.

Feeling Role - F

Involve people, Winning commitment, Awareness of human values/ needs, Inspire, Persuade, Help, Motivate.

Judging Role-J

Organize, Structure, Conclusion, Time-Conscious.

Perceiving Role-P

More options, Probing, Openness, Quality, Flexibility, Taking in new information, Adapt, Adventure, Process-focus.

Can you imagine if an organization has all Intuitives and no Sensors or vice versa? In the first case practical execution may suffer and in the second case, innovations would suffer.

This Sensing CEO Never Appreciated the Intuitive

ABC was established about 70 years back and used to be a great name in its product line and type of business. It had started a down turn in profits and the staff was highly demoralized with a feeling of stagnation. In my survey of the organizational culture I found that the CEO was a true `Sensing Type'. It was also observed that he hardly allowed any new idea to emerge and used to subdue simply by asking examples or evidences of effective implementation. Furthermore, he was so methodical and detailed that even small purchase, of say a table chair, had to pass through him and he used to enjoy grilling his staff for escaping minute details. As a result employees had stopped taking any risk or suggesting anything new. CEO would always shoot down the new idea by simply asking whether it has been implemented somewhere else. This was enough to kill the innovative spirit of the think tank or 'Intuitives'. When MBTI was used, he could find the reason of this company not diversifying for the last 70 years. As a great insight he rather started respecting the other types of nature/ opinions compared to his unconscious favoring of his own types. He restructured the whole company. Saving of millions was reported within 6 months through Kaizen (continuous improvement) and the company had planned diversification as well.

Using type difference at work

Though everyone can learn skills in non-preferred areas, co-workers can benefit from the natural focus and skills of colleagues with preferences different from their own.

While no one should use the personality type theory to avoid tasks or to excuse unacceptable or insensitive behavior, in works settings it would be an advantage to utilize the natural strengths of various types in the following manner.

- The clearest vision of the future usually comes from an Intuitive type.
- The most practical realism usually comes from a Sensing type.
- The most incisive analysis usually comes from a Thinking type.
- The most skillful understanding and handling of people usually comes from a Feeling type.

The constructive use of differences

This is a step beyond recognizing and accepting differences as it enables us to value and integrate other perspectives. Steps in applying the constructive use of differences:

- Becoming aware of the differences and realize that differences can help us to grow if we can utilize them constructively.
- Learning about the other preferences and their preferred way of working.
- Appreciate and acknowledge the value of others viewpoints.
- Involving others in the task/team and seeking them out.

Leveraging the diversity as a team

The Vice President of a reputed company once narrated the following story to me.

"Surender was one of my deputies and a strong `Judging' type by nature whereas I was a typical case of 'Perceiving'. On any new proposal regarding training or an HR intervention, I would keep exploring to great depths so as to find the best solution out of visible and invisible possibilities. Surender, on the other hand, after receiving a proposal would like to finish it as early as possible. He was ignorant that many times it was actually a premature decision, which he was pushing without fully exploring the options. He was a scheduled person who enjoyed closing the pending issues as early as possible. He used to tell others that as a boss I am not a fast decision-maker. Knowing his nature, its strengths and likely pitfalls, I told him. 'Surender, you are an excellent closer which I am not, but I am a good explorer and you mostly close the decisions without fully exploring other options. Can we not pool our strengths and avoid pitfalls? That will happen only when we start respecting the values we can provide as a team. With this understanding and leveraging of diversity, we emerged as a good team and could execute many innovative things with quality and within the time frame."

The "Best Part" of Types

ISTJ-ISFJ

Respecting and relying on internally stored, realistic, and complete data about actual events and people who are important to them.

INFJ-INTJ

Developing and relying on clear, complex inner insights about the present and future.

ISTP-INTP

Logically organizing vast amounts of data or concepts into systematic explanatory structures.

ISFP-INEP

Assessing everything by strong inner values about honoring and supporting human beings.

ESTP-ESFP

Delight in action, experience, get stimulated by interaction with the world and people.

ENTP-ENFP

Scanning the environment for new stimulation by interaction with the world and people.

ESTJ-ENTJ

Decisively, logically, and efficiently structuring the external environment to achieve goals.

ESFJ-ENFJ

Structuring the external environment to meet the needs of people and to adjust it with their own values.

Use of type in choosing a career or work areas

It has been observed that generally people with a particular type would enjoy more naturally certain areas of work or profession as it can utilize his or her inherent strengths. The classification is listed below.

ST	SF	NF	NT
Apply these by being			
Practical & analytical	Sympathetic & Friendly	Insightful & enthusiastic	Logical & analytical
And can find more scope for their interest in:			
Technical skills with objects and encouraging facts	Practical help and service for people technical	Understanding and people	Theoretical& frameworks
And may have natural preference for careers in:			
Applied Science	Healthcare	Psychology	Physical science
Business	Community Service	Human resources	Research
Administration	Teaching	Teaching	Management
Banking	Supervision	Research	Computers
Law enforcement	Religious services	Literature	Law
Production	Support services	Religious service	Engineering
Construction	Sales	Healthcare	Technical work
		Arts & music	

While all human beings have the ability to adjust as per situations irrespective of their nature and type, people can develop the maturity to excel in other areas as well. It takes awareness and practice to work perfectly in our non-preferred areas. However it is still advised to find certain elements/areas of natural preference so that work can be enjoyed rather than suffer it as a burden. Excellence can be achieved only when work is enjoyable.

Typical Types Biases

You exhibit type bias when:

- You don't recognize the validity and value of the ways naturally followed by another type for doing things.
- You are critical of someone who is doing something "true to its type".
- You value only what you understand, what is natural to you.
- You project onto an opposite type, an area of yourself that you neglect or feel uncomfortable with.
- You label opposite preferences as limiting or limited.
- You attribute motive and intention to opposite preferences, instead of understanding how they function for that person.

Examples of common type biases

- E's may believe I's are "intentionally withholding information" when they are actually processing the information internally and reflecting on their thought process.
- I's may believe E's are not interested in the conversation when they are distracted by some external activity or person.
- S's may see N's as grandiose or trying to change the subject when they "leap" or use gut feelings.
- N's may see S's are trying to "shoot down their ideas" when they raise practical questions regarding implementation and draw on their past experiences.
- T's may see F's as "always talking about people and their grievances." Resisting change when F's want to process the emotional impact of a decision on people.
- F's may see T's as being critical and unkind when T's are trying to analyze objectively and solve the problem.
- J's may see P's as lazy or trying to sabotage a project when P's are not yet ready to move to conclusion as they are still probing/exploring further for betterment.

- P's may see J's as trying to "straight-jacket" them when J's are trying to keep a discussion on track and in accordance with the schedule/ agenda.

Different Drums and Different Drummers

If my wants are different from your, please don't consider me wrong. Or if I believe other than you, at least pause before you correct my view.

Or if my emotion is less than yours, or more, given the same circumstances, try not to ask me to feel more strongly or weakly. Or yet if I act, or fail to act, in the manner of your design for action, let me be.

I do not, for the moment at least, ask you to understand me. That will come only when you are willing to give up changing me into a copy of you.

I may be your spouse, your parent, your offspring, your friend, or your colleague. If you will accept me without changing my personality, one day you will realize, that my ways are not wrong and they may suits me.

To put up with me is the first step to understanding me. Not that you embrace my ways as right for you, but that you are no longer irritated or disappointed with me for my seeming waywardness. And in understanding me you might come to prize my differences from you, and far from seeking to change me, preserve and even nurture those differences.

Story of a China Girl-- Li-Li

A long time ago in China, a girl named Li-Li got married and went to live with her husband and mother-in-law. In a very short time, Li-Li observed that she couldn't adjust with her mother-in-law at all. Their personalities were very different, and Li-Li got furious by many of her mother-in-law's habits. In addition, she criticized Li-Li constantly.

Days passed and weeks passed. Li-Li and her mother-in-law never stopped arguing and fighting. But what made the situation even worse was that, according to ancient Chinese tradition, Li-Li had to bow to her mother-in-law and obey her every wish. All the anger and unhappiness in the house was causing Li-Li's poor husband great distress.

Finally, Li-Li could not bear her mother-in-law's bad temper and dictatorship any longer, and she decided to do something about it. Li-Li went to see her father's good friend, Mr. Huang, who sold herbs. She told him the situation and asked if he would give her some poison so that she could solve the problem once in a moment. Mr. Huang thought for a while, and finally said, "Li-Li, I will help you solve your problem, but you must listen to me and obey what I tell you."

Li-Li said, "Yes, Mr. Huang, I will do whatever you ask me to do." Mr. Huang went into the back room, and returned in a few minutes with a package of herbs. He told Li-Li, "You can't use a quick-acting poison to get rid of your mother-in-law, because that would cause people to become suspicious. Therefore, I have given you a number of herbs that will slowly build up poison in her body. Every other day prepare some delicious meal and put a little of these herbs in her serving. Now, in order to make sure that nobody suspects you when she dies. You must be very careful to act very friendly towards your mother-in -law. Don't argue with her, obey her every wish, and treat her like a queen." Li-Li was so happy. She thanked Mr. Huang and hurried home to start her plot of murdering her mother-in-law. Weeks went by and months went by, and every other day, Li-Li served the specially treated food to her mother-in-law. She remembered what Mr. Huang had said about avoiding suspicion, so she controlled her temper, obeyed her mother-in-law, and treated her as her own mother.

After six months, the whole household had changed. Li-Li had practiced controlling her temper so much that she found that she almost never got mad or upset. She hadn't had an argument with her mother-in-law in six months because she now seemed much kinder and easier to get along with. The mother-in-law's attitude toward Li-Li changed, and she began to love Li-Li like her own daughter. She kept telling friends and relatives that Li-Li was the best daughter-in-law one could ever find. Li-Li and her mother-in-law were now treating each other like a real mother and daughter.

Li-Li's husband was very happy to see what was happening. One day, Li-Li came to see Mr. Huang and asked for his help again. She said, "Dear Mr. Huang, please help me to keep the poison from killing my mother-in-law! She's changed into such a nice woman, and I love her like my own mother. I do not want her to die because of the poison I gave her."

Mr. Huang smiled and nodded his head. "Li-Li, there's nothing to worry about. I never gave you any poison. The herbs I gave to you were vitamins to improve her health. The only poison was in your mind and your attitude toward her, but that has been all washed away by the love which you gave to her."

Have you realized that how you treat others is exactly how they will treat you?

> *There is a wise Chinese saying: "The person who loves others will also be loved in return."*

Instead of being bent upon changing people first understand them and their perspectives and fair chances are that you will also be understood in due course of time.

Summary

- Each individual and type has special gifts. There is no right or wrong type, no better or worse combination of types in work or relationships
- Everyone uses each of the preferences to some degree. Our type is made of those we prefer.
- Type does not explain everything. The human personality is too much complex. Self-empowerment by developing appropriate qualities for success, matters more in life than merely being of a particular type.

- If your type is that of Mahatma Gandhi or Bill Gates it does not mean that you are now Gandhi or Bill Gates. To become Gandhi or Bill Gates you need to develop qualities in yourself, which have been explained in various parts of this book. Type, of course, can provide you a natural advantage in your working in a desired way.
- You may use type to understand and forgive yourself, but not as an excuse for doing or not doing anything.
- Become aware of your types biases (we all have them!) to avoid negative stereotyping.

Chapter

5 Transformation

- Power of silence – first and essential step to transformation
- Empathic listening
- Power of acceptance
- Managing resentment
- Managing resentment – Forgiveness
- Power of agreement
- Power of gratitude
- Managing emotions
- Managing relationships
- Managing relationships-deposit chart
- Living in abundance
- Power of alignment
- Discovering our lost qualities
- Power of humor
- God's delay is not god's denial
- Equanimity in life-a wise person is happy even in bad times
- Power of softness and forcefulness
- The marks of maturity

Stuck is…Having only one way to see the situation…… and not liking what you see.

- Anonymous

Oh God give me the courage to change the things which can be and ought to be changed. Give me the serenity to accept the things which cannot be changed but give me the wisdom to know difference.

- Anonymous

Start With Yourself!

'When I was young and free and my imagination had no limits, I dreamt of changing the world.

As I grew older and wiser, I discovered the world would not change, so I shortened my sights somewhat and decided to change only my country.

But it, too, seemed immovable.

As I grew into my twilight years, in one last desperate attempt, I settled for changing only my family, those closest to me, but alas would have none of it.

And now as I lie on my deathbed, I suddenly realize: If I had only changed myself first, then by example I would have changed my family'.

From their inspiration and encouragement, I would then have been able to better my country and, who knows, I may have even changed the world.

- Anonymous

In this chapter I will present various powers that can transform our life and recreate a life that is powerful and chosen by us.

Power of Silence — First and Essential Step to Transformation

Silence is a condition of a quiet mind, not being so noisy with judgments and opinions. It is an art that puts to rest all judgments and opinions and prevents energy loss.

Observing silence can prevent our inner self from being affected by the environment.

Silence should be one of the most important qualities for us to acquire, as wisdom often accompanies it. To reflect and learn from a particular experience effectively, one should not be preoccupied with negative thoughts. The mind must be silent in order to see clearly the hidden messages behind that experience, which often leads to priceless realizations.

Since the mental noise is created by thoughts, one needs to know how to quieten the thoughts. One way to do this is to allow the mind to focus on one particular thing. It can be an object or the work that you are doing whereby your whole being is involved in it.

Another way to satiate the mind is to become an observer to every thought that is flowing through the mind. It is similar to watching a movie where one is not involved with the events taking place in the movie.

Knowing the meaning of silence is different from experiencing it. Those who have experienced the power of silence will know the value of observing it. Silence holds the key to clear thinking, positive action and higher productivity.

Meditation also helps in developing the power of silence.

Stop your inner dialogue and provide some silent spaces

A truly silent person is one who can look at the present and see the future.

In fact, we are nowhere close to it. In a few quick moments our mind has leapt beyond the present to childhood, to college, to club, to spouse, to boss, to America, to Hawai and so on.

While our minds wander across the globe, we end up not being present in the moment at all. We are missing from the very moment in which we think we exist. That moment has become dead, as we are absent in it.

When we look at the object and suspend our thoughts for a while, we enter a new, rejuvenated world. We are then fully present to see the object as it is not as we may describe it in our imagination or in our memories. We make no judgement or choices. We feel no regrets. No worry.

This simple exercise of suspending thought in order to see an object can refresh us and bring joyous meaning into a tired day. The more thoughts we chain together by association, the stronger the bridge becomes for the mind to walk upon.

When we cut back on the inner dialogue, we break down some links in the chain and allow for silent spaces between our thoughts. If we learn to stay intensely aware while in those silent spaces, we begin to see and hear the world in a newly vibrant and dynamic way.

Try to imagine what our lives could become if every moment we were fully conscious of everything around us. We will never get bored; no experience would ever be stale. We would literally be reborn fresh every moment of our existence.

That great walk in Rishikesh

Dr. Paula Horan the International Rekii Master, during the Core Empowerment Training at Rishikesh in the Himalayas took us for one hour nature walk everyday. The exercise was to watch, observe the natural creations, flowers, insects, tree, flowing Ganga river, blue sky, chirping and flying of birds, whatever comes within our observations. All was to be observed and felt as it was appearing to us without projecting any meaning to it. No judgment, no evaluation, just acceptance without a thought or a label. It was a great bliss inside. It was a happy and a powerful moment because it was without any evaluation. It reminded me of the joy a child gets when he is without any label. Is it not true that we are more stressed today due to so much labeling?

Reality is not what it seems

The ultimate reality may be different from your perceived reality. The world appears to us as it does because of the particular instruments we use in seeing it. We make just two categories right or wrong, positive and negative. Do we look into the naked reality without judgment or label? Once you start doing it, your life will become more natural, lighter and blissful.

Power of Truth

When you consciously say something inaccurate, those lies become something unrelated in the mind and create disharmony.

- Telling a lie means not narrating the things as you see them. The mind gets clouded and such a mind cannot be decisive. It is not rational.
- If you want to strengthen your mind and clarify it, do not say anything unrelated or inaccurate.

The benefit of following the time-honored values of living in truth is a tranquil mind. When we diverge from the standards of ethical conduct, our minds suffer from increased agitation. Let us take the example of telling the truth versus lying. When we lie, one part of the mind knows what the truth is and the other half knows just the opposite of it. Those two halves then live in tension.

Power of knowledge

A person is walking in a dark forest at twilight. He's alone, and the shadows around him are getting darker and darker. He sees an obstruction on the narrow pathway in front of him and stops dead in his tracks. "A snake" he gasps, and his heart starts pounding furiously.

He retraces his steps and races back to his village. He returns with a village friend who has brought along a lamp. His friend shines the light of the lamp towards the fearsome snake and the frightened man discovers that what he had seen as a snake is merely a rope, twisted in the shape of a slithering, fearsome reptile.

The pounding in his heart recedes. He proceeds on his way with a smile on his face.

Only knowledge of the reality behind the appearance can dissipate the effect of those appearances.

- Initially it was accepted that the Sun rotates around the Earth. Its reverse was proved after the discovery of telescope. Similarly the earth was believed to be flat rather than round and most of fishermen were told not to go far away into the sea fearing that they might fall at the end.

We live in our own reality made from our own experience and background. With our limited knowledge, we are not wrong. But after acknowledging the naked reality our view get broaden and then the whole paradigm may possibly shift.

Power of seeking

A seeker is a person with the following qualities:

An acknowledgement that he knows very little

Many people think they know everything. They get stuck in their limited knowledge. They never learn. The first thing a seeker knows is that he knows very little.

A willingness to learn

Many people acknowledge that they do not know, but they are not ready to learn.

Non-judgmental and open-minded

Some people would like to learn, but their narrow-minded and judgmental attitudes do not allow them to learn.

A total, one-way commitment to the path

Some people are open-minded, but they lack commitment and determination towards their goal. They keep hopping here and there and never progress on one path.

Always puts truth and service before pleasure

Sometimes even committed and determined people stray from the path in pursuit of momentary pleasures.

Patience and perseverance

Some people are committed, determined, and are not swayed by pleasures, but if they lack patience and perseverance, they become restless and dejected.

Are you a seeker? You are the best judge.

Empathic Listening

Empathic listening is the ability to understand others and requires us to listen without prejudice. People often say:

"How can you appreciate me when you do not even understand me".

"How will I open up with you unless you understand me and my unique situation/feelings? You may not know how to advise or counsel me".

Most people do not listen with the intent to understand. They listen with the intent to reply. They are either speaking or are preparing to speak.

Empathic listening is to understand by getting inside the other persons' frame of reference and know how they are feeling.

Empathic listening is deeply therapeutic and healing. It gives the other person a psychological atmosphere and once that need is met, you can focus on problem solving. It is depositing in the "Emotional Bank Account".

Selective listening-The opposite to empathic listening

We hear what we want to hear and have already decided, irrespective of what is really being said. How can then the other person feel that satisfaction of being listened? We also lose the opportunity of knowing the reality.

To give you an example of selective listening, let me share with you a story I heard in an Indian state where prohibition was introduced with lots of public opposition and a renowned medical expert was to address a group of alcoholics. He wanted to make a demonstration that would be powerful enough to make people realize that alcohol was injurious to health. He had two glasses, one with pure water and the other with pure alcohol. He put an earthworm into the water glass and it swam beautifully and came up to the top. He put another earthworm into the alcohol glass and it disintegrated before their eyes. He wanted to prove that this was what alcohol did to the internal body. He asked the group what was the moral of this exercise? A person from the back replied immediately "If you drink alcohol then you won't have worms in your stomach." Was that the message doctor wanted to convey? Of course it was not. That was selective listening.

Common obstacles of listening

Some of the common obstacles to proper listening are following:

- *Being judgmental*–(You listen only to seek support for the negative image you already have)
- *Rehearing*–Creating arguments against the speaker's view.
- *Mind Reading*–Disregard what he is saying and try to surmise what he really means.
- *Advising*–Advising instead of listening to make you feel needed. Distancing from his true feelings.
- *Pleasing*–Being so nice that you may end interrupting.
- *Filtering*–Hear something but not everything.
- *Deflecting*–You redirect by changing the subject or telling a joke when the topic is uncomfortable to you.

The awareness of these obstacles will help you to overcome them with practice.

Observing the other side—Essential step to empathic listening and mutual understanding

Empathy has been described as walking in another's shoes. It means to understand another person from his or her point of view. Observing the other side is an essential interpersonal skill. Without it, you cannot hope to get along with people.

Many in today's fast-paced busy society, are often taught to believe that it is right to persuade others to adopt their particular point of view. One must be "right" about the subject at hand, then bombard the opponent, long and hard with as many "facts" as one may find to support his position.

This "narrow mind" approach can lead only to confrontation, argument, and a hardening of positions, since the other person thinks in his mind and feels in his heart that he is right. And of course, from his own perspective, he is. In this scenario, you are giving the other person only two choices: surrender or use force in return. Neither results in a "win-win" situation.

It shouldn't be surprising that this approach is seldom successful, for "a mind convinced against its will is of the same opinion still."

The reality is that everyone wants to be right, at least a little bit right about what he or she believes. People want to be accepted and recognized for their basic intelligence, ideas, and opinions. And it is seldom the case that one person is totally right about something and another persor is totally wrong.

The point to realize is that people who believe they are right are never going to accept the fact that you are right until you find something that is right about their point of view. In other words, people will maintain a closed mind until you demonstrate that you do understand something about their position. Other people are more likely to open up their mind a little as well and begin to consider the value of your arguments only if you made them free to speak. In the process, you both learn something about each other's thought and act the way you do. Unfortunately, most people don't communicate effectively with each other. They just take turns talking.

When two people open up their mind to the other's views, they are well on their way to coming to mutual agreement. Alternatively, two people with closed minds are likely to continue endless arguments without getting on any conclusion.

Diagnose before you prescribe

- We should first understand the other person, i.e., diagnose before we prescribe. Those doctors who don't listen to patients fail to diagnose properly. The problems remains with the patient as he has hardly been understood.
- Understand the perception of the other and consider that the other person may not be sharing our paradigm. Even in the case of difference in perspective, you can evolve a win-win solutions.
- When we really deeply understand each other, we open the door for creative solutions and the third alternative. The differences then become the milestone to synergy.

Effective listening

Normally a person speaks at the rate of about 125 words per minute, whereas the mind functions at a rate between 450 to 500 words per minute. This allows your mind to think about other things for about two-thirds of the time when it is not being fully utilized. Your mind naturally tends to wander when it is not properly utilized. When you try to listen and think simultaneously, you end up doing neither very well. The trick for effective listening is to use this spare time to concentrate more closely on what the other person is saying.

Here are some additional tips to facilitate effective listening:

1. Be intensely interested in the topic being discussed. Many times we think that we already know everything about a given subject, but this is seldom case. If you really think the subject is boring and of no interest to you, even then start showing a sincere interest, and after a few minutes, you'll find that it offers many interesting things. Even if the speaker lacks proper speaking skills, ignore his shortcomings and instead focus on the words as they are being spoken as well as their meaning.
2. Be patient and don't form fixed opinions about the topic. Too often we jump to conclusions before people have stated their actual position.
3. Pause before replying to collect your thoughts and ensure that the speaker has finished what he wanted to say. People need adequate time to express themselves fully before responding to questions and criticism about their views from others.
4. Be broad-minded and empathize with the speaker from his point of view. Everyone has a right to speak. You may not like the particular person or what he represents, but nothing is gained if ideas cannot be communicated. A person's physical gestures, dress, or use of certain words may offend you. For some of these same reasons, you may offend the other person also. With an open mind and a sincere interest in the other person, each has a good chance of learning from the other.
5. There are times when one need emotional support. To talk as an outlet for stored-up thoughts about a problem on the job, a relationship with another, some other concern about the behavior of a family member, close friend or the spouse.

Expressing these feelings can be an exhilarating accomplishment. The feelings may relate career progress, personal victory, a great idea for the future, or an adventure in living. A person in this mood does not want to be challenged, judged, advised, debated, interrupted or ignored.

The person is saying "Please listen to me, I need to share my thoughts and feelings, with you. In such a situation I need your patience and tolerance because I might not be logical, clear, or correct and I need to understand myself. But wait until I've completely ventilated my feelings before you point out to me, or give me feedback or advice".

What would you do if someone wants you to listen:

- Was too busy?
- Started preaching and advising?
- Disagreed with the first things you said?

6. Have you ever been the listener when someone wanted to express their feelings, but didn't want your advice or comments? Was it easy to listen without offering solutions or advice? Could you play the role of an effective listener in this situation?
7. It is felt that the quickest way to impair a relationship and to cut off good communication is not to function as a listener when a person close to you feels the need to talk. How do you feel about this?

Power of Acceptance

Acceptance is an attitude. It's a mood, mental state. It is one's general policy on relating to the world at large. It is an active reaching out and approving the way things are.

- Acceptance means to acknowledge things as they are.
- It is the inner strength to accommodate the imperfections around us.
- It is not an act of agreeing with the imperfections.
- We may disagree with a person's point of view without getting upset. We can disagree without being disappointed.
- Acceptance is a mental condition showing maturity and strength by accepting the imperfections of the world. This is a good antidote for reactive behavior.
- Acceptance outburst the energy that got struck while hurt or frustrated.

When people don't get into the habit of accepting, acknowledging or embracing life, they never feel affirmed, wise or lively also. This is the cause of many problems.

- Healers teach us that all healings begin with acceptance.
- Being angry and frustrated about something (or someone)

diminishes your power. But acknowledging it and granting forgiveness, brings ease with it, and then power returns back to us with self-empowerment.

- This isn't resignation; rather, it's our capacity to just accept things as they are. It is our capacity for truth.
- Acceptance is saying yes, yes, yes to life.

Start accepting events as they occur. Don't demand or expect that events should happen as you would wish them to. Accept events as they actually are. This will not only make you more peaceful but also more balanced in your responses.

As an exercise you can write down 11 imperfections in your life (in yourself, in others, in your spouse and your organization) and then auto suggest the following statement and say it truly from the bottom of your heart in relation to any specific person "accept you as you are for I know that you are simply a victim of your own conditioned mind".

Find the good in whatever happens

A king along with his minister went to a forest for hunting and accidently injured himself by cutting his hand. The minister tried to console him, `Sir whatever happens just happens for something good. There should be something good in this as well'. The king was bleeding and was upset by his minister's response. He threw him in a deep well as mark of punishment for inappropriate remarks. He then proceeded for hunting in the forest but was caught by a group of tribesmen who were looking for a human sacrifice for their deity. When the king was presented to the chief priest for the sacrifice, the priest refused to kill him as the person was not a perfect sacrifice as he was already injured. It was necessary that the person for sacrifice should be healthy and without any injury. The king was thrown away and asked to disappear. The king thanked God for the injury caused to him and on his way rescued the minister by puffing him up from the deep well. He narrated the incident to the minister and said 'it was good that I was injured which really saved my life. But what was the good part in my throwing you in this deep well? The minister replied 'it was the best thing that could have happened to me in life. Had I not been thrown in the well, I would have accompanied you for hunting and in that case, would have been the perfect sacrifice for the deity'.

Make full use of whatever has happened to you. You never know what good it contains

Most of the difficulties which we face in life actually present us with an opportunity to turn inward and to invoke our own submerged inner resources. The trials we endure can and should lead us to our hidden strengths. Successful people look beyond the incident itself and try to form the habit of putting it to good use. You possess strengths you might not realize you have. Find one. Use it. If you encounter an opportunity against your values, then self-restraint is the resource needed; if pain or weakness, then stamina; if verbal abuse, then patience is what needed more.

We may not have control over what happens to us in life, but we do have control over how we react to what has happened or happens to us. How we meet life defines the difference between a happy person and sad one, a successful person and a failure. This point is simply illustrated by the following inspiring examples.

- Stephen Hawking had suffered by the devastation of Lou Gehrig's disease (amyotrophic lateral sclerosis), each day rapidly losing his ability to use his muscles, speech and the slightest movement of his hands. He earned an international reputation as the most brilliant theoretical physicist since Albert Einstein.
- Greek orator Demosthenes overcame a weak voice and an ineffective speech delivery to become one of the greatest orators. He practised at the seashore with pebbles in his mouth in order to improve the strength of his speech delivery.

Managing Resentment

The following incident narrated by a friend of mine will give an idea of what resentment can be and how it gets created as well:

"In the capacity of President of a large professional association, I was the convenor of a national level conference. I had invited the articles/papers from more than hundred speakers, experts and wanted them to be published in the form of a book. I was leading a large team of volunteers and asked three of my professional friends who were also the members of the executive body to form an editorial committee and sort out the articles for publication. I had worked on the articles to some extent and had negotiated the price of the book from one of the reputed publishers and then got engaged in other committees being the in-charge of the conference. My involvement with the book had started few months back and now I was keenly awaiting its release and was looking forward to see my name in it. When I received the latest edition of the book before it was to be launched in the conference, I was bitterly disappointed as my name was not even listed in it or even properly acknowledged. My three colleagues whom I had asked to supervise the publication, were listed as authors of the book along with their profiles. I was fuming inside all upset and angry. Just a one line acknowledgement from the trio in the book did not pacify my anger. The conference was rated as one of the best of its kind at the national level and as convenor I received all praise for my efforts to make it a great and successful event.

Despite all this praise for the conference, my thrill of doing the best conference got diminished soon, as I felt the trio had cheated me. The trio who were otherwise good friends of mine suddenly became my worst enemies and biggest cause of resentment. I was angry inside but pretending to be okay, could not say anything to them (looking good trap).

The friendship and trust was getting lost. The trio was possibly unaware of this storm inside me and ignorant of my feelings. Even if someone praised me for my innovative and remarkable contributions to the conference, it would just remind me of the injustice caused and the cheating by my dear colleagues. Unable to bear it any longer one day I just exploded on Rajan, one of the three and gave him a full taste of my pent-up anger. While expressing my anger he got clarity of my expectations that were never met by trio. Rajan agreed and admitted that my contributions for the book deserved a better acknowledgement and it was a mistake on their part which was out of ignorance rather than with any intention. Rajan said, 'we would have been delighted to include your name had I spelled my desire for the same'. I realized my mistake and the lapse on my part. I had simply worked on assumptions and was expecting something without clarifying my expectations. It was the frustration of undelivered communication. `Intentions created but not expressed'. Furthermore, I had simply assumed that I was entitled to be a member of editorial team in my capacity as convenor of the conference since in such earlier conferences of this professional body the convenor was given this status. Therefore, I felt there was no need to explicitly express my desire. They should have understood it.

While we will discuss later on this topic what this person did to get rid of this resentment and how he handled it, let us first consider some aspects of resentment.

- Resentment is an energy sucking act reflected in bitter or angry feeling one holds within when insulted, ignored, injured, etc.
- Resentment is normally directed at a person or a thing. Behind all resentment there is always an expectation. Both expectation and resentment go hand in hand. We usually have an expectation of how something should be or how someone should behave and if they do not comply with our expectation, we harbor resentment towards that person or situation.
- Resentment may also occur when someone harms us with or without intention in some way and make us feel hurt and angry. The interesting thing is that person who has hurt us may not even be aware of it but we may carry this tinge of sadness around us wherever we go or interact with anyone.
- Once the feeling of resentment is impressed in our subconscious mind, it will eventually get expressed through our behavior, verbal and non-verbal communication. In other words, we will display the same characteristics which we resent in another person and we may not be aware of it at all.
- Medically there is enough proof that energy suckers, particularly resentment, affect our immune system causing many ailments and doing more harm as the years go by.

According to Dr. Wayne W. Dyer, "Resentment creates invisible inner world blocks. Our success gets blocked. Sometimes we get angry at the way people treat us".

> *Instead of being angry at the way we were treated, regardless of how horrible we have assessed it to be, we need to learn as well as view that treatment from another perspective. "They did what they knew how to do, given the conditions of their lives. They operated from their conditioned mind".*
>
> *Most of obnoxious acts are cries for help.*
>
> *As an exercise think of a person whom you resent most. Auto suggests the following statement with true feelings. "I forgive you from the bottom of my heart for I know that you were simply the victim of your own conditioned mind".*

Managing Resentment — Forgiveness

Forgiving others is the best way to manage resentment. All religions advise us to practice this as it is the best remedy. Let us see how. Forgiving others is an act of magnanimity

- People who forgive others are those who are fully aware of their own as well as other's limitations. By forgiving, they are actually acknowledging that perfection is a very relative term and nobody can be expected to be perfect in this world from everybody's point of view. They are also acknowledging that all imperfections are only circumstantial, highly temporary and can change with time.

  Forgiveness becomes extremely difficult if we have traces of the energy suckers particularly resentment, revenge, blame, judgments, hatred etc.
- People suffer because of their inability to forgive truly from the bottom of their hearts.
- True benefit of forgiveness is that when we forgive someone, we stop blaming him or her any more and the relationship is back to normal. This improves teamwork and interpersonal effectiveness at work.
- Forgiveness is the key that unlocks the door of resentment and the handcuffs of hate. It is that power which breaks the chains of bitterness and the shackles of selfishness.

> *"Forgiveness is an act of self love. If we want to live an awakened and enlightened life we must put the principle of forgiveness into work on a continuous basis."* Dr. Wayne W. Dyer

Forgive others but do take corrective action to improve the matter like clearing the situation, learning out of the incident, making a new resolution etc. This will help you to look into future possibilities instead of being stuck in the present.

- Don't be angry inside.
- Health is not what you eat but it is also what is eating you up.

In the example narrated earlier about the publishing of a book, the person did the following to deal with the situation and learn from it:

1. He discussed the issue with the trio and expressed his true feelings in a non-provocative but sincere manner.
2. He learnt a big lesson in not carrying the frustration of undelivered communication. He resolved to work on his expectation and express it so well that something can be done about it. The introspection led him to be more assertive in his communication and expressing clearly the expectations.
3. He practiced forgiveness. He realized that the trio might have acted as per the best choice available to them. People usually don't have bad intentions to damage us or work against us. It just happens. They would like to take their best course of action as per their reality/perception. They have acted as per their own conditioning of mind so best way is to forgive them for your own sake'.
4. The incident actually served to inspire him to start writing a new book. Since he had a strong desire to be author of a book, he started writing his own book. When he successfully wrote this book, he was thankful for the incident as whatever had happened, it just happened. The reconciliation with the trio helped him clear the upset, abandon his anger and rather in a gratifying manner he proposed Rajan as next President of the association in his place after his tenure.

Excerpts from the book-"You will see it when you believe it" by Wayne W. Dyer

These are the excerpts regarding the incident of forgiving his father while standing at his grave by Wayne W. Dyer. His father had deserted his family when Wayne was just two years old and he has seen his mother's suffering from this desertion and had developed great resentment against his father as Wayne had to spend his precious years in foster house. Wayne used to be very angry whenever he heard a word called 'father'. He was always upset and fuming against his father whom he had never met again for next two decades, till this specific incident happened, which totally transformed his life. The incident is about his feelings when he came to know that his father against whom he had so much anger had died recently and he goes at his graveyard to converse with him.

"When I finally stood looking at the marker on the grass, MELVIN LYLE DYER, I was transfixed. During the next two and half-hours I conversed with my father for the very first time. I cried out loud, oblivious to my surroundings. And I talked out loud, demanding answers from a grave. As the hours passed I began to feel a deep sense of relief, and I became very quiet. The calmness was overwhelming. I was almost certain that my father was there with me. I was no longer talking to a gravestone, but was somehow in the presence of something, which I could not and still cannot explain.

When I resumed my one-way conversation, I said, "I somehow feel that I was sent here today and that you had something to do with it. I don't know what your role is or even if you have one, but I am sure that the time has come to abandon this anger and hatred that I have carried for so long. I want you to know that from this moment, all my anger has gone. I forgive you. I don't know what motivated you to continue your life as you did. I am sure that you must have felt many forlorn moments knowing that you had three children that you would never see. Whatsoever had been going in your mind but I am no longer angry on you. When I think of you it will be with compassion and love. I am letting go of all this disorder that is inside me. I know in my heart that you were simply doing what you knew how to do given the conditions of your life at the time. Even though I have no memory of having seen you, even though it was my fondest dream to someday meet you face to face and hear your side, I will not let those thoughts ever hold me back, feeling of love is all I have for you." As I stood at that lonely grave marker in southern Mississippi I said words I have never forgotten, because they signified how I would be conducting my life from then onwards: "I send you love . . . I send you love . . . honestly, I send you love."

In one pure honest moment I have experienced the feeling of forgiveness for the man who was my father, for the child I had been who wanted to know and love him. I felt a kind of peace and cleansing that was new for me. Though I was unaware of it at that time, that simple act of forgiveness was the beginning of an entirely new level of experiencing life for me. I was on the threshold at a stage of my life that was to - encompass worlds that I could not even imagine in those days."

Later on Wayne W. Dyer became one of the best-selling authors in USA and is transforming the life of millions of people across the world. That is the power of forgiving others which is although usually difficult but very useful and gratifying.

Forgiving ourselves

If forgiving others is difficult, forgiving ourselves is even harder. Many people spend their whole lives punishing themselves mentally and physically for what they believe to be their own shortcomings. By not forgiving the self, many persons systematically destroy all their relationships; some live a life of poverty or sickness. At the root of this suffering can be a belief system which says, "I have done a lot of naughty things", "I am guilty", or "I don't deserve to be healthy and happy". You may be surprised at how many sick people there who are not convinced that they deserve to be healthy and happy!

If you were feeling guilty I would suggest that you have endure enough. Why prolong it? If you were to feel guilty for an extra year or two, it wouldn't help things.

Throw out your guilt. It's not that easy to throw it out. Maintaining a healthy mind takes a lot of effort as does maintaining a healthy body. But it is worth the effort.

Power of Agreement

Let us consider this example narrated by a bank manager.

"I had been invited by one of my office staff member to attend the birthday party of his son. The party was arranged at his village which was 18 km away from the city and I promised to be there at 7.30 pm along with my family as he had requested my presence and I too was keen. I had all intentions to go there while getting ready for the same my friend gave tickets of a famous charity show, which he had managed in the VIP rows. I told him of my engagement but I was tempted to accompany him to the show neglecting somewhere about the evening birthday party.

On the other hand, the staff member kept on waiting anxiously for long as I was supposed to be his chief and most important guest in the village. The whole village waited for me to arrive. When questioned, the staff kept on defending me saying that I might be stuck in the traffic and should be on the way. After a prolonged, fruitless and humiliating period of waiting, he finally cuts the cake.

On first working day (Monday), I presented a nice gift to him for his son and made a good excuse for not attending the function on account of some reasons. He stated the whole incident and said that even a timely phone call would have saved him from the humiliation caused due to his absence. I realized the blunder I had made. The person appears now to have forgotten the incident. But something has got damaged inside me when I remember of his humiliations. My self-respect is lost. My trust with him was lost, as I had not kept my word."

An agreement is a declaration or a commitment or promises that we make to honor our words. It expresses an intention. When you make an agreement with someone, it creates an expectation and the other person to some extent becomes dependent on you.

Every role that we play in life has its own agreement. For example, we play roles in our lives such as father, mother, son, manager, husband, wife, etc. which has their own implied agreements.

Some of the agreements we break may involve:

a. Family b. Ourselves c. Friends

d. Workplace e. Spirituality f. Society

- When we make an agreement, we give a commitment which has power, so never take it lightly. When we break an agreement, a part of the self gets affected. It affects our self-image.

Agreement plays a large role in our lives and in our ability to stay in balance and in harmony with ourselves as well as others. All agreements are promises we make to ourselves and to others. <u>When we keep a promise we get rewarded and when we break a promise we need to pay a price.</u>

Price that we usually pay for breaking an agreement.

i. Loss of self trust
ii. Loss of trust from others
iii. Loss of self-esteem, respect and confidence
iv. Relationship deteriorates
v. Lack of clarity

Is it possible to keep all your agreements?

In life it is not possible to fulfill all agreements because everyone is living at different levels of expectations. However one can reduce the breaking of agreements to the least by observing the following rules:

1. Make only those agreements, which are very important to you. Avoid making agreements that are only important to someone else, but not so important to you. In order to avoid hurting others' feeling either you may;

i. break the agreement later, and create a feeling of hurt, or

ii. keep your agreement but hurt your feelings.

Therefore it is better to say on the spot so that the other person can be clear and take the right course of action from the beginning.

2. Write down your agreements with others in a diary so that you can be reminded of your commitments or agreements.
3. Any agreement that you make, regardless of how small it may be value it. Never take any agreement lightly.
4. As soon as you know that you are unable to keep an agreement, inform the other person. Rework/renegotiate the agreement if you cannot honor it. Make an apology and render it respectfully and graciously.
5. If you have broken an agreement due to some unforeseen circumstances, forgive yourself and apologies to the other party.
6. Avoid making agreements that you are not sure of keeping. If you are uncertain, it is better to inform the other person by saying a straight "No". If you can still make it, then it would be a benefit.
7. Consider all agreements that you might have broken. What can you do now to correct the situation? A sincere apology sometimes may create wonders.
8. Also consider in your relationships, the agreements that you need to reinforce now, while there is still time.

When you have done something wrong or made a mistake

- Explain the position with complete details (focus on situation with maturity, rather than reacting to it in an impulsive manner.
- Show your true feelings. The wronged person be more likely to calm down if you look upset. If you admit you are at fault, he will be generous and stop his grudging, disciplining or unnecessary preaching you further.
- Passing the comments is usually an ineffective approach as it sounds of excuse making. So be wary of excuses.
- Make a joint restitution to correct the mistake or at least avoid it in future.

- After the apologies and excuses, you must act to compensate the damage you have done.
- Token gifts can do something but material gestures, are not always appropriate.
- Give an assurance of not repeating and think of a new system that will recompense the mistake and solve other problems also.
- Many great things including transformations just happen when we resolve to do things differently after learning from our blunders.
- Think finally that it was an accident and bound to happen. Hence do not carry the guilt for long (treat it as fate).

They say the best men are moulded out of faults. Consider the goof ups as a prime opportunity for self development. Mistakes can make us wiser if we learn from them. While the fool keeps on repeating mistakes, the wise person learns from the mistakes, not only of his own but that of others too.

Power of Gratitude

A person must have a deep sense of gratitude for all things.

- Gratitude means being profoundly thankful. It is an emotional experience within for having or receiving something. When we have gratitude in our hearts, we feel good.

> * *A sense of gratitude in a person is very important. No man can live entirely off his wits alone.*
>
> * *We did not create the abundant natural resources we need to survive. Every individual's work depends on the cooperation of other people. In other words, we owe our daily lives to the blessing of nature and the goodwill of our fellow men. It is important to be aware of this, to feel deep gratitude, and to repay the kindness of others. Do so, and you become a source of abundance energy.*

- The feeling of gratitude creates happiness, satisfaction and peace within oneself. In other words, it develop optimism.
- The constant feeling of thankfulness is therapeutic. It also upgrade the energy suckers such as greed, hatred and jealousy.

- We should be grateful to our creator, parents, the universe and our ancestors for the world they gave to us to live into. We ought to be grateful for many other things such as oxygen, having a healthy body, food, etc. in life.
- When we do a favor to somebody and he is thankful for it, and he acknowledges and appreciates us, the chances are that we will help him again. Similarly when we give thanks to the universe for all the things that we have, it will give us more.

The thought or feeling of thanks is said to create a strong magnetic field, which attracts further things into our life. Gratitude is an excellent quality to cultivate, and it is particularly important to grow in life. When all of us attain this state of mind, we shall see the birth of a world, which is truly prosperous in a material and spiritual sense.

- An expression of gratitude increases the value of things. If you perceive somebody's gift as a trifle, you attach very little value to it. But if you appreciate it, its value will seem proportionately greater and you will be able to make better use of it.
- Remember that a thankful heart can turn lead into gold.

If we have little capacity to appreciate, then we will become resentful and discontented for no good reason. This will give us a jaundiced outlook and make us liable to hurt others. On the other hand, a strong sense of appreciation will help us find something good in everything, making us light-hearted and at peace with others. In this state of mind, we will find it easy to follow the old phrase, live and let live.

So practice having a grateful attitude and you will be happy.

Write down one achievement of which you are very proud

- Now make a list of all the people, known or unknown, who helped you accomplish your task.
- Re-read your list and think about it.
- Mentally send a 'thank you' to each person who helped you in your endeavor. In some cases a negative action by a person may have spurred you on to increased activity in your task. Include that person in your thanks note.

Attitude of gratitude

We should be thankful for what we have, not only from a spiritual point of view, but also from a scientific point of view. The great spiritual preachers; Krishna, Jesus, Buddha, Mohammed and others have taught that we should count our blessings. The wisdom behind this is that our mind is a magnet and we gravitate towards what we think about the most.

If Amrik continues to grudge that no one has supported him, that there is never enough money, nobody likes him, he always gets the rotten jobs and life is tough, then he will overlook opportunities, refuse offers of assistance, and continue to propel himself into financial and emotional bankruptcy. On the subconscious level he will repel opportunity and attract one drama after another as he sees his world unfold precisely as anticipated. Amrik's picture of things is that he misses out and goes without reward and he will create a life for himself in accordance with his own thinking.

It is said that the universe is essentially fairly forgiving, but that if a person consistently concentrates on what he doesn't have, he will get less and less of what he wants. I have also found that those people who have the most beautiful friendships are those people who value them very highly. Those who lead active and fulfilling lives are the people who are consistently rejoicing in what life gives them.

In many cases we may have been conditioned to look at the negative side of life. If there are ten things going right and one thing wrong, we tend to draw attention to what is wrong. When your son gets eleven out of twenty in a math's test, we don't concentrate on the eleven he got right but on the nine that he missed. When we have a headache, we don't say "My chest, stomach, legs and arms feel great!" We say, "My head aches!" Too many people believe that focusing on faults is being realistic and being rational.

There is a positive side to everything! If you are miserable about all the things you want but haven't got, think also about all the good things you never expected and have still got it.

* My primary school teacher in the village Mr. Balbir Singh had always been a source of inspiration to me, as he used to encourage me regularly. I awfully adore him the most. After attaining fairly a prosperous career, I was keen to meet him personally to express my gratitude for his inspiration. I had managed to search his present address and went to

meet him along with my wife and children. I felt the charm of positive vibes when I touched his feet as an Indian culture of expressing gratitude and respect to acquire his blessings. My both sons also touched his feet in order to acquire the blessings from the same person who had shaped the life of their father. I still cherish those moments, which always provide me and my family an inspiration and impetus energy to boost my aplomb. Although I went to express gratitude for my own sake but that unseen power got transmitted to my family as well from his blessings.

It is truly said *'The magic of expressing gratitude not only benefit you but it spread the positive energy all over and charges your surroundings entirely'.*

Feel blessed

Break through all the barriers and feel you are blessed. This is the one and only step you have to take. The rest will all happen.

This deep sense of feeling 'I am blessed' can help you overcome all obstacles in life. You receive courage and confidence and you will open up for grace to pour in.

The moment you realize you are blessed, then:

- All complaints disappear
- All grumbling disappears
- All insecurities disappear
- A sense of being ignored disappears
- Expectation of being praised disappears

To make a difference in your life, feel you are blessed.

Managing Emotions

Energy suckers are the harmful negative emotions present in us. They trap the mental energies in the subconscious mind. This does more harm to as the years go by. The energy suckers will hinder a person's emotional progress in life and his well-being.

At a scale from 0-10, grade yourself for each of these qualities. Zero will mean the absence of the quality and 10 will mean the quality is very strong in you.

Energy suckers

- Worry	- Resentment	- Sadness
- Anger	- Confusion	- Laziness
- Hatred	- Insecurity	- Boredom
- Jealousy	- Guilt	- Emptiness
- Revenge	- Pain	- Loneliness
- Fear	- Tiredness	- Depression
- Bitterness	- Helplessness	- Greed
- Anxiety	- Worthlessness	- Embarrassment
- Rejection	- Frustration	- Regret

Exercise

- List down three of your prominent negative qualities that if removed, can cause a major positive change in your life.
- Also recall three incidents when you displayed these negative qualities.
- You will find that for each incident, it was some expectation that you had which caused these feelings although many times you might have not even worked on these expectations or even communicated them properly to the concerned person.

Avoid adopting the negativity of others

Don't sabotage yourself by unwittingly adopting negative, unproductive attitudes through your associations with others. Other people's views and troubles can be contagious.

When you encounter a downhearted friend or a colleague, who suffer a sudden reversal of fortune, be careful not to be influenced by the apparent misfortune. Remember to discriminate between events themselves and your interpretation of them. Remind yourself: "What hurts this person is not the occurrence itself, for another person might not feel oppressed by this situation at all. What is hurting this person is the response he or she has uncritically adopted towards this incident."

To join them in indulging in wrongheaded, negative feelings is not a demonstration of kindness or friendship to the people we care about. We can do a better service to others and ourselves by remaining detached and avoiding such response. In such conversations with someone who is depressed, hurt or frustrated, show him or her kindness and give them a sympathetic ear, but don't allow yourself to be swayed in emotions.

It is our view of events or people that hurts us, not the events or people

People don't have the power to hurt you. If someone irritates you, it is only your own response that is irritating you. Things themselves don't hurt or hinder us. It is our attitudes and reactions that give us trouble. Therefore, when anyone seems to be provoking you, remember that it is your judgment of the incident that provokes you. Try not to merely react in the moment. We cannot choose our external circumstances, but we can always choose how we respond to these circumstances.

Mistreatment comes from false impressions and is your own interpretation

When other persons insult you or speak unkindly about you, remember that they do so in terms of their impression that it is right to do so. It is unrealistic to expect people to see you as you see yourself. If people reach conclusions based on false impressions, they are the ones hurt rather than you, because it is they who are misguided. When someone interprets a true proposition as a false one, the proposition itself isn't hurt, only the person who holds the wrong view is deceived and thus damaged. Once you clearly understand this, you will feel less hurt and can remain more positive.

Techniques to overcome negative emotions

1. *Experience*: Go through the experience. Acknowledge it.
2. *Observe*: Step aside and objectively observe the situation and yourself as a spectator, rather than a participating agent. This will make you understand the various issues clearly.
3. *Learn*: What is this experience teaching me.
4. *Accept*: Ability to embrace the experience and be thankful for the lesson.

Managing Relationships

Let us use the word `Relationship Account' to understand relationships. In accounting practice, the Bank Statement has credit and debit columns. Credit represents deposit and debit represents withdrawal from the bank account.

Bank Statement

Date	*Particulars*	*Debit*	*Credit*	*Balance*
1/1/01	Deposit		15000	15000
2/1/01	Withdrawal	1000		5000

Our Relationship Account, like the bank account above, may have a net positive balance or overdrawn balance depending on the transactions we have had with others.

Some examples of Deposits/Withdrawals in a relationship are as follows:

Relationship Account

Deposit	**Withdrawals**
1. Courtesy	Discourtesy
2. Kindness	Unkindness
3. Supportiveness	Unsupportiveness
4. Helpfulness	Helplessness
5. Keeping promises	Breaking promises
6. Listening	Not listening
7. Appreciation	Finding Fault
8. Apology	Pride
9. Loyalty	Duplicity
10. Encouragement	Discouragement
11. Smile	Scowl
12. Acknowledgement	Ignore
13. Honoring expectations	Violating expectations
14. Recognition	Non-recognition

Just like a bank, when an account is overdrawn in our relationship, the trust is lost and real problems start.

- Write down all those relationship accounts that have been overdrawn by you.
- List down all relationships where you need to deposit to restore the trust.

In the case of a relationship account, unlike accounting transactions, which have specific values, the deposits and withdrawals are very subjective. However, one can feel if the balance is positive or negative. In our daily life when people work together, or stay together, invariably withdrawals will take place.

By acting positively you can build a reservoir of trust in the relationship account, as you never know when the need for withdrawal may arise.

When the account is overdrawn the trust is lost and problems will start.

Basically most of the problems are relationship problems.

Someone said, "There are no business problems; only relationship problems". All problems in business can be traced to relationship difficulties. Business is about people and if there is a problem, it is invariably a human problem. No matter what others tell you, when you lose business it is always a relationship constraint or an excessive withdrawal.

Giving is the crux in relationships

A little girl and her father were crossing a bridge. The father was kind of scared person so he asked his little daughter, "Sweetheart, Please hold my hand so that you don't fall into the river." The little girl said, "No, Dad. You hold my hand." "What's the difference?" asked the puzzled father.

"There's a big difference," replied the little girl. "If I hold your hand and something happens to me, chances are that I may let your hand go. But if you hold my hand, I know for sure that no matter what happens, you will never let my hand go." In any relationship, the essence of trust is not in its bind, but in its bond. So hold the hand of the person whom you love rather than expecting them to hold yours.

Power of Smile

A smile costs nothing, but gives much.

It enriches those who receive, without making poorer those who give.

It takes a moment, but the memory of it sometimes lasts forever.

None is so rich or mighty that he can get along without it, and none is so poor, that he can be made rich by it.

A smile creates happiness in the home, fosters good will in business, and is the countersign of friendship.

It brings rest to the weary, cheer the discouraged, sunshine to the sad, and it is nature's best antidote for trouble.

Yet it cannot be bought, begged, borrowed, or stolen, for it is something that is of no value to anyone, until it is given away.

Some people are too tired to give you a smile;

Give them one of yours, as none needs a smile so much as he who has no more to give.

Tell the people you love and care for, that they are special and important. Tell them, before it is too late.

One day Maths teacher asked her students to list the names of the other students in the room on two sheets of paper, leaving a space between each name. Then she told them to think of the nicest thing they could say about each of their classmates and write it down. It took the remainder of the class period to finish their assignment, and as the students left the room, each one handed over the papers. That Saturday, the teacher wrote down the name of each student on a separate sheet of paper, and listed what everyone else had said about that individual. On Monday she gave each student his or her list. Before long, the entire class was smiling. "Really?" she heard whispered. "I never knew that I meant anything to anyone!" and, "I didn't know others liked me so much," were most of the comments.

No one ever mentioned those papers in class again. She never knew if they discussed them after class or with their parents, but it didn't matter. The exercise had accomplished its purpose. The students were happy with themselves and one another. That group of students moved on.

Several years later, one of the students was killed in "Kargil" war and his teacher attended the funeral of that special student. She had never attended Funeral of a serviceman before. He looked so handsome, so mature. The place was packed with his friends. One by one those who loved him took a last walk. The teacher was the last one to bless. As she stood there, one of the soldiers who acted as pallbearer came up to her. "Were you Sanjay's maths teacher?" he asked. She nodded: "yes." Then he said: "Sanjay talked about you a lot." After the funeral, most of Sanjay's former classmates were there. Sanjay's parents were there, obviously waiting to speak with his teacher.

"We want to show you something," his father said, taking a wallet out of his pocket "They found this in Sanjay pocket when he was killed. We thought you might recognize it. "Opening the bifold, he carefully removed two worn pieces of notebook paper that had obviously been taped, folded and refolded many times. The teacher knew without looking that the papers were the ones on which she had listed all the good things each of Sanjay's classmates had said about him.

"Thank you so much for doing that," Sanjay's mother said. "As you can see, Sanjay treasured it." All of Sanjay's former classmates started to gather around. Arjun smiled rather sheepishly and said, "I still have my list. It's in the top drawer of my desk at home." Puneet's wife said, "Puneet asked me to put this in our wedding album." "I have mine too," Rashmi said. "It's in my diary"

Then Deepali, another classmate, reached into her pocketbook, took out her wallet and showed her worn and frazzled list to the group. "I carry this with me at all times," Deepali said and without wetting an eyelash, she continued: "I think we all saved our lists" That's when the teacher finally sat down and cried. She cried for Sanjay and for all his friends who would never see him again. The density of people in society is so thick that we forget that life will end one day. And we don't know when that one day will be.

So please, tell the people you love and care for, that they are special and important. Tell them, before it is too late.

The Story of 3 Old Men

A woman came out of her house and saw 3 old men with long white beards sitting in her front yard. She did not recognize them. She said, "I don't think I know you, but you must be hungry. Please come in and have something to eat."

"Is the man of the house home?", they asked.

"No", she replied. "He's out."

"Then we cannot come in", they replied.

In the evening when her husband came home, she told him what had happened.

"Go tell them I am home and invite them in!"

The woman went out and invited the men in".

"We do not go into a House together," they replied.

"Why is that?" she asked.

One of the old men explained: "His name is Wealth," he said pointing to one of his friends, and said pointing to another one, "He is Success, and I am Love." Then he added, "Now go in and discuss with your husband which one of us you want in your home."

The woman went in and told her husband what was said. Her husband was overjoyed. "How nice!!", he said. "Since that is the case, let us invite Wealth. Let him come and fill our home with wealth!"

His wife disagreed. "My dear, why don't we invite Success?"

Their daughter was listening from the other corner of the house. She jumped in with her own suggestion: "Would it not be better to invite Love? Our home will then be filled with love!"

"Let us heed our daughter's advice," said the husband to his wife.

"Go out and invite Love to be our guest."

The woman went out and asked the 3 old men, "Which one of you is Love? Please come in and be our guest."

Love got up and started walking toward the house. The other 2 also got up and followed him. Surprised, the lady asked Wealth and Success: "I only invited Love, Why are you coming in?"

The old men replied together: "If you had invited Wealth or Success, the other two of us would've stayed out, but since you invited Love, wherever he goes, we go with him. Wherever there is Love, there is also Wealth and Success!!!!! !"

Stop blaming in your relationships

A boy was born to a couple after eleven years of marriage. They were a Loving couple and the boy was the gem of their eyes. When the boy was around two years old, one morning the husband saw a medicine bottle open.

He was late for office so he asked his wife to cap the bottle and keep it in the cupboard. His wife, preoccupied in the kitchen totally forgot the matter. The boy saw the bottle and playfully went to the bottle fascinated by its color and drank it all. It happened to be a poisonous medicine meant for adults in small dosages. When the child collapsed the mother hurried him to the hospital, where he died. The mother was stunned. She was terrified how to face her husband.

When the distraught father came to the hospital and saw the dead child, He looked at his wife and uttered just six words.

Questions:

1. What were the six words?
2. What is the implication of this story?

Answer:

The husband just said. "I am with you my Dear".

The husband's totally unexpected reaction is a proactive behaviour. The child is dead. He can never be brought back to life. There is no point in finding fault with the mother. Besides, if only he had taken time to keep the bottle away, this would not have happened.

No one is to be blamed. She had also lost her only child. What she needed at that moment was consolation and sympathy from her husband. That is what he gave her.

If everyone can look at life with this kind of perspective, there would be much fewer problems in the world. Take off all your envies, jealousies, unforgiveness, selfishness, and fears. And you will find things are actually not as difficult as you think.

Moral of the story

Love people unconditionally. Separate people from their qualities. Sometimes we spend time in asking who is responsible or whom to blame, whether in a relationship, in a job or with the people we know. By this way we miss out some warmth in human relationships.

As you sow so shall you reap

Newton discovered the law of cause and effect: in other words, that *for every action there is an equal and opposite reaction*. We only get back what we put in. If we plant tomatoes, we won't reap thistles. It is important to remind ourselves that this principle affects everything we do and every experience we have.

In addition, what we have in our life at the moment is a result of sowing we have been doing until now. If we currently enjoy warm friendships and loving relationships, it is because we have prepared the ground and planted the seed. If our business or profession is currently flowering, it is because we've expended the effort to get the results.

If we talk about others, we'll be talked about. If we speak well of others, they will speak well of us. If we rip people off then we will be ripped off. If we rejoice in the success of others, we will be more likely to enjoy success ourselves. If we tell lies, we will be told lies. If we criticize, we will be criticized. If we love, we beloved.

> *Confucius said, "What you would not want to be done to yourself, do not do to others."*
>
> *Aristotle said, "We should behave to the world as we wish the world to behave towards us."*

The wonderful thing about nature is that it gives us back much more than we put in. When you plant a pumpkin seed, you don't just get back one seed!. You actually get much more.

- Nature is very generous.
- Plant a few seeds and you may end up with a truckload of pumpkins. Again, this principle works with everything we do, but first we need to get out in the fields and dig!
- The universe is fair and just. We get back from life only what we put into it.

Adding value in relationships by recognizing the need of others.

In essence, good human relations involve adding value to other people, because they, like you, deserve it. It is giving people something they want - recognition, in return for something you want - their cooperation.

- When you increase the self-esteem of others, you are showing them respect and that you expect the best from them, thereby helping them perform their best.
- We all possess valuable, intangible assets that others desperately want. We all have acceptance, approval, appreciation, respect, and encouragement in unlimited quantity to give!
- Unfortunately, few people appreciate the fact that you have to give in order to receive.

People will give you what you want to the degree you give them what they want first. If you show others respect and acknowledge their importance, they usually will do the same for you.

List down the relationships that require you to put deposits. Plan out the kind of deposits that are appropriated for each of the account.

Seven major deposits in our Emotional Bank Account for better interpersonal relationship.

With continuing expectations, old deposits evaporate.

Keep on depositing, as you never know when you may need a withdrawal.

1. Understand the individual.
2. Attending to little things (kindness and courtesy, take care of feelings).
3. Keeping commitments (massive withdrawal is to make a promise to someone that is important to him and not keep it).
4. Clarifying expectations (do not work on different assumptions). Never assume that our expectations are self-evident and are clearly understood. It can lead to personality clashes and communication breakdown.
5. Showing personal integrity (it leads to trust).
   - Be loyal to those who are not ever present.
   - Avoid duplicity and practice honesty.
   - Have courage and confront the real issue.
   - Do not disrespect the dignity of others, do not deceive.
6. Apologize sincerely when you make a withdrawal. Say
   - 'I was wrong'.
   - 'I showed you no respect, I am deeply sorry.

People usually forgive mistakes but not bad motives.

7. Law of giving and loving unconditionally - let people and those in your relationships live independently without conditions/strings and their natural growth process gets encouraged.

More about relationships

We should know the beliefs/values/rules of people with whom we interact. If we are not sensitive we must be prepared for pain. We may like or love somebody but if that person continues to break our rules and values, inevitably it will result in upsets and stress. Every upset with another human being is an upset rule.

- When you increase the self-esteem of others, you are showing them respect and that you expect the best from them, thereby helping them perform at their maximum.

People frequently enter into a new relationship for the purpose of benefiting or getting something. This automatically creates a lot of expectations. When these expectations are not met, the relationship is affected. The only way a relationship can last is to view it as a place to give rather than to take and you can make more deposits in it.

As we know whatever we focus on, will expand. When we focus on what is wrong in a relationship, we will ultimately experience it. This is the law. So, if you focus on the positive side of relationships, you will find a lot which is positive in it and vice versa.

Managing Relationships-deposit Chart

We make deposits in our relationships with the following three levels of awareness:

1st Level - Indifference to Deposit

2nd Level - Conditional Deposit

3rd Level - Unconditional Deposit

Indifference to deposit

At the first level, people feel and say that deposit is not important to get things done. They may not be aware that people are emotional beings and are sensitive to how they are being treated. The reason for the failure to have good teamwork and a shared vision in an organization is often due to lack of deposit within team members. When one feels mistreated or his/her genuine credit for work denied, he or she can get upset and may hold a resentment, which puts a brake to one's co-operation, commitment and communication with others.

Conditional deposit

At this level people are aware that the feelings of others have to be taken care of and deposits are important for excellence, teamwork and harmonious working relationship. However, these deposits are based on some conditions. When the conditions are not met they will refrain from placing deposits in that account.

Some examples:

(a) You should care for me, and then I will care for you.

(b) You should be polite to me, and then I will be polite to you.

(c) You cooperate with me, only then I will cooperate with you.

When the conditions are not fulfilled one moves down to the first level.

- If the love between a husband and wife is based on some conditions, then there is no security in that deposit. Many divorce cases are due to conditional deposits.

Unconditional deposit

Deposits that are not based on any conditions are called unconditional deposits. The deposit is part and parcel of the individual's nature which is not dependent on the environment or other's behavior. If one is giving unconditional commitment, it need not be based on the superior or others' behavior, remuneration, facilities, systems and procedure in the office, etc. Wherever this person is present he or she will be committed without any condition. Let it be at home or at the office, only when committed does the person feel truly satisfied. People who operate from the Third Level of Awareness are few and they are very special. They emanate a very harmonious vibration to their environment, which can attract others towards them. It is only natural for these people to progress fast in their career path and life.

A great ability seen in such persons is that they can raise others' level of deposits towards them in the long run. If we give unconditional love to someone who hates us, soon it will hit him back in the form of guilt and naturally the guilt will push the person to love us. The height of happiness attained through unconditional deposit is intensely emotional and cannot be expressed in words. It is also therapeutic. Others find security and peace in those people who operate with unconditional deposit. Such persons are always needed and are highly esteemed in the organizations and society.

Self expansion and Self-contraction

Reactive choices are deemed to bring negative consequences. What are the causes for all the reactive choices that we make in our lives? And why do we make reactive choices?

Reactive choices are the effect of energy suckers present in a person. Energy suckers remove one's ability to rationalize and understand a person or a situation. It has also been clinically proven that physical ailments are the effect of energy suckers.

Unfulfilled expectations or demands are the major causes behind every energy sucker. These expectations are merely conditioning from one's past experience in life. The conditioning can be deeply rooted in the subconscious mind. Owing to this one becomes a victim of one's conditionings. To become aware of one's expectations or demands is very important for the development of oneself. Constant reflections on these expectations and demands are very therapeutic. In deep contemplation one will be able to see these expectations or demands stemming from three types of centers. They are predominantly the Sensation, Security and Power centers as shown below.

Examples of expectations produced by the Sensation center:

1. There should not be any traffic jams when I am on the road.
2. I must smoke a cigarette after my meal or when I am in the toilet.
3. My car should not be scratched by anyone whenever I park it anywhere.
4. My chair must be comfortable.
5. Others should praise me or others should not criticize me.

Examples of expectations produced by the Security center.

1. I must have a secure income.
2. My organization must be stable.
3. If others are promoted I must be promoted too.
4. I must not be retrenched.
5. I must not lose my money in the shares I have bought.
6. There must not be any war or any kind of disaster.
7. There must always be enough money in my bank account.

Examples of expectations produced by the Power center:

1. I must be given a higher position.
2. Others must respect me (especially my subordinates).
3. My opinions must be appreciated and agreed by others.
4. I must have more money than others.
5. My subordinates must carry out my instructions implicitly without any hesitation.

6. I must always make the final decision.
7. I must drive a better car than my friends.

Addiction to expectations can turn into pain

Addiction towards these expectations or demands, which come from the three centers, can turn into pain when they are not fulfilled. This is the law of life, which any individual can discover for oneself during his or her lifetime.

Expectation – addiction – suffering

If the expectation is realistic it is good. It contributes to one's better health and better relationship. However, the difficulty to overcome some deeply ingrained expectations, is due to deep-rooted centering or Self-Contraction. In deep silence we can observe the suffering that we see around us is because we have been conditioned to serve our expectations first. Man has been conditioned to believe that he is a separate entity by himself and he needs to care of himself first.

Such expectation forms the perimeter for oneself. The perimeter can be contracted or expanded. The way to relax the addiction towards one's expectation is to expand oneself beyond one's own perimeter. This is called Self-Expansion. When one expands to the family perimeter, he or she will be able to relax his or her self-demands. Such people are able to care for their family as if they are caring for themselves. Acceptance and forgiveness towards people within the perimeter becomes easy. The expansion can further move towards a bigger perimeter like society, country, and mankind.

Self-expansion leads a person to become a natural leader, wherever he or she may be.

Self-expansion is also a continuum of maturity in a person. It is really the evolution of the heart to feel and yearn for more and more aspects of creation. The beauty of self-expansion is that the person would be able to harmonize and attract every other being within the perimeter.

Self-expansion is therapeutic because by being able to relax personal expectations, one will not be threatened by the energy suckers, thus enabling one to lead a healthy practical life. Those who are leading a happy life are the examples of self-expansion.

The Tale of two Seas

Sitting in the Geography class in school, I remember how fascinated I was when we were being taught all about the Dead Sea. As you probably recall, the Dead Sea is really a Lake, not a sea. It is so high in salt content that the human body can float easily. You can almost lie down and read a book! The salt in the Dead Sea is as high as 35% - almost 10 times the normal ocean water. And all that saltiness has meant for no life at all in the Dead Sea. No fish. No vegetation. No sea animals. Nothing lives in the Dead Sea. And hence it is named as: Dead Sea.

While the Dead Sea has remained etched in my memory, I don't seem to recall learning about the Sea of Galilee in my school Geography lesson. So when I heard about the Sea of Galilee and the Dead Sea and the tale of the two seas - I was intrigued. Turns out that the Sea of Galilee is just north of the Dead Sea. Both the Sea of Galilee and the Dead Sea receive their water from river Jordan. And yet, they are so different.

Unlike the Dead Sea, the Sea of Galilee is pretty, resplendent with rich, colorful marine life. There are lots of plants. And lots of fish too. In fact, the sea of Galilee is home to over twenty different species of fish.

Same region, same source of water, and yet while one sea is full of life, the other is dead. How come?

Here apparently the question is why? The River Jordan flows into the Sea of Galilee and then flows out. The water simply enter through the Sea of Galilee and then goes out - and that keeps the Sea healthy and alive with marine life.

But the Dead Sea is so far below the sea level, that it has no outlet. The water flows in from the river Jordan, but does not flow out. There are no outlet streams. It is estimated that over a million tons of water evaporate from the Dead Sea every day. Leaving it salty. Too full of minerals. And unfit for any marine life.

The Dead Sea takes water from the River Jordan, and holds it. It does not give.

Result? No life at all.

Think about it.

Life is not just about getting. It's also about giving. We all humans need to be a bit like the Sea of Galilee.

We are fortunate to have wealth, knowledge, love and respect. But if we don't learn to give, we could all end up like the Dead Sea.

The love and the respect, the wealth and the knowledge could all evaporate. Like the water in the Dead Sea.

Excess of anything, will lead to destruction! If we get the Dead Sea mentality of merely taking in more water, more money, more everything the results can be disastrous. It would be good to make sure that in the sea of our own life, we also have outlets. More outlets the better. For love and wealth - and everything else that you get in your life. We should ensure we don't just get (receive), we give too. Keep the taps open. And it will open the floodgates to happiness.

Make that a habit, to share, to give and experience life. Experience the magic of true happiness.

Living in Abundance

A belief in scarcity, for example, that there isn't much abundance in the world is a fatal error. A person who holds this belief sees life as a pie with just so many pieces. If you get a piece of the pie, this means there is one piece less for someone else. Or if others have the slice that you have set your eyes on....too bad, it is already taken!

A logical extension of such thinking is to believe that if you succeed, another must fail. If you are prosperous, someone else must be poor. After all, there isn't enough of everything to go around. This also means that you can't have more of what you now want unless you take it away from someone else.

Another misbelief is that you must be careful to protect what you already have because others are surely after it. The safe approach then is simply to trade. Give a little to others of what they want in return for receiving a little of what you want. But at all costs, never give first! You may never get repaid! By using this cold, calculating approach, you end up living in a prison of your own making, and the prison bars represent misbelief.

And you readily identify with them because they reinforce what you already believe reflects reality.

By focusing repeatedly on life's negative events, you tend to adopt a more negative outlook on everything. Negative news will always bring you down to its destructive level.

It can never lift you up to a more creative level.

- Scarcity is the mother of selfishness, jealousy, aggressiveness, and resentment. All of its effects are negative.
- Abundance is the mother of prosperity, creativity, kindness and love. All of its effects are positive.
- Abundance means health, wealth and happiness all in balance. It is contrary to the common belief that abundance means having a lot of money.
- Abundance is celebrating every moment of life.
- The prerequisite for abundance is that we must do what we love and love what we do.
- The question is, are we doing what we love?

Power of Alignment

Alignment of thought-feeling-action

Thought, feeling and action are involved in every activity of ours. They are a part and parcel of us. Thoughts and feelings are our inner-side, while actions are the outer and perceptible side.

* There are cases where the thought will say, "this is the right thing to do!" but the feeling says, "I don't like doing this!" and the action will either follow the thought or the feeling, whichever is the stronger.
* Whenever there is a clash between these three components (thought, feeling and actions) it is called a non-aligned or disjoined state. A non-aligned state is a stressful state. It invites energy suckers and makes the work activity a burden or a chore.

We cannot be effective in our lives if we are not aligned

If there is no alignment then there will always be stress and achieving the set goals will be a struggle. A lot of effort will be required to move and accomplish things. Alignment gives freedom and power to act. More things can be done and less energy will be spent to accomplish a particular task. There will be joy in the act and creativity will also emerge. It is just like a car- if the wheels are not aligned it will soon be reflected in our driving and on the tyres.

The danger of non-alignment

The state of non-alignment in oneself can very often be easily detected through the pressure or stress produced in the self. This pressure comes from the conscience within to push a person to correct and get himself aligned quickly. The danger persists when the non-alignment is not corrected immediately. If one repeatedly gets oneself into non-aligned activities, and does not correct them, soon non-alignment will become a pattern and thus the person becomes a non-conformist, disobedient and a problem.

A person is said to be inflexible when he or she is not sensitive to the pressure caused by his or her non-alignment. Every activity will be done as a burden and without interest and life will seem stressful. The person will conclude that life is drudgery. Constant complaining and blaming others will become a behavioral characteristic of the person.

Your desires also impact on your alignment

Our desires and aversions are mercurial rulers. They always crave satisfaction. Desire commands us to run off and get what we want. Aversion insists that we must avoid the things that repel us. Typically, when we don't get what we want, we are disappointed, and when we get what we don't want, we are distressed.

Desire and aversion, though powerful, are but habits. We can prepare ourselves to adopt better habits. Restrain the habit of being repelled by all those things that aren't within your control, and focus instead on combating things within your power that are not good for you. Do your best to rein in your desire. For example if you desire something out of your reach, disappointment will surely follow. You might neglect the very things that are accessible and worthy.

Of course, there are times when for practical reasons you must go after one thing or shun another, but do so with grace, accuracy, and flexibility.

Areas of Control /Areas Beyond Control

Life is a series of events. We face various problems, situations, events or circumstances in life where we need to act. Before we act, it will be to our advantage to categorize the problems, situations, events or circumstances into categories, which we can control either directly or indirectly by our choices or those situations over which we have no control.

- Area of control (AOC)
- Areas beyond our control (ABC)

A. Problems or situations, which we can control, are in AOC, which require our own effort to change them. For example 1. Reducing body weight 2. Improving job skills.

B. The issues, problems or situations/circumstances over which we have no control (ABC) are those which we can do nothing about such as our situational realities, and things which were in our past.

As an example we cannot change the breakfast which we ate one hour earlier, similarly we cannot change our past events.

- I know of a person who is still carrying guilt because 10 years back he could not decide on buying a house whose worth has now culminate. The more he remembers past incident, the more he feels guilty. The best way is to take present responsibility and learn to accept and live with certain situations even though we don't like them. In this way we have better control over our lives.

Exercise

1. Write down some of the problems which have been bothering you.
2. Identify one major problem and write all actions that you need to do which are within your control to handle effectively.
3. In the above problem, write down what is beyond your control.

Know what is in your access and what is not? What you can control and what you can't?

Our freedom and happiness begin with a clear understanding of one principle: some things are within our control, and some things are not. It is only up to you to adopt this fundamental rule so as to distinguish between what you can and can't control. That inner tranquility and outer effectiveness then become possible.

Within our control are our own opinions, aspirations, desires, and aversions. We have domain over such areas and though they directly influence us. We always have a choice about the contents and character of our inner lives.

Outside our control, however, are such things as what kind of body we have, whether we're born into wealth or strike it rich, how we are regarded by others, and our status in society. We must remember that those things are externals and are therefore not our concern. Trying to control or to change what we can't access, will only results in torment.

We should remember that the things within our power are naturally at our disposal, free from any restrain or hindrance; but those things outside our power are weak, dependent, or determined by the whims and actions of others. Remember, too that if you think that you have free rein over things that are naturally beyond your control, or if you attempt to adopt the affairs of others as your own, your pursuits will be thwarted and you will become a fault-fording, anxious, and frustrated person.

Power of choice

- Choosing an act makes all the difference to the inner-side of a person.
- There is a lot of significance in choosing. Making a choice in our context means participating in a favorable act with interest and commitment.
- An act without the element of interest or love is called a `Have to' activity which means that the act itself is an unfavorable choice.
- A person who is performing a `Have to' act will carry a negative attitude in him while he who chooses his act (favorable choice) will carry a positive one.
- Every choice that we make has its own consequences, following the law of cause and effect.
- If one is suffering, it is due to one's wrong or inappropriate choices made in the past.
- We are the direct product of our choices that we made in our life.
- Life is full of choices.

Exercise

What are the "HAVE TO DO" activities in your life that you can change to "CHOOSE TO DO" activities? You can see the difference in your life, once you decide and implement this.

It is my choice to act. How can others impact me if I have chosen?

Buddha was once walking with his disciples when a passer-by looked at the group angrily and shot a malicious insult at Buddha.
Buddha went on smiling, paying no heed to the assailant.
His disciples were aghast. "Why didn't you say something? He insulted you without any reason."
Buddha answered, "The man may have thrown the insult, but I didn't catch it."

Why do you choose to become angry?

The power of choice says that whenever you first decide to accept responsibility, you are able to control or make an impact. Like, the pilot of an airplane or the driver of a bus is able to control the operation of the vehicle. And he knows he must accept full responsibility for whatever result his actions bring about.

Failure to accept full responsibility for your thinking machine, the streering wheel of your life, will also lead you in frustration and unhappiness. There will always be unexpected events in your life over which you have little or no control.

Empowering of your life requires accepting 100 per cent responsibility for all your thoughts and actions. There is no way you can gain control over your thoughts and actions without accepting full responsibility for them. Exercising the power of choice is essential in maintaining a high level of energy, peace of mind, self-confidence, and positive emotions.

Being Proactive

Proactivity means our ability to choose our response, based on our values and principles, no matter what we are subjected to.

According to the above definition, there are two parts to proactivity:

(a) We have choice no matter what happens.

(b) The choice is based on values and principles.

Stimulus response behavior model

In life we face many kinds of stimuli, which can provoke us to get angry or activate any of the energy suckers. Knowing how to handle these stimuli can make our lives more meaningful and joyful.

Otherwise we can be bogged down by the problems of life. The misery in one's life may be due to our inability to effectively confront the problems of life.

The stimulus response behavior model shows how a proactive person utilizes his freedom of choice to stay calm and stable during moments of crisis. A reactive person reacts to stimuli automatically without using the freedom of choice and this will bring forth misery.

Stimulus →	Conscious mind →	Subconscious mind →	Action	
Proactive	– Freedom to choose	– Experience – Observe – Learn & Accept	– Calm & – Stable	**Proaction**
Reactive	– Freedom to choose not Activated (Automatic)	– No learning	– Energy sucker	**Reaction**

Can we make life more joyful and avoid being bogged down by the problems of life? To do this, we need to adopt the proactive approach. What we say in various situations itself reveals whether we are proactive or reactive.

Reactive language	Proactive language
1. There's nothing I can	Let's look at our alternatives
2. That's just the way I am	I can choose a different
3. He makes me so mad	I control my own feelings
4. They won't allow that	I can create an effective presentation
5. I have to do that	I will choose an appropriate response
6. I can't	I choose
7. I must	I prefer

Living in the present

All you have is now. Our personal effectiveness, happiness and peace of mind are determined by how much we are able to live in the present. Regardless of what has happened in the past and what is going to happen in the future, NOW is where you are.

- One of the beautiful things about young children is that they absorb themselves totally in the present moment. They manage to induldge themselves completely in whatever they do, whether it is watching TV, drawing a picture, building a sandcastle or whatsoever they choose to devote their energies to.

As we become adults, many of us learn the art of thinking about and worrying about several things at once. We can allow past problems and future concerns to crowd into our present such that we become miserable and ineffective.

We also learn to postpone our pleasures and our happiness, often developing a notion that sometime in the future everything will become much better.

- The high school student thinks, "When I'm out of this school and need not to follow instructions, then everything will be great." He complete school and suddenly recognizes that he won't be happy until he has left home. He leaves home and starts university and soon decides, "When I would have got my degree, then I'll be really happy!" Eventually he gets his degree at which time he realizes that he can't be happy until he has a job.
- He gets his job and has to start at the bottom of the heap. You guessed it. He can't be happy yet. As the years roll by, he postpones his happiness and peace of mind until he gets engaged, gets married, buys a house, gets the kids out of school, retires . . . and he drops dead before he allows himself to be blissfully happy. All his present moments were spent planning for a wonderful future, which never arrived.

Do you relate at all to this kind of story? Do you know anybody who has postpond the happiness in future? The thing about being happy is that you have to be totally involved with the present.

If you have postponed spending time with the people who mean the most to you, then you are not living in present.

* Why not we decide to be happy on journey and not just when we reach our destination? If you have been to any shrine like Vaishno Devi for example, then you can realize that the journey was more satisfying and enjoyable than merely being on the top. This may be the reason that walking up many

kilometers on the hill is possibly more satisfying than flying by helicopter.

* A study was carried out some years ago in the USA where the object was to determine how much quality time middle class fathers spend with their young children. The participants had microphones attached to their shirts to monitor how much communication took place between father and child each day.

The study showed that the average middle class father spent about thirty seven seconds quality time per day with his child. No doubt many of the fathers involved had great plans for spending time with their loved ones "when the house is finished", "when the pressure is off at work", "when there is more money in the bank"... The point is that none of us has a guarantee that we will be here tomorrow. 'NOW' is all we have got.

- Living in the present also means that we enjoy whatever we are doing for its own sake, and not just for the end result. If you happen to be painting your front verandah, you can make a point of enjoying every stroke of the brush, of learning everything there is to know about how best to do the job, all the while being aware of the breeze on your face, the birds singing in the trees and everything else that is happening.

Living in the present is about expanding our awareness to make the current moment more memorable rather than shutting it. If you have worries like that of losing a job or doing less in business, it is not easy to empty out your mind and find peace. The easiest way to improve your mental state is to take action, get involved and participate.

- Living in present is about taking action without fear of the consequences.

Waiting for things

Have you ever noticed that when you are just waiting for a taxi, it never seems to arrive? The same seems to be true for other things that we wait for. Similarly, you may have found yourself waiting too long for a phone call. After waiting for what seemed like hours, you decided to busy yourself with something else and the call came. Whenever we sit and wait for letters, people, the right job, the perfect partner, some wonderful adventure or anything else we want, it takes a long time to arrive. Sometimes it never comes.

* There is a principle operating here which is telling us, "Get on and live your life in the present moment and don't hold your breath for things to happen."

Let go and relax

You might have noticed what happens when you are trying really, really hard to remember something or solve a problem? Invariably, you don't get the results you want.

Most people may have noted that in their search for ideas and solutions to problems they have their greatest success, while they are naturally relaxed like in shower, bath, bed, toilet.

To understand this scientifically when we relax, our brain rhythms move into a slower mode-the alpha mode-where we are far more capable and creative. Results come easily. When you step into a warm shower, you naturally relax. In bed, the same happens, and hence you will come up with new ideas! You can be very creative in the bedroom. You are open to ideas in the toilet, because you have to relax in there just to get the job done!

Physical relaxation is also important for peak performance. As we relax our physical body, our whole metabolism comes into balance; our blood pressure, our breathing becomes deep and easy, and the organs in our system work harmoniously.

We get the best results in our life when we are prepared to go with the flow. This means finding the delicate and elusive balance between effort and relaxation, between attachments and letting go. It is not easy to achieve!

Again, we can learn from nature. The birds and the animals work, but they don't work day and night. They know when they have had enough. Try talking a sparrow into a little nightshift! Sparrows know when it's time to have a break. Even the soil needs a rest so often. Patience pays.

When I was a child, we used to sow the mango seeds in the evening taking care of the soil and water. The next morning we would dig the soil to know how much seeds have grown. It took years together to realize that it takes natural time for all our actions to mature even if the action has been performed in the right manner and the surroundings are favorable.

Discovering Our Lost Qualities

Qualities like being approachable, cheerful, present minded, forgiving, happy, energetic, innocent, open, focused, lovable, non-judgmental, fun oriented etc. are positive ones that were present at childhood.

The intensity of these qualities could have deteriorated through time due to contamination of negative thoughts entertained while we grew up into an adult. We were programmed to compare and compete seriously with each other as we grew up to face the challenges of adulthood and life.

We became more self centered and are addicted to our own expectations that allows energy suckers to rule our life.

Positive qualities are called "child-like qualities", but are far different from being childish. Childish is negative and child-like is positive. Childish has the nature of stubbornness, dependency on others for our happiness, and child-like is being cheerful, happy and self reliant.

- Recent work in the field of management, especially in having better teamwork and productivity, shows that work and play must go hand in hand. Every human being has a child in them that needs fun at some point of time. When this is curtailed, we will have a very serious and grumpy person, who in turn will be sapping away energy from others to have his expectations fulfilled. He cannot be an effective team player.
- Teamwork with fun is like driving a car towards destination with good lubricating oil. A team of serious people with a serious relationship is bound to find their journey in achieving their goals a rough one. This is the reason why many people are restless at work place.

List down all positive qualities that were present in your childhood. Which of these qualities are totally or partially lost in you?

Power of Humor

When you laugh, all kinds of wonderful things happen to benefit your body and mind. Endorphins are released in your brain which gives you a "natural like" and your respiratory system gets the kind of work-out that it may get from jogging.

Laughter relieves pain. You can only laugh when you are relaxed and the more relaxed you are, the less pain you feel, so funny books and movies are ideal pain relievers. In fact, you can't get ulcers and laugh at the same time-you have to choose one or the other. The same goes for other illnesses. We often get sick by taking ourselves and life too seriously. We just need to laugh for being healthy.

The art of being happy means ability to laugh at difficulties as soon as possible after they happen. One person, involved in the above situation, would resist laughing for two years. Another may decide that after two weeks it is the time to stop crying and start laughing. Therefore, the first person chooses to stay miserable fifty times longer than the other one.

> We all suffer misfortunes. *Happy people choose to avoid waiting too long to see the funny side of their disappointment.*

Periodically, let us remind ourselves that we are human and that we will do stupid things. If you expect to be perfect you don't belong to this planet. Let's remember that our own troubles always seem much bigger to us than to anyone else. If no one else is losing sleep, may be we don't need to either.

- Children can teach us a lot about laughing. Happy youngsters will laugh at almost anything, naturally and boldly. They seem intuitively to know that daily a good laugh keeps them healthy and balanced. They come equipped with an insatiable thirst for joy and fun. It is a shame that by the time many reach adulthood this attitude has been replaced by one which says: "Life is all seriousness." Grown-ups spend their time telling children when not to giggle and when not to laugh-"Don't laugh in class, don't giggle at the dinner table"-until much of their natural spontaneity is gone.

One of our major responsibilities toward others is to enjoy ourselves! When we are having fun, we feel better, we work better and people want to be around us. Life is not that serious. Let's take humor more seriously.

Who am I-Searching your real self. Need to shift the thinking.

We mostly define ourselves by what we do or what we have done.

- I'm Senior Executive in a leading MNC.
- I've been a President of large professional association.
- Last year I published 20 new titles.
- Under my leadership our factory output raised by 50% in the last 5 years.

Our lives consist of citing names, titles, and lists to prove that all those things we've done are worth created. And our self image is tied up in this.

But where was I in all these restless hours? And where did I disappear once the work is done? Now when my job is done, am I still a worthwhile person to be discussed, respected, adored and praised? How do I define myself now?

Most of us spend many years searching for ourselves-for our personal truth-outside ourselves. We seek that truth in a career, in parenthood, in climbing steep mountains, in undertaking impossible challenges. When careers get short-circuited in a demotion or layoff, when the youngest child leaves home for colleges, we are forced to stare nakedly at our own face and apprehend our essential identity.

We continue to add new layers of complexity to our lives as soon as any one layer falls away by accident or intention. We have barely left one job before we feverishly clutch onto the next opportunity.

We don't allow life to become simpler. In fact, we've become experts in complicating it-and then we suffer from the ensuing worries, stresses, and endless complexities.

Once we make that stop and re-establish our inner balance, we can then continue to undo the frenzy-over and over again, while remaining in the midst of an active life. We do that by learning to use the mind in a new way.

You are what you think. If your identity is defined by the thought, "I'm a talented software engineer," and then if that identity is further enhanced by the thought (probably never expressed out loud), "I'm a worthwhile person because my talent has led me to achieve a respected position in my company"-you are never with yourself, never centered in your own being.

Position gone, identity destroyed. Position improved, self-worth soaring.

Thus, we dance like marionettes obedient to the strings pulled by the thrusts and changes of the world around us.

The trick is to learn to think in such a way that we remain centered in our being no matter what changes take place in the roles we happen to play or how intense the peace of activity around us may become.

We just need to shift our thinking and start enjoying everyday, every moment of our life.

Know and discover first the real you

Twelve people were walking on foot from one village to another. On the way, they had to cross a river. Reaching the other shore, they wanted to be sure all had crossed safely. Each one counted only eleven and left himself out. They were very distraught and began to cry for the loss of the twelfth.

A wise man came along and asked them "Oh, my dear friends, why are you crying?"

"We were twelve but now we are only eleven," they replied. The wise man saw that they were twelve, so he made them stand and count. To the last person he said, "You are the twelfth!" They all rejoiced for having regained the twelfth.

When you lose sight of the Self, then the Master comes and shows you that you are the twelfth! Or you can discover it by introspection, meditation, or seeking true knowledge from the Source.

Recognizing yourself makes everything truly joyful.

One should find more about others, but first find your true self also.

Shun Your Ego If You Want To Be Happy

There is an ego?

1. When you don't get attention.
2. When you seem to be losing attention.
3. When you get attention.

   Ego causes heaviness, discomfort, fear, and anxiety. Ego doesn't let love flow.

> Ego is separateness, alienation, wanting to prove and to possess.
>
> Often you feel either contempt or jealousy towards someone with an ego.
>
> Instead you should have compassion.

Ego has a positive aspect: ego drives one to do work. A person can do a job out of joy, compassion, or out of ego.

Most of the work done in the society is for boosting the ego. In service, work is done out of love.

When you wake up and see that there is nothing to be proved and nothing to possess, the ego dissolves.

God's Delay is not God's Denial

In the present-day context we're so focused on instantaneous gratification that our short-term solutions often become long-term problems. Our kids have trouble paying attention in school long enough to think, memorize, and learn partly because they've become addicted to instantaneous gratification from constant exposure to things like video games, TV commercials, and MTV. As a part of society now we have the unrelenting pursuit of the quick fix, like fast food, this can be deadly dangerous.

Deciding to commit yourself to long term results rather than short term fixes is very important in life. What appears to be impossible in the short term may eventually turn into a phenomenal example of success and happiness in the long term. Remember always through extremely tough times: God's delay is not God's denial.

Power of Decision

Decision-making is a great power

1. Decision makes the real difference and is a great power if we use it judiciously.
2. Committing to something is hard but a true decision.
3. Make decisions more frequently.
4. Learn from your decisions.
5. Stay committed to your decisions but with flexibility in your approach.
6. Decision making can be a joy.

Know that it is your decision, not your condition, which determines your own destiny.

Equanimity in Life—A Wise Person is Happy Even in Bad Times

People who have the sense of service will have good times even in bad times.

When there is famine or war, Red Cross people will feel fine because they are serving. The more relief they can bring to others, the happier they feel. It is not that they wish such disasters to happen in order to serve. Rather they know that nature works on its own and there are many things out of our control. Hence they accept the verdict of nature and still do whatever they can.

On the other hand, selfish people who just want to enjoy themselves will be miserable even in good times.

Even in good times people often lose their temper at small matters. Guests often do not come, or some little thing went wrong.

A wise person is happy even in bad times. A stupid person is unhappy even in good times.

You make the time good or bad. People usually blame the bad time and then wait for a good time. But even if an astrologer says you are in a hopeless time, you can make it good.

Power of Softness and Forcefulness

Often people are soft, due to lack of courage and forcefulness. They suffer a lot. And at some other time, they become volatile without any justified reason and may suffer again.

Yet there are some people who possess a softness that comes from maturity, magnanimity, and the knowledge of the Self.

There are also two types of forcefulness in people: aggressive and assertive. Aggressive people are forceful out of weakness or out of fear. Assertive people are forceful out of care, love, and compassion.

The Marks of Maturity

Mature is our, who is patient, who is willing to give up immediate pleasure in favor of the long-term gain.

Mature is, who has the ability to settle differences without resentment or anger.

Mature is, who perseveres despite setbacks.

Mature is one, who knows that life is too short to be wasted in prejudices.

Mature is one, who has the capacity to face disappointments and adversity without becoming bitter.

Mature is one, who is humane, and who responds to the needs of others with compassion.

Mature is one, who has the humility to say, "I was wrong" and the self-control not to say, "I told you so" when he is proved right.

Mature is one, who does not complain that the rosebush has thorns but rejoices that it bears roses.

Mature is one, whose deeds conform to his thoughts and words.

Mature is one, who lives in the present without being shackled by the dead past or the upcoming future.

Mature is one, who strives to change the things he can and who lives in peace with the things he cannot.

Mature is one, who gently and constantly questions himself, "Am I mature?"

Chapter 6

Understanding and Developing Emotional Intelligence

- What is emotional intelligence?
- Emotions
- Rational and emotional brains
- Emotional hijacking
- Impact of EQ in career, success and life
- The blind spots
- Study of EQ working at Bell lab
- Dangers of emotional illiteracy
- It is EQ that gets you promoted
- Emotional competencies
- Can EQ be developed?

"IQ (Intelligence Quotient) gets you hired but EQ (Emotional Intelligence) gets you promoted.

..... Time Magazine

Emotional intelligence is the foundation of success and happiness in life, relationship and career. It is our ability to manage our emotions rather than letting emotions to control us when we feel challenged by uncertainty, fear, frustrations, stress, lack of balance in work and life.

Research studies indicate that approximately 1-20% of our success comes from our intelligence quotient (IQ) and the other 80-99% comes from other factors. Many of these other factors relate to how we apply our wisdom to manage our emotions in our quest to achieve balance to cope up with many and varied workplace challenges. It is necessary for people to be knowledgeable, skilled, and competent in these areas if they have to achieve the best possible results for their time, money, energy and talent.

The need to be emotionally intelligent is particularly acute during emotionally charged times, those times when we feel fearful, frustrated, and fatigued. Fearful of workplace and career uncertainty. Frustrated at having lost our "voice" and our place. Fatigued from dealing with workplace, career and relationship challenges. People who are emotionally smart are at the very heart of successful organizations. Leading organizations the world over are investing time and money to increase the emotional intelligence of their personnel to improve company's bottom line.

What is Emotional Intelligence?

To understand emotional intelligence, let us consider the simple statements given below:

- This CEO does not understand the feelings of employees.
- He is jealous of his colleagues.
- The new boss, is too sensitive; he takes everything too personally.
- He is always in a hostile mood.
- The operation manager is always nagging others and criticizing them.

These statements refer to various blends of emotions, moods or lifestyles as reflected through personality characteristics. Emotional intelligence is also the ability to understand oneself and others hence work effectively.

Emotional Intelligence refers to the capacity for recognizing our own feelings as well as others, for motivating ourselves, for managing emotions well in ourselves and in our relationships.

Emotional Intelligence is the ability to build fruitful and productive relationships. It is essential to work productively with other people. The more emotional and social intelligence, common sense and smart we are, the easier it is to be efficient and successful in our daily lives. It includes components like self-awareness, ability to manage disturbance, motivation, empathy and social skills such as cooperation and leadership. It is believed that various problems of maladjustment at the workplace have their origin in poorly developed emotional awareness at early childhood and the way we are brought up.

Successful CEOs, managers, salespersons, politicians, bureaucrats, professionals and entrepreneurs are all likely to have high levels of emotional intelligence. On the other hand, persons with low emotional intelligence are judged to be misfits.

Emotional Quotient (or EQ) is used interchangeably with Emotional Intelligence (EI) that refers to emotional awareness and emotional management skills. It is a measurement of our ability to balance emotion and reason so as to maximize long-term happiness.

Emotional intelligence involves the ability to monitor your own and others' emotions. To discriminate between these emotions, one must use them effectively for guidance. Emotion refers to a feeling with its distinctive thoughts, psychological, biological states and ranges of propensities toward action.

Emotions

Emotions are the impulse to act out instant plans for handling various situations in our day-to-day lives. There are hundreds of emotions, along with their blends, variations, mutations and nuances. Each emotion plays a unique role in our life as emotions prepare us for specific kind of response.

Anger

The expressions of anger can be in the form of resentment, fury, outrage, wrath, exasperation, indignation, acrimony, animosity, annoyance, irritability, hostility and at the extreme violence. In the state of anger blood flows to hands, heart rate increases and rush of hormones such as adrenaline generates a pulse of energy for strong action.

Fear

Expression of this emotion can take the form of anxiety, apprehension, nervousness, concern, misgiving, worrisome, qualm, dread, fright, terror, phobia and panic. In the case of fear, the blood goes to long skeletal muscles such as legs, making it easier to flee. Hormones are generated that put the body on general alert to fix attention on the immediate threat.

Happiness

This emotion gets expressed by the feelings of joy, relief, contentment, bliss, delight, amusement, pride, sensual pleasure, thrill, gratification, satisfaction, euphoria, ecstasy and, at the extreme stage, a mania. In case of happiness the biological reaction is an increased activity in the brain center that inhibits negative feelings and fosters an increase in available energy therefore quitting of worrisome thoughts. Such a state offers the body a general rest, as well as readiness and enthusiasm for the tasks at hand to plan goals.

Love

Trust, kindness, affinity, acceptance, friendliness, devotion, adoration and infatuation can express love as an emotion. Love and tender feelings generate a state of calmness, of contentment conducive to relaxation and cooperation.

Shock

Surprise can take the shape of shock, astonishment, amazement and wonder. In case of surprise, raised eyebrows allows a larger visual sweep and permits more light to the retina thus allowing more information about the unexpected event. This facilitates to figure out what is going on and decides the best course of action.

Sadness

Feelings like grief, sorrow, gloom, melancholy, self-pity, loneliness, dejection, despair and depression express sadness as an emotion. In this state the body's metabolism gets slowed down as a biological reaction to compensate any significant loss. There is a corresponding drop in energy and enthusiasm levels which actually creates an opportunity to introspect, to mourn, to grasp the consequences of the event so that when energy returns, a new beginning can be made.

Other blend of emotions

Doubt, boredom, jealousy, disgust, shame, hope, faith, courage, forgiveness, and equanimity are many other blends of emotions. And the list is incomplete as psychological research on how to classify emotions continues. These biological propensities to act are shaped further by our life experiences and culture. Emotions enable human beings to respond appropriately to a variety of environmental situations.

Our two minds

Someone's watering eyes may mean he is sad but his words or actions may appear contrary to his act. One is an act of emotion and the other is that of reason. One that thinks and one that feels: heart and head.

- Knowing something is right in the mind can be different from feeling that it is right in the heart. This is the emotional/ rational dichotomy.
- With the harmony in both aspects of the mind, emotional and rational. The rational mind refines and sometimes vetoes the inputs of emotions. These are interconnected and yet semi-independent faculties. Generally both aspects of the mind are well coordinated; feelings are essential to thoughts, thoughts to feelings.
- But when passion surges, the balance tips: it is the emotional mind that captures the upper hand then, swamping the rational mind.

That the thinking brain develop from the emotional; reveals much about the relationship of thoughts to feeling; there was an emotional brain long before there was a rational brain.

Rational and Emotional Brains

There are two ways of looking at anything, the rational and the emotional, neither way is superior in comparision. When we favor one way above another, the repressed function usually becomes unconscious. Whatever is repressed usually returns to haunt us in another form. If we repress thought and subjugate it, then our emotions go out of hand. This can be dangerous and chaotic. Our ability to think will be stuned and will be confined to make rational actions. If you want to do something badly enough, you will always find logic for it somewhere. If we repress emotions, then our thoughts become dry and colourless. We will lack motivation and imagination as well as the inspiration to take the next logical steps. Our feelings will go underground, only to come up in another, often disguised location where they are far harder to deal with.

The relationship between emotions and rational intelligence is a complex one. It is important to appreciate how these interact. Through conscious effort, emotional responses can be regulated and used appropriately; it is when such awareness is lacking that emotional reactions over power rational thought. To understand this, let us first study the evolution and working of these two brains.

Flight and fight or something else

Incidents of attack on lone persons or ladies by unknown persons were reported in some parts of Delhi. In case of sudden entry into a house by an intruder, many inmates get perplexed and lose their ability to analyze the situation appropriately so act accordingly. One lady in Vasant Kunj acted wisely by remaining calm and engaging the intruder in a smooth conversation. Later on she locked him up in a room. How could she decide on a better course of action and save herself as compared to others? The working of the two brains and deciding an options other than flight or fight can explain this better.

Fight or flight were the emotional responses resorted in earlier times to enable both animals and human beings to survive. Choosing simply between fight and flight were the only possible and relevant responses in case of difficulties. In those days when predators could strike any moment and natural calamities like floods or droughts threatened our survival more frequently. The options were limited to human beings. With the advancement of society in the course of human evolution, the odds for survival began to change dramatically and our choice for responses have broadened a lot.

In the course of evolution, the developed neocortex in Homo sapiens has provided a distinct identity to human beings. Neocortex as the seat of thought, puts together and comprehends what the senses perceive. It adds feeling to what we think about and allows us to have feelings about ideas. The addition of neocortex and its connection to the limbic system has helped human development. It enables us to decide what is right or wrong, which is rationality.

Reptiles, who have no neocortex lack material affection and have been found to eat the young ones when they hatch. With a larger size of neocortex in human beings as compared to other mammals, the interconnections of brain circuitry develop better, allowing the possibility of more responses. This is the reason that humans are able to display a greater range of reactions in emotions as well as flexibility in behaviour.

However these centers of higher thinking and rationality still do not govern our emotional life specially when there is an emotional crisis. In such a situation, the emotional centers generate overwhelming force which influences the functions of the rest of our brain including that of the thought center. In case of emotional explosion, the center of limbic systems usually declares an emergency and utilizes immediately the rest of the brain to deal with the situation. Before the neocortex, the thinking brain could have had a chance to know and decide what is happening, the reactions due to emotions that have already taken place.

Another important center in the case of emotions is the Amygdala. This is a part of our limbic system in the brain and it is the main center for emotions. If the Amygdala is removed from the brain, the person cannot assess the emotional significance of events and may become emotionless. Such a person may become uninterested in people and relationships and may prefer to function without feelings. All passions depend on it. Animals that have the Amygdala removed lack fear or rage and lose the urge to compete or co-operate. Tears are also triggered by Amygdala. Without Amygdala, our life gets stripped of personal feelings. Amygdala has a crucial role in our emotional brain and it can take control over what we do even as the thinking brain, the neocortex is still coming to a decision.

The working of Amygdala and its interaction with neocortex constitute the heart of Emotional Intelligence. During an emotional emergency, the Amygdala's extensive web of neural connections captures and drives the rest of brain including the rational brain. It gets a privileged position to hijack the brain as the survival of the person is at stake.

Usually the sensory signals from eye or ear travel first in the brain, the thalamus, and then-across a single synapse-to the Amygdala; a second signal from the thalamus is routed to the neocortex-the thinking brain. This branching allows the Amygdala begin to respond before the neocortex, which mulls information through several levels of brain circuits before it fully perceives and finally initiates its more tailored response. This explains the overwhelming power of emotion over rationality.

From the neocortex most of the time the signals are sent to the limbic brain and from there the appropriate response radiates out through the brain to rest of the body. Joseph Le Doux, a neuro scientist at the center for Neural Science at New York University has discovered that a smaller bundle of neurons that leads directly from the thalamus to the Amygdala allows it to receive some direct inputs from the senses and start a response before they are fully registered by the neocortex. Hence Amygdala does not entirely depend on signals from neocortex to formulate its emotional reactions. Via this emergency route, the Amygdala can lead us immediately to actions while the slightly slower, but fully informed neocortex unfolds its more refined plan of reactions. Hence some emotional reactions and emotional memories can be formed without any conscious, cognitive participation at all. This can explain the incidents of fear/phobias where one incident affects our whole life without much reason. The shortcut from thalamus to Amygdala completely bypasses the neocortex. In the first few milliseconds of our perceiving something we not only unconsciously comprehend what it is, but also decide whether we like it or not (form an opinion about). Hence our emotional mind can have an opinion different from our rational mind.

Le Doux further established that Amygdala can take control of our brain and over what we do even as the thinking brain, the neocortex, is still coming to a decision in an appropriate response. The emergency route from ear or eye to thalamus to Amygdala is crucial as it saves time in an urgent situation when an instant response is needed. In real emergencies such working can be justified but if it becomes a normal phenomena, then it creates a problem.

While Amygdala works as storehouse for unconscious opinion in the form of emotional memories, the registration and making sense of perceptual patterns is done by the hippocampus. It remembers the hard facts but the Amygdala retains the emotional flavor that goes with these facts. Hippocampus provides a memory of context, which forms the base for emotional meaning. Hippocampus also recognizes the differing significance of real or apparent threat i.e. the lion in a zoo or a forest. If we missed an accident on the road, the hippocampus will retain the specifics of the incident i.e. with which speed the car was running, who was the other person etc.

But the Amygdala thereafter will always send us a surge of anxiety in similar situations. The hippocampus is crucial in recognizing a face but it is the Amygadala, which adds whether you like or dislike him. The more intense the Amygdala arousal, stronger would be the imprint: the experience that scares us the most or thrills us the most, is among our most indelible memories. In fact the brain has two memory systems, one for ordinary facts and one for emotionally charged ones. One drawback of such neural alarm is that the urgent message which Amygdala sends is sometimes, out of date or inappropriate to the situation. The Amygdala scans experience, comparing what is happening now with what happened in the past through associative memory. When one key element of a present situation is similar to the past, it can call it a "match" and acts before there is full confirmation.

Many times we react to the present in ways that were imprinted long ago with thoughts, emotions, reactions learned in response to the events not dimly similar but close enough to alarm the Amygdala. While the hippocampus retrieves information, the Amygdala determines if that information has any emotional relevance. Both work hand-in-hand. In the childhood or early age the hippocampus, which is crucial for narrative memories and the neocortex, seat of rational thought, have yet to become fully developed. While the Amygdala, which matures very quickly in the infant's brain is much closer to be developed at birth; the hippocampus keeps developing throughout life. This explains why interactions in our earliest years lay down a set of emotional lessons.

Working of Amygdala and Neocortex

When a message is received by our senses like eye or ear, it is first sent to the thalamus. Then the thalamus translates the nerve impulse into the brain language. A major part of the message then goes to visual cortex where it is analyzed and assessed for meaning and appropriate response. If that response is emotional a signal goes to Amygdala to activate emotional centers. A smaller portion of the original signal goes straight from thalamus to Amygdala in a quicker transmission, allowing a faster (though less precise) response. Thus the Amygdala can trigger an emotional response before the cortical centers have fully understood what is happening.

The emergency route from eye or ear to thalamus to Amygdala is crucial; it saves time in an emergency. But this circuit carries only a small portion of the sensory message and hence what registers in the Amygdala via this express route is at best a rough signal just enough for a warning. This primitive, minor brain system in mammals is the main brain system in non-mammals. It is quick but not a precise process. Such imperfection in, a squirrel, is fine since it leads to erring on the side of safety but in human dealing, it may be disastrous in terms of inappropriate responses. This type of feeling prior to thought, called precognitive emotion, is the triggering of reactions before there is a full confirming evidence of the nature of the external stimulus or event.

Emotional Hijacking

Emotional hijacking involves two dynamics; the triggering of Amygdala and a failure to activate the neocortex process that usually keeps emotional response in balance. At these moments the rational mind is swamped by the emotional mind. The prefrontal cortex acts as an efficient manager of emotions-weighing reactions before acting.

Indeed the intellect cannot work at its best without emotional intelligence. This does not mean that we are doing away with emotions and putting reason in front but instead to find an intelligent balance between the two. It is to harmonize head and heart, the rational and emotional.

Amygdala Hijack-Case of Mike Tyson

In 1997 the boxer Mike Tyson became enraged in the course of his fight and bit off the ear of his opponent Evander Holyfield. This act later on cost him $30 million. It was a clear case of amygdala hijacking, as Tyson was a victim of alarming of brain centers. Through the natural superhighway, the Amygdala gets linked to prefrontal areas to alarm the brain for survival. The creation of this superhighway is triggered by any memory of past happening. In this case, Tyson again was butted by Holyfield and this flooded him with rage as he did the same thing eight months earlier, in a match that Tyson had lost. Then he got upset and filed a complaint against Holyfield for the same but has to face unjust. This emotional alarm reminded Tyson that he might again lose the match by this unfair play of Holyfield. As a victim of this alarm Tyson simply suffered emotional hijacking as his impulse took over and swamped rationality.

Impact of EQ in Career, Success and Life: Examples

Goleman, the author of the book 'Working with Emotional Intelligence' has cited many examples illustrating how EQ affects our performance in life and career.

- The reason for firing a chief operating officer. 'He was extraordinarily talented, brilliant conceptually, a very powerful mind. That's how he become chief operating officer. But he was not a brilliant leader, even particularly likeable. He was often brutal in his responses. In groups he was socially awkward; he had no social grace, or even a social life. At 45, he had no near and dear ones. He worked all the time. He was one-dimensional and I had to fire him.'

Clear differences in terms of emotional competence have been noticed between successful managers and those who failed. Specific competencies where differences have been observed are listed below.

Self-control

Unsuccessful managers handled pressure poorly and were prone to moodiness and angry outbursts. Successful managers on the other hand were able to bear stress, remained calm, confident and dependable in case of crisis or turmoil.

Conscientiousness

The unsuccessful group reacted to failure and criticism defensively denying, covering up, making excuses or even passing on the blame. The successful ones assumed responsibility by admitting their mistakes and failures hence took appropriate action to correct the situation.

Trustworthiness

Those who got derailed, typically, were overly ambitious and too ready to get ahead at the expense of other people. Successful managers on the other hand had high integrity, with a strong concern for the needs of their subordinates and colleagues, for the demands of the task on hand, giving higher priority to these issues.

Building bonds and leveraging diversity

Due to their insensitive and manipulative manner the failed group was unable to build a strong network of cooperatives, mutually beneficial relationships needed for support. Successful managers on the other hand were able to get along with all types of people by leveraging the diversity.

Flexibility

The unsuccessful managers were unable to adapt their style to make changes in the organizational culture, or were unable to take in or respond to feedback regarding the traits they needed to change or improve. They could neither listen nor learn. They were rigid and could not change their style as per the need while the opposite group was flexible.

Relationship

The single most frequently mentioned factor descriptive of those who failed was that they were too harshly critical, insensitive, or demanding, and as a result they alienated those who worked with them. They lacked empathy and could not motivate others.

These negative traits are fatal handicaps even for brilliant executives with strong technical expertise. One executive described a derailed colleague in the following words: 'He is a great strategic thinker and he has high ethical standards, but he lashes out at people. He is very smart, but he achieves superiority through demeaning others. Many people have tried to help him work on this flaw, but it seems hopeless.'

Other examples

While citing the examples of two college students, Goleman explained the different levels of performance despite high IQ but differing EQ.

- A college student had perfect scores on his college admissions tests a pair of 800s on the verbal and math sections of the SAT, and a 5 on each of three-advanced placement tests. Despite this he was unmotivated, often skipped classes. He dropped out for a while, finally graduating after 10 years. He simply ended working as a one-man computer consulting business.
- The second one was a math's prodigy who entered high school at the age of 10, graduated at 12, and got his doctorate in theoretical mathematics from Oxford at 18. In high school he was a bit short for his age because he was so young-about a foot shorter than the others. He was also about twice as bright

as anyone else among many students resented him for it. He was often taunted and bullied. But despite his diminutive stature, he didn't back down. Like a little fighter, he stood his ground against the bigger hulks at school. He had the assertiveness to match his intellect-which may explain how he became the head, of one of the most prestigious mathematics departments in the world.

Low EQ can lead to negative feelings such as

Failure, anger, victimization, guilt, lethargy, fear, disappointment, resentment, frustration, loneliness.

These energy suckers do not allow us to reach the peak performance.

A high EQ usually leads to positive feelings like

Motivation, self-control, peace, satisfaction, appreciation, friendship, fulfillment, and freedom. These feelings lead us to happy, healthy and successful relationships in life.

Such a person merges himself in the execution of his assignment and can be called emotionally present. An emotionally present employee is fully attentive and completely involved in his work and performs at the peak. Others perceive him as accessible, engaged, see how he contributes his creative ideas, energy and intuitions. Being present in one's current job requires total attention to and immersion in the task on hand. Presence begins with self-awareness. When fully present, you are more attuned to those around you, to the needs of the situation, and you are 'in flow'. You may be thoughtful, funny or self-reflective, drawing on whatever capacity or skill you need at the moment.

The opposite of this is all too familiar, employees go through their work as a routine, obviously bored, or otherwise disconnected. Take the case of a front office executive in a company who hates her job. She says, 'Sitting up here, smiling, typing and being friendly-it's all useless. These eight or nine hours are a waste. There isn't any satisfaction in it for me.'

People with varying levels of EQ may react differently to similar situations

The art of influencing others and making a positive or negative impact on situations can make one either a star performer or a failure.

Daniel Coleman quotes the example of the merger of two of the largest financial firms in the US. The press heralded the event as a crowning achievement. Within weeks of the announcement, numerous meetings were held in two firms, detailing just how the two big companies would merge into a single giant. As it is usual in the case of such mergers, hundreds of employees were expected to lose their jobs since many functions would be duplicated between the two companies resulting in surplus manpower. But how could this news be conveyed to the employees without aggravating the situation? Let us see what happened.

One manager conveyed his message in the worst manner. He gave a gloomy speech: `I don't know what I'm going to do, but don't expect me to be nice to you. I have to fire half the people here, and I'm not exactly sure how I'm going to make that decision, so I'd like each of you to tell me your background and, qualifications so that I can start firing you.'

The manager in the other company did better. His message was very encouraging:

- We think this new company will be an exciting platform for our work, and we're blessed with talented people from both organizations to work with. We'll make our decisions as quickly as we can, but not until we're positively sure we've collected enough information to be fair. We'll update you within few days on how we're doing. And we'll decide both on the basis of objective performance data plus qualitative abilities, like teamwork and other such factors.

One can imagine the impact made on the employees by the two managers. In the former company everyone was underestimated. What they heard was `I'm not being treated fairly.' They were bitter, demoralized and said, `I don't know if I even want to work for, this company any more.' In the second organization, the employees were more productive, because they were excited about the prospects. They knew that even if they did not end up with a job, the decision certainly would be fair.

Both managers were influential-but in completely opposite ways. Star performers are skilled at sending emotional signals, which makes them powerful communicators, and enables them to sway an audience, i.e., makes them leaders. Apart from this, they have high EQ. On the other hand, those who fail to understand the emotions of others have generally low on EQ and bring about poor management results and discouragement.

The Blind Spots

Blinds spots are those weak areas of our personalities, which impact on us adversely but we may not even aware of them, still doing it unconsciously and consistently. Kaplan has identified some of the more common and costly 'blind spots' on the basis of a study of 42 otherwise highly successful executives. A wide range of employees were studied, from department heads to CEOs, and certain common problems were identified as listed below.

Blind ambition

Such persons have to win or appear 'right' at all costs; they compete not cooperate; they exaggerate their own value, contribution, are boastful and arrogant. They perceive people in terms of black and white, i.e., as enemies or allies.

Unrealistic goals

They set overly ambitious, unattainable goals for themselves, the group or the organization; they are unrealistic about what it takes to get jobs done.

Relentless striving

These individuals are compulsively hardworking at the cost of everything else in life. They only live for their work and can't balance their life.

Driving others

Such persons push others too hard, burning them out; they micro manage and take over instead of delegating. They become ruthless and insensitive to the emotional harm caused to those whom they manage or influence.

Power hungry

They seek power for their own interest rather than that of the organization; they push their personal agenda regardless of other perspectives and exploit others for their own good or status.

Insatiable need for recognition

They are addicted to glory; they take credit for others efforts and blame them for mistakes. They sacrifice follow-through and proper execution in pursuit of the next victory.

Preoccupation with appearances

Need to look good at all costs and overly concerned with their public image.

Need to seem perfect

These persons are enraged by criticism, even if realistic. They blame others for their failures and cannot admit personal weaknesses or their mistakes.

Study of EQ Working at Bell Lab

A study of star performers at the Bell Labs was conducted by Robert Kelly and Janet Caplan so as to ascertain the reason for difference in performance between the star performers and average workers. Bell Lab is the world famous scientific think tank near Princeton. Engineers and scientists who are all at the top in the academic IQ tests work in the lab. But within this pool of talent, some emerge as stars, while others are only average in their output. What makes the difference between the stars and the average is not their academic IQ, but their emotional EQ. They are better able to motivate themselves, and better able to work their informal network into their adhoc teams.

The stars were studied in one division at the lab. The study focussed on the unit that creates and designs the electronic switches that control telephone systems-a highly sophisticated and demanding piece of electronic engineering. Because the work is beyond the capacity of any one person to tackle, it is done in teams that can range from 5 to 150 engineers. No single engineer knows enough to do the job alone; getting things done demands tapping other people's expertise. To find out what made the difference between those who were highly productive and those who were only average, Robert Kelly and Janet Caplan had managers and peers nominate the 10 to 15 per cent engineers who stood out as stars.

They compared the stars with everyone else. The most dramatic observation at first was the paucity of differences between the two groups. "Based on a wide range of cognitive and social measures, from standard tests for IQ to Personality inventories, there is little meaningful difference in innate abilities", Kelly and Caplan wrote in the Harvard Business Review. "As it develops, academic talent was not a good predictor of on-the-job productivity. Nor was IQ."

But after detailed interviews, the critical differences emerged in the internal and interpersonal strategies "stars" used to get their work done. One of the most important factors was a rapport with a network of key people. Things go more smoothly for the standouts because they put time into cultivating good relationships with people whose services might be needed in a crunch situation. These people were a vital part of an instant adhoc team to solve a problem or handle a crisis. "A middle performer at the Bell Labs talked about being stumped by technical problems" Kelly and Caplan observed. "He painstakingly called various technical masters and then waited, wasting valuable time, while calls went unreturned and e-mails unanswered. Star performers rarely face such situations because they do the work of building reliable networks before they actually need them. When they call someone for advice, stars almost always get a faster answer.

Informal networks are especially critical for handling unanticipated problems. "The formal organization is set up to handle easily anticipated problems," one study of these networks observes. "But when the unexpected problems arise, the informal organization kicks in. Its complex web of social ties forms every time colleagues communicate, and solidify over time into surprisingly stable networks. Highly adaptive, informal networks move diagonally and elliptically, skipping entire functions to get things done."

Beyond a mastery of these essential networks, other forms of organizational savvy the Bell Labs stars had mastered included effectively coordinating their efforts in teamwork; being leaders in building consensus; being able to see things from the perspective of others, such as customers or others in a work team; persuasiveness; and promoting cooperation while avoiding conflicts. While all of these rely on social skills, the stars also displayed another kind of knack: taking initiative, being self motivated enough to take responsibilities above and beyond their stated jobs-and self management in the sense of regulating their time and work commitments well. All such skills, of course, are aspects of emotional intelligence.

As knowledge based services and intellectual capital become more central to corporations improving the way people work together will be a major way to leverage intellectual capital, making a critical competitive difference. To thrive and not just survive, corporations would do well to boost their collective emotional intelligence.

Emotional Illiteracy

A person with low emotional intelligence may display the following problems:

- Lack of empathy. He does not show emotions.
- Distances oneself from others or is withdrawn.
- Can't view things objectively.
- Always takes things, personally.
- Poor interpersonal skills.
- Often hurts others and can be arrogant.
- Takes rash decisions.
- Is self centered and self seeking.
- Low self motivation.
- Has huge inertia.
- Does not know his potential/ weakness.
- Too hungry for recognition.
- His performance depends on the surroundings.
- No space for others.
- Loses will to compete or survive.
- Indulges in self-pity.
- Too reactive. Gets affected by anything that happens around him.

How the organization suffers when its employees have low EQ:

- Under performance.
- Wastage of time and energy.
- Lack of focus on organizational goals.
- Inter-personal problems.
- Lack of team spirit. Inability to be a team member.
- Insecurity in the organization due to unpredictability.
- Mood swings in the team.
- Disruption of organizational peace or industrial relations.
- Too much work stress.
- People not enjoying their work.
- Undercutting/internal politics. Unhealthy competition amongst employees.

People who are emotionally intelligent help the organizations to grow. That is the reason leading global organizations are investing time and money to increase the emotional intelligence of their personnel.

It is the EQ That Gets You Promoted

IQ gets you hired, but EQ gets you promoted. Chief Executive of a company was asked to rank the top performers working with him. The results showed that they were not necessarily those with the highest IQs; they were those whose e-mails got answered. They had better networks therefore could influence others quickly and effectively.

Employees who are good in networking, collaborating and mixing with their colleagues are more likely to get the cooperation they need to achieve their goals. It has been observed that employees most often failed because of an interpersonal shortcoming rather than because of a technical inability or functional deficiency. Many fatal flaws in career are related to classic emotional failing, such as poor working relations, authoritarianism or excessive ambition and conflict with the top management. EQ has given a new dimension to business, industry and career counselling. It is increasingly being used in customer service training as the customer is at the centerstage in today's competitive business environment. The customer is saying, `I don't care if every member of your staff is from IIT, IIM, Harvard or Stanford. I will go where I am understood and treated with respect.' The employer also similarly wants to promote those who deliver results, not those who have merely passed from elite institutions. Many MBA schools have started testing for EQ during MBA entrance as those with high EQ are likely to succeed more.

One may be an excellent doctor in terms of technical knowledge. However, if his temper is more painful to bear than his treatment, so despite his professional expertise, he loses patients very easily. People with low EQ do have feeling, and these feelings can reach till such an intensity that they can erupt. These persons are more likely to become emotionally overwhelmed than those who consistently recognize the physical signals of emotions, because suppressed emotions can eventually rise to the surface, causing unexpected emotional outbursts and physical ailments. Self-awareness is one of the important constituents of emotional intelligence.

Five Basic Emotional Competencies

Emotional intelligence means managing the feelings so that these are expressed appropriately, effectively, enabling the self and others to work smoothly. Competence is a personal trait or a set of habits that enables us to be more effective or achieve better job performance either at the workplace or in our relationships with others. Goleman has grouped a common core of personal and social abilities as the key ingredient in success under the umbrella of emotional intelligence.

Self-awareness

Knowing what we are feeling in the moment, and using those preferences to guide our decision making; have a realistic assessment of our own abilities and a well-grounded sense of self-confidence.

Self-regulation

Handling our emotions so that they facilitate rather than interfere with the task at hand; being conscientious and delaying gratification to pursue goals; recovering well from emotional distress.

Motivation

Using our deepest preferences to move and guide us toward our goals, to help us take initiative and strive to improve, and to persevere in the face of setbacks and frustrations.

Empathy

Sensing what people are feeling, being able to take their perspective, and cultivating rapport and attunement with a broad diversity of people.

Social skills

Handling emotions in relationships well and accurately reading various social situations and networks; interacting smoothly; using these skills to persuade and lead, negotiate and settle disputes, promoting cooperation and teamwork.

The Emotional Competence Framework

Personal competence (Self-mastery)

These competencies determine how we manage ourselves

1. Self Awareness

Knowing one's internal states, preferences, resources and intuitions.

- *Self-awareness is the vital foundation skill for three emotional competencies*: Emotional awareness: Recognizing one's emotions and their effects.

- *Accurate Self-assessment*: Knowing one's strengths and limits.
- *Self-confidence*: A strong sense of one's self worth and capabilities.

Emotional awareness

People with this competence

- Know which emotions they are feeling and why.
- Realize the links between their feelings and what they think; do and say.
- Recognize how their feelings affect their performance.
- Have a guiding awareness of their values and goals.

Self-confidence

A strong sense of one's self-worth and capabilities. The courage that comes from certainty about our capabilities, values and goals. People with this competence

- Present themselves with self-assurance.
- Can voice views that are unpopular and go out on a limb for what is right.
- Are decisive, able to make sound decisions despite uncertainties and pressures.

Accurate self-assessment

Knowing one's inner resources, abilities, and limits. A candid sense of our personal strengths and limits, a clear vision of where we need to improve, and the ability to learn from experience.

People with this competence are:

- Aware of their strengths and weaknesses.
- Reflective, learning from experience.
- Open to candid feedback, new perspectives, continuous learning, and self-development.
- Ability to show a sense of humor and perspective about themselves.

2. Self-regulation

The two primal skills-handling impulse and dealing with upsets-are at the core of five emotional competencies relating to self-regulation. It has five elements:

- Self-control: Managing disruptive emotions and impulses effectively.
- Trustworthiness: Displaying honesty and integrity.
- Conscientiousness: Dependability and responsibility in fulfilling.
- Adaptability: Flexibility in handling change and challenges.
- Innovation: Being open to noble ideas, approaches, and new information.

Self control

People with this competence:

- Manage their impulsivê feelings and distressing emotions well.
- Stay composed, positive, and unflappable even in trying moments.
- Think clearly and stay focussed under pressure.

Trustworthiness and Conscientiousness

Maintaining integrity and taking responsibility for personal performance.

People with this competence:

For trustworthiness

- Act ethically and are above reproach.
- Build trust through their reliability and authenticity.
- Admit their own mistakes and confront unethical actions in others.
- Take tough, principled stands even if they are unpopular.

For conscientiousness

- Meet commitments and keep promises.
- Hold themselves accountable for meeting their objectives.
- Are organized and careful in their work.

Innovation and adaptability

Being open to noble ideas and approaches, and being flexible in responding to change.

People with this competence:

For innovation

- Seek out fresh ideas from a wide variety of sources.
- Entertain original solutions to problems.
- Generate new ideas.
- Take fresh perspectives and risk in their thinking.

For adaptability

- Smoothly handle multiple demands and shifting priorities.
- Adapt their responses and tactics to fit fluid circumstances.
- Are flexible in how they see events.

3. What motivates us?

Emotional tendencies that guide or facilitate in reaching goals:

- *Achievement Drive*: Striving to improve or meet a standard of excellence.
- *Commitment*: Aligning with the goals of the group or organization.
- *Initiative*: Readiness to act on opportunities.
- *Optimism*: Persistence in pursuing goals despite obstacles and setbacks.

These motivational competencies typify outstanding performers:

Achievement drive

Striving to improve or meet a standard of excellence.

People with this competence are:

- Result-oriented, with a high drive to meet their objectives and standards.
- Set challenging goals and take calculated risks.
- Pursue information to reduce uncertainty and find ways to do better.
- Learn how to improve their performance.

Commitment

Aligning with the goals of a group or organization.

People with this competence

- Readily make sacrifices to meet a larger organizational goal.
- Find a sense of purpose in the larger mission.
- Use the group's core values in making decisions and clarifying choices.
- Actively seek out opportunities to fulfill the group's mission.

Initiative and optimism

Displaying pro-activity and persistence. People with this competence.

For initiative

- Are ready to seize opportunities.
- Pursue goals beyond what's required or expected of them.
- Cut through red tape and bend the rules when necessary to get the job done.
- Mobilize others through unusual, enterprising efforts.

For optimism

- Persist in seeking goals despite obstacles and setbacks.
- Operate from hope of success rather than fear of failure.
- See setbacks as due to manageable circumstances rather than a personal flaw.

4. Empathy

These competencies determine how we handle relationships for empathy

Awareness of others' feelings needs and concerns.

- *Understanding others*: Sensing others' feelings, and perspectives, and taking an active interest in their concerns.
- *Developing others*: Sensing others' development, needs and boosting their abilities.
- *Service orientation*: Anticipating, recognizing, and meeting customers' needs.

- *Leveraging diversity*: Cultivating opportunities through different kinds of people.
- *Political awareness*: Reading a group's emotional currents and power relationships.

Understanding others

People with this competence

- Are attentive to emotional cues and listen well.
- Show sensitivity and understand others' perspectives.
- Help out others based on understanding of their needs and feelings.

Developing others

People with this competence

- Acknowledge and reward people's needs for further growth.
- Offer useful feedback and identify people's needs for further growth.
- Train, give timely coaching, and offer assignments that challenge and foster a person's skills.

Service orientation

People with this competence

- Understand customers' needs and match them to services or products.
- Seek ways to increase customers' satisfaction and loyalty.
- Gladly offer appropriate assistance.
- Grasp customers' perspective, act as a trusted advisor.

Leveraging diversity

People with this competence

- Respect and relate well to people from varied backgrounds.
- Understand diverse worldviews and are sensitive to group differences.
- See diversity as opportunity, creating an environment where diverse people may thrive.
- Challenge bias and intolerance.

Political awareness

People with this competence

- Accurately read key power relationships.
- Detect crucial social networks.
- Understand the forces that shape views and actions of clients, customers, or competitors.
- Accurately read organizational and external realities.

5. Social skills

Adeptness at inducing desirable responses in others. Social skills, in the essential sense of handling another person's emotions artfully, underlie several competencies. These include:

- Influence: Wielding effective tactics for persuasion.
- Communication: Listening openly and sending convincing messages.
- Conflict management: Negotiating and resolving disagreements.
- Leadership : Inspiring and guiding individuals and groups.
- Change catalyst : Initiating or managing change.
- Building bonds: Nurturing instrumental relationships.
- Collaboration and cooperation : Working with others towards shared goals.
- Team capabilities: Creating group synergy in pursuing collective goals.

Influence

People with this competence

- Are skilled at winning people over.
- Fine-tune presentations to appeal to the listener.
- Use complex strategies like indirect influence to build consensus and support.
- Orchestrate dramatic events to effectively make a point.

Communication

People with this competence

- Are effective in take and give, registering emotional cues in attuning their message.

- Deal with difficult issues in a candid and straightforward manner.
- Listen well, seek mutual understanding, and welcome sharing of information fully.
- Foster open communication and stay receptive to bad news as well as good.

Conflict management

People with this competence

- Handle difficult people and tense situations with diplomacy and tact.
- Spot potential conflict, bring disagreements into the open, and help to de-escalate the situation.
- Encourage debate and open discussion.
- Orchestrate win-win situations.

Leadership

People with this competence

- Articulate and arouse enthusiasm for a shared vision and mission.
- Step forward to lead as needed, regardless of position.
- Guide the performance of others while holding themselves accountable.
- Lead by example.

Change catalyst

People with this competence

- Recognize the need for change and remove barriers.
- Challenge the status quo to acknowledge the need for change.
- Champion the change and enlist others in its pursuit.
- Model the change expected of others.

None of us can be perfect in all competencies. We have strengths and limitations. The extent of competencies needed for a particular profession also varies. *The aggregate of EQ in all related competencies might be more important for overall success rather than a high score in one or two competencies.* Our strengths are usually spread in many areas and there are many paths to excellence.

Can EQ be Developed?

Experience and research clearly demonstrate that while some aspects of our personality are fixed, we may choose the way we want to act them out. It is never too late to make changes in your life, or help others do the same.

Emotional intelligence, unlike IQ, can be improved throughout life. One can tone up the emotional competence at any stage. Normally with our growth in life, emotional intelligence tends to increase since we learn to be more aware of our moods. We are also able to effectively handle distressing emotions, listen and empathize. To a large extent, maturity itself describes this process of becoming more intelligent about our emotions, the interplay of thoughts and feelings.

While certain personality characteristics are inherited from parents, most of competencies falling under emotional intelligence can be developed as this kind of intelligence is not fixed at birth. Scientists have not yet discovered an emotional intelligence gene as such. It is something you have learnt or not learnt. It is a lot of common sense and related to wisdom which may come with maturity.

Our emotional development is closely related to our childhood. The healthy emotional development of children is vital to both their ability to learn when young as well as to their success and happiness as adults. However, experience shows that the emotional development of children has by and large been neglected in the present age of information and knowledge. As a result, children often bear the brunt of emotionally unskilled individual parenting, rigidity and blind preaching.

A child's mental frame can actually be sculpted by parental example during the formative stage. Parents need guidance in recognizing and nurturing emotional intelligence in their children, both within the home and outside. Intelligence, measured as IQ, is certainly an asset. The current system of education may produce intelligent children, but if something else very important is overlooked, success and happiness in life may suffer. To excel in life, a child needs to master the art of compassion, impulse control, self-motivation, influencing others effectively and many other related aspects.

In today's world, although a high IQ is desirable yet EQ is becoming increasingly important for growth and success. In many advanced countries, traditional education is increasingly tilted towards cognitive achievement, and as a result children may have to face a great deal of emotional pressure and frustration. The historical and cultural emphasis on moral and emotional education is one of the reasons that Asian immigrants in the West have done reasonably well in terms of emotional intelligence and making a place for themselves despite many hurdles.

Whatever may be your current level of EQ, you can learn to develop it. The process of developing EQ is not that difficult. Emotional intelligence impacts you in all aspects whether work, relationship or family life. It affects how good you feel, how much you can achieve, the quality and richness of your relationships. It impacts parents as well as children, all of us. What is important is that, one can develop EQ through a step-by-step process. Increasing EQ offers quick dividends and opens many avenues for success and happiness.

People are fast realizing that the ability to feel is as vital to their well being as the ability to think. You need to understand the critical importance of your raw emotions, but often you do not know how to do so. How do you learn to master complex and confusing emotions? Developing emotional competencies is the answer. Human beings are not equally emotional all have varied natural temperaments. Awareness, feedback and support can change the way you act out, express yourself and utilize your emotions significantly. Unlike IQ, emotional intelligence can be developed with practice.

Emotional learning-raising the EQ

When we experience an emotion it offers an opportunity to learn, if we start becoming aware of our emotions. We go through a learning cycle. Emotion is triggered by an event, which may be highly dramatic or so trivial that it is hardly noticed. The response could be an uncontrollable rage, grief, a bitter feeling of guilt, depression or something else. Or it could be a feeling of love, the beginning of hope or a fleeting sensation of joy. Whatever the emotional response, it gives us an opportunity of looking at life in a new way and examining some of our assumptions, values and beliefs. After doing this, we may modify some of our thoughts that led us to this emotional state. This can then result in fresh attitudes and possibly new behavior. If we learn the lesson revealed by our emotion then we can jump off the cycle of reactive patterns and choose a new response by proactively deciding it. If we don't, it tends to repeat itself as a negative feedback loop.

Stage 1 : An event or happening, a trigger.

Stage 2 : Emotional response.

Stage 3 : Opportunity to revise emotional response by examining assumptions, values and beliefs.

Stage 4 : If revised, then new attitude, action and behavior.

Stage 5 : New life chosen by us. Revised emotional response.

If values, beliefs or assumptions are not revised then there is a possibility of repetition of the same undesirable behaviour or something that had upset us in the past.

Coaching on emotional intelligence

He was a marketing executive and could take criticism: but when he felt his idea or character is being attached, his anger flared up and he said things he felt ashamed of later on. But he was determined to improve his emotional self-control. His plan for improvement as follows:

1. Learn and master steps for better self-control, such as anticipating hot-button situations and preparing himself so that he won't "lose it".
2. Changing the inner interpretations and reminding himself, what he sees as "criticism" or an "attack" is most often feedback that is meant to be helpful for him.
3. Decide a course of action for future situations.
4. Practice those responses at every opportunity. Mentally rehearse them twice a month.
5. Enroll fellow colleagues to role-play troubling situations so that one can try out new self-control strategies and new responses.

6. Have a fellow member agree to signal when he sees him being stubborn, inflexible, or otherwise overreacting, to remind him to exercise self-control.

Coaching for skills that are vital

With awareness, feedback, introspection, practice and support one can choose to respond in a desired manner rather than reacting as an automatic habit. Some of the areas one can work to improve along with suggested methods are listed next.

1. Taking initiative by being a risk taker

People who are good at taking the initiative know that taking certain calculated risks will greatly improve the quality of their lives. When they take the initiative to face challenges and opportunities, they reap rewards. It doesn't always work out, but the cliche "nothing risked, nothing gained" is true. Here are some steps to help you move towards more initiative and risk taking.

When considering a potentially risky action,

- Determine the risks and obstacles.
- List all the things that may go wrong.
- Find the chances of things going wrong.
- Assess how serious it would be.
- Know why you should do it.
- Calculate your payoffs for achievement.
- Estimate the costs for not attempting it.

List positive reasons to go ahead

List all the positive, upbeat reasons to take the risk. Focus on the possible win instead of the loss

1. Develop an action plan.
2. Dates and action steps to accomplish the goal.
3. Practice and preparation.
4. Attempt first steps or practice in a safe environment.
5. Support systems and reinforcement techniques.
6. Arrange support form others. Reward progress.

Use these steps to work through a risky opportunity. You may have not taken the initiative to pursue such an opportunity so far. It might be buying a new house, taking on a major assignment at work, making an investment, changing to a new job or starting a new business. Consider an opportunity where you must take some initiative to start.

What is the risky opportunity you face?

1. What are the benefits of success? List at least three.
2. What could go wrong?
3. What would be your first steps show initiative and start tomorrow?
4. Who could provide you support to move ahead?
5. Are you the kind of person who focuses on pleasure or pain? Use pleasure or pain motivation to galvanise you into action as discussed in earlier chapters.

2. Listening better through empathy

Good listeners have empathy for the person they are listening to. They know it isn't necessary to agree or even sympathise with someone's views or feelings. It is just important to understand the other's feelings and the reason for those feelings. Learning empathic listening takes practice. Some steps for it are;

- Let the person speak.
- Try not to interrupt, to give advice, or interpret.
- Let the speaker finish what he has to say.
- Listen to hear what they emphasize and what kind of examples they use.
- Listen with all your senses.
- Listen to words , observe body language, sense feelings.
- Check for meaning whenever you don't understand.
- Satiate queries.
- Learn, when not to ask.
- Ask clarifying questions sparingly to help with shared understanding.
- Try being silent and wait for the speaker to summarize.

Example: An irate customer calls to complain about a late delivery

- Listen without interrupting.
- Observe non-verbal behaviour.
- Reflect back to check meaning.
- Reflect back to check understanding.
- Be patient to allow the total message to emerge.

3. Becoming stress free and being determined to succeed

We can be more effective by making commitments to take action, to change habits, to let go of certain attitudes or to think differently. This will enable you to be stress free and happier. For example:

- Take action-ask for a raise or agreed commitment.
- Change habits-stop smoking.
- Let go of an attitude-`He can never think positive about me.'
- Think differently-`I can be very successful with this assignment.'

It takes self-confidence and determination to fulfill commitments. If you have trouble following through once you've decided to change, consider the Determination Spectrum. It defines the stages of commitment.

Stage 1: I won't do it. I don't want to. Not determined.

Stage 2: I can't do it.

Stage 3: I want to do it.

Stage 4: I will try to do it.

Stage 5: I can do it.

Stage 6: I commit. Will do with determination.

Stage 1 is characterized by anxiety, fear and doubt. When you add know how and positive thinking, you gain self-confidence which characterizes stage 6. Here are some things you can do to replace anxiety, fear and doubt with self-confidence.

- Develop self-esteem by recognizing your skills and accomplishments. One way is to write down and regularly review an achievement list for yourself.
- Develop a habit of rewarding yourself when you work hard.

- Use affirmations (short positive statements) daily to build your confidence.
- Affirmations are a way of flooding your mind with "positive self talk".
- Encourage confidence by recognising success.
- Make a note of things you do well.
- At the end of everyday, record your successes in a diary.
- Seek the support of others.
- Stay away from negativity. Start a "mutual admiration society" with your friends to raise each others' spirits.
- Keep a list of things you want and the goals to be achieved.
- Whenever you achieve one, you cross it off the list.
- Keep both lists visible; what you have achieved and what you still want to achieve.

4. Integrating new behaviours into your life

Any change requires adaptation to new set of behaviours. People who are good at managing change are not afraid to adapt, as it is essential.

A formula to bring change and promote adaptability includes

- a picture of what the results will look like,
- a plan to get there, and
- a lot of practice.

Why do we need so much practice? Because new behavior takes time to be internalised, or transform nature. Here's what happens to you when you are trying to integrate a new skill:

- *Resistance*-natural tendency to stay with the familiar.
- *Being unsure*-when we start to apply new skills and behaviors, we feel phoney and uneasy.
- *Assimilation*-with practice, we start to feel familiar with new skill or behavior.
- *Transference*-able to apply behavior or skill to a new setting.
- *Integration*-automatically and unconsciously performing new skill or behavior.

Questions

In this exercise, think of the behaviour that you want to change or improve. Get a picture in your mind of what success will look like. Make this picture stronger in your mind. Then as part of a plan to achieve that success, schedule opportunities to practice.

Examples

Skill to improve.

Become better at listening to colleagues.

How success will look like.

Be calm while listening and not interrupt.

Plan to get there.

Take time everyday to work on listening and ask for feedback.

Practice schedule.

Everyday, just before lunch, I'll find a staff member and ask them for an update. My agenda will be to practice listening without comment and interruption.

5. Effective coaching by celebrating success

Great coaches look for opportunities to celebrate success. This makes individuals and teams feel like winners. Encouragement produces motivation and spirit. Success can be team "wins", such as achieving milestones or recognition of an individual's achievement such as passing a test.

How to celebrate?

- Team wins lend themselves to team events.
- A special social occasion, for example.
- Personal wins should get broad recognition as well.
- Deliver the praise in person and make it public.
- Recognizing a person in front of their peers is always better.
- Praise in public and best to criticize in private. Never embarrass someone in front of others.

Consider a leadership or coaching situation that you are part of.

Enter your responses to the following:

1. What events have happened recently that are worthy of celebration?
2. How can the team be rewarded?
3. How might an individual be rewarded?
4. Which accomplishments are worth celebrating?
   * For a team?
   * For an individual?
5. What are good team rewards?
6. What are good rewards for individuals?
7. None of us is as strong as all of us-Better teamwork

We benefit from alliances and teamwork. Good team members are quick to ask for support when they're in stressful circumstances or need help. They are also quick to offer and give help.

Examples of 'when to ask for help'?

- In a new or strange situation.
- When you need advice.
- When you're stressed out.
- When you need objective feedback.
- When you don't understand.
- When you're in trouble.

Who are the people you go to ask for support? Who are some others you could go to? Consider organised groups, like teams at work, clubs as well as individuals.

I usually ask for help when: ------------------

I could also ask for help when: ----------------

When I need support/ help I usually go to -------

Now I can also go to ------------------

EQ Test No. 1

The following questions, answered honestly, will give you a rough idea of what your EQ is:

1. **You are on an airplane that suddenly hits extremely bad turbulence and begins rocking from side to side. What do you do?**

A. Continue to read your book or, watch a movie, paying little attention to the turbulence.

B. Become vigilant for an emergency, carefully monitoring the stewardesses and reading the emergency instruction card.

C. A little of A and B.

D. Not sure-never noticed.

2. You have taken a group of 4-year olds to the park, and one of them starts crying because the others won't play with her. What do you do?

A. Stay out of it-let the kids deal with it on their own.

B. Talk to her and help her figure out ways to get the other kids to play with her.

C. Tell her in a kind voice not to cry.

D. Try to distract the crying girl by showing her some other things she could play with.

3. Assume you're a college student who had hoped to get an A in a course, but you have just found out that you got a C on the midterm. What do you do?

A. Sketch out a specific plan for ways to improve your grade and resolve to follow through on your plans.

B. Resolve to do better in the future.

C. Tell yourself it really doesn't matter how much you do in the course, and concentrate instead on other courses where your grades are higher.

D. Go to see the professor and try to talk her into giving you a better grade.

4. Imagine you're an insurance salesman calling prospective clients. Fifteen people in a row have hung up on you, and you're getting discouraged. What do you do?

A. Call it a day and hope you have better luck tomorrow.

B. Assess qualities in yourself that may be undermining your ability to make a sale.

C. Try something new in the next call, and keep plugging away.

D. Consider another line of work.

5. **You're a manager in an organization who is trying to encourage, respect for racial and ethnic diversity. You overhear someone telling a racist joke. What do you do?**

   A. Ignore it-it's only a joke.

   B. Call the person into your office for a reprimand.

   C. Speak up on the spot, saying that such jokes are inappropriate and will not be tolerated in your organization.

   D. Suggest to the person telling the joke that he go through a diversity-training program.

6. **You're trying to calm down a friend who has worked himself up into a fury at a driver in another car who has cut dangerously close in front of him. What do you do?**

   A. Tell him to forget it-he's okay now and it's no big deal.

   B. Put on one of his favourite tapes and try to distract him.

   C. Join him in putting down the other driver, as a show of rapport.

   D. Tell him about the time something like this happened to you and how you felt as mad as he does now, but then you saw the other driver was on the way to a hospital emergency room.

7. **You and your life partner have gotten into an argument that has escalated into a shouting match; you're both upset and in the heat of anger, start making personal attacks you don't really mean. What's the best thing to do?**

   A. Take a 20-minute break and then continue the discussion.

   B. Just stop the argument-go silent, no matter what your partner says.

   C. Say you're sorry and ask your partner to apologize, too.

   D. Stop for a moment, collect your thoughts, and then state your side of the case as precisely as you can.

8. **You've been assigned to head a working team that is trying to come up with a creative solution to a nagging problem at work. What's the first thing you do?**
   A. Draw up an agenda and allot time for discussion of each item so that you make the best use of your time together.
   B. Allow people to take out time and know each other better.
   C. Begin by asking each person for ideas about how to solve the problem while the ideas are fresh.
   D. Start out with a brainstorming session, encouraging everyone to say whatever comes to mind, no matter how wild.

9. **Your three years old son is extremely timid and a bit fearful of new places and people, virtually since he was born. What do you do?**
   A. Accept that he has a shy temperament and think of ways to shelter him from situations that would upset him.
   B. Take him to a child psychiatrist for help.
   C. Purposely expose him to lots of new people and places so that he can get over his fear.
   D. Engineer an ongoing series of challenging but manageable experiences that will teach him how to handle new people and places.

10. **For years you've wanted to get back to learning to play a musical instrument you tried in childhood, and now, just for fun, you've finally gotten around to starting. You want to make the most effective use of your time. What do you do?**
   A. Hold yourself to a strict practice time each day.
   B. Choose pieces that stretch your abilities a bit.
   C. Practice only when you're really in the mood.
   D. Pick pieces that are far beyond your ability, but which you can master with diligent effort.

Know your answers

1. Anything but D - that answer reflects a lack of awareness of your habitual responses under stress (A-20, B-20, C-20, D-0).

2. B is best. Emotionally intelligent parents use their children's moments of being upset as opportunities to act as emotional coaches, helping their children to understand what made them upset, what they are feeling and alternatives the child can try. (A-0, B-20, C-0, D-0).
3. A. One mark of self-motivation is being able to formulate a plan for overcoming obstacles and frustrations and implementing it. (A-20, B-0, C-0, D-0).
4. C. Optimism, a mark of emotional intelligence, leads people to see setbacks as challenges they can learn from, and to persist, trying out new approaches rather than giving up, blaming themselves, or getting demoralized (A-0, B-0, C-20, D-0).
5. The most effective way to create an atmosphere that welcomes diversity is to make clear in public that the social norms of your organization do not tolerate such expressions. Instead of trying to change prejudices (a much harder task), keep people from acting on them (A-0, B-0, C-20, D-0).
6. D. Data on rage and how to clam it show the effectiveness of distracting the angry person from the focus of his rage, empathizing with his feelings and perspective, and suggesting a less anger provoking way of seeing the situation (A-0, B-5, C-5, D-20).
7. A. Take a break of 20 minutes or more. It takes at least that long to clear the body of the physiological arousal of anger-which distorts your perception and makes you more likely to launch damaging personal. attacks. After cooling down you'll be more likely to have a fruitful discussion. (A-20, B-0, C-0, D-0).
8. B. Creative groups work at their peak when rapport, harmony and comfort levels are highest-then people are free to make their best contribution (A-0, B-20, C-0, D-0).
9. D. Children born with a timid temperament can often become more outgoing if their parents arrange an ongoing series of manageable challenges to their shyness. (A-0, B-5, C-0, D-20).
10. B. By giving yourself moderate challenges, you are most likely to get into the state of flow, which is both pleasurable and where people learn and perform at their best (A-0, B-20, C-0, D-0).

Where you stand?

0 – 100 - You really need to work on your emotional responses.

100 – 150 - Not bad. But you have certain blind spots in your emotions.

150 – 200 - Your emotional quotient is good. But this does not mean that you cannot do better.

EQ Test No. 2

This test measures some areas of your personal and professional life. This is a psychological test, which will help you learn more about yourself. The questionnaire given below will measure your emotional reactions to different situations. Answer honestly and do not spend too much time on any one item. Usually your first response is the best response. Do not leave any question unanswered and complete the test in a single sitting.

The questionnaire

1. You have just learnt that you have been ignored for a promotion by the management for which you were eligible. Moreover, one of your junior has been selected for the same promotion. You are upset and feeling frustrated. What do you do?
   (a) Ignore it–it was your bad luck.
   (b) Talk it over with your boss, bringing out the facts about your contribution and ask for reconsideration of the management's decision.
   (c) Start abusing the colleague who superseded you, leveling allegations of manipulation and corruption against him and speak against the decision-maker.
   (d) Move to court and obtain a stay order and vow to teach a befitting lesson to the management through legal battle.
   (e) Resign from the organization.
2. A freshly recruited smart first-class professional graduate joins your organization as a management trainee. After a few weeks she complains to you that her superiors and subordinates were not taking her seriously. What will you suggest to her?

(a) Suggest that she handle the situation herself and not to bother you about trivial matters.

(b) Tell her that such behavior is typical of most organizations and she should ignore it.

(c) Suggest that she undergo behavioral training to learn interpersonal skills.

(d) Empathize with her and help her figure out ways to get others to work with her.

(e) Tell her to look for another job.

3. As a manager you are taking a weekly review meeting which also has some women employees. You overhear a male employee telling an offensive joke about women employees. What do you do?

(a) Ignore it–it is only a joke.

(b) Call the employee in your office after the meeting and pull him up.

(c) Send the employee to attend a sensitivity training program for overcoming his prejudices.

(d) Ask the women employees to protest in writing so that you can take appropriate action.

(e) Announce on the spot that such jokes are inappropriate and shall not be tolerated in your organization.

4. In a fit of anger, you undergo an argument with your colleague that has led to personal attacks from both sides. The entire office has witnessed the unpleasant episode. You and your colleague had actually never intended to tarnish the image of each other. How will you tackle this ugly situation?

(a) Sit calmly and consider what triggered the argument between you and your colleague and was it possible to control your anger at that point of time.

(b) Avoid arguments and leave the scene.

(c) Apologize and ask your colleague to apologize too.

(d) Continue with the argument till you reach some definite conclusion.

(e) Complain to the management against your colleague.

5. Imagine you are an insurance salesperson approaching prospective clients to purchase insurance policies. A dozen people in a row have shut the door on your face and you are feeling frustrated. What will you do?

(a) Blame yourself and stop work for the day.

(b) Reassess your capabilities as an insurance salesperson.

(c) Come out with fresh strategies to overcome similar failures in future.

(d) Think of changing your job.

(e) Contact the clients again some other day.

6. Imagine you are a site engineer of a large construction company. A worker suddenly slips down and dies. There is a violent reaction and agitated workers surround you. What will you do?

(a) Call the police/management and let them decide the further course of action.

(b) Threaten the agitating workers with dire consequences if they do not cool down immediately.

(c) Reason with the workers and explain the safety measures you had taken to prevent such incidents.

(d) Call the agitated workers for a discussion and ask for their suggestions so that such incidents do not occur in future.

(e) Find an opportunity to slip away from the scene.

7. You accompany your friend from Delhi to Agra in his car. You notice another car loaded with children suddenly overtaking your car and cutting sharply in front of your car. Your friend, who is driving the car, gets nervous, as he had to apply the brakes immediately to avoid hitting the other car. What would be your reaction at that time?

(a) Tell your friend to stop and relax for some time rather than continue driving.

(b) Tell your friend to chase the other car and stop it.

(c) Yell at the driver of the other car.

(d) Tell your friend to smile and thank God that everyone is safe.

(e) Just ignore what had happened as a very minor incident.

8. You are on an aircraft and suddenly the pilot announces that it has been hijacked by terrorists. Everyone is in a state of shock, nervousness, and utter confusion. What will be your reaction?

(a) Blame yourself for choosing an inauspicious day for traveling.

(b) Attend to the instructions of the pilot/air hostess and ask the other fellow passengers to do the same.

(c) Continue to read your magazine and pay little attention to the incident.

(d) Cry out and vow not to travel by air in future.

(e) Falsely claim that you are a heart patient needing medical attention and beg the hijackers to release you.

9. Imagine that you are a police officer posted in a sensitive area. You get information that there have been violent ethnic clashes between two religious communities and a large number of people have been killed from both sides and property has been damaged. What action will you take?

(a) Decide not to visit the spot personally, as there may be danger to your life from the fury of the public.

(b) Take your time to respond-in any case this is not the first time riots have occurred.

(c) Try to handle the situation tactfully-assuage the feelings of both communities-tracking down the reasons for the clash, and taking all desired remedial measures.

(d) Send your subordinate inspector to study the situation.

(e) Arrange to hand over the dead to the respective families after getting the postmortem done.

10. You have a grown-up son who starts arguing with you every now and then on matters relating to your personal and social life. One day he tells you that you have dictated your terms to the family for very long and cannot continue to exercise the authority anymore. He also tells you that as a father you cannot impose your outdated attitudes and irrelevant values on him. He further confronts you and says that he is an adult and henceforth he will take all major decisions. You are disturbed at his defiant behavior. How will you tackle him?

(a) Accept his statement in helplessness and take a low profile position in the family.

(b) In disgust, tell him to leave home and find a separate place for himself.

(c) Send him to a psychologist to learn to adjust with his environment.

(d) For the time being delay the arguments, manage your feelings, sit with him and explain your point of view as patiently as possible without making the situation tense.

(e) Ignore his hostile comments and change the topic of discussion.

11. This morning an old man was driving his old car on the wrong side with his little grandson on his lap. He was too careless to switch on the indicator before turning the car and in the process dashed onto the bonnet of your new car, which you were driving. How will you behave at this time?

(a) Just smile at the old man and ask him to be grateful to God for his grandson, who was safe.

(b) Get annoyed at the old man and shout at him.

(c) Ask for compensation for the damage.

(d) Give the old man a long lecture on how to drive safely

(e) Call the police.

12. Imagine you are a doctor and you have operated upon a cancer patient in the morning. When you go home for lunch you receive a call that the patient has developed some complications and you decide to rush back to the hospital. On your way back to the hospital you are held up at the traffic light, as the signal is red. You wait impatiently and when the signal turns green you start your car without noticing a scooterist in front and hit him. He loses his balance but regains it with great difficulty. What will you do now?

(a) Immediately stop the car, get out, introduce yourself and apologize.

(b) Ignore him and keep moving.

(c) Thank God that nothing serious had happened.

(d) Stop for a moment, collect your thoughts and move towards the hospital.

(e) Tell the scooterist what has happened and continue driving.

13. You are a general manager of a large production company. Next week there is a board meeting and your department is expected to prepare the annual report. You get a call from one of the production units in another state that there is a strike and your presence is urgently required to negotiate with the union. You delegate the responsibility to your assistant general manager (AGM) to get the report prepared for the board meeting on time and leave the city. When you return you are perplexed to find that your AGM has not prepared the report and the board meeting is scheduled for the next day. What do you do?

(a) Feel remorse for your decision to delegate work to the wrong person.

(b) Get worked up and fire the assistant general manager for failing to carry out your instructions.

(c) Complete the work yourself to avoid embarrassment before the board.

(d) Understand the difficulties faced by the assistant general manager in getting the work completed, motivate him saying that it could still be done and make a plan to sit long hours to complete the job on time.

(e) Send the assistant general manager for further training to sharpen his managerial skills.

14. You are a professor in a college and while taking a class one of your students comments that your style of teaching is not good, that you have not prepared the topic properly and also that you are just passing time. How will you react?

(a) Report to the principle of the college about the behaviour of the student.

(b) Ask him to leave the classroom and tell him in strong words that you cannot change your style:

(c) Ask him to meet you after the class in your chamber.

(d) Heed to the need of the class and promise to prepare the topic properly in future.

(e) Ignore him and continue with your lecture.

15. As the CEO of a company you are involved in a meeting with the union leaders on their pending demands. During the meeting one of the union leaders shouts at you saying that you are a big liar and levels serious allegations of corruption and favoritism against you. You are very upset. How will you react to the remarks of the union leader?
    (a) Just ignore what he said, continue with the discussion and listen to their demands with a cool frame of mind.
    (b) Suspend him from the job.
    (c) Cancel further negotiations and ask him to apologize first.
    (d) Advise him not to make personal remarks.
    (e) Leave the room after assigning the responsibility to your subordinate to continue with the negotiations.

Question	Response	Score	Explanation
1.	a b c d e	0 20 0 5 0	Under frustration people tend to respond in ways which are emotionally not intelligent. In this situation response B is most suitable and emotionally intelligent.
2.	a b c d e	5 0 5 20 0	Getting along with others and having healthy interpersonal relations is an important emotional competence. Empathizing and helping people in distress reflects high EQ. Response D is best.
3.	a b c d e	0 5 5 0 20	One cannot change prejudices of people overnight. An emotionally intelligent response will be to create a healthy environment and not to tolerate offensive remarks. Response E is best.

Contd....

4.	a b c d e	20 5 0 0 0	Psychologists have now proved that taking some time off from angry situation helps to cool down your temper. Response A is best under such circumstances.
5.	a b c d e	0 10 20 0 5	The situation measures the levelofoptimism,animportant emotional competence. The sales person who sees failure as a challenge and comes out with fresh strategies without getting demoralized will act similar to response C.
6.	a b c d e	5 0 20 20 0	Only a manager with high EQ will be able to handle a threatening and stressful situation tactfully. Responses C and D are best.
7.	a b c d e	20 0 0 10 5	Avoiding habitual response and taking cool decisions under irritating and annoying situations reflect high EQ. Response A is best.
8.	a b c d e	0 20 15 0 0	Response B indicates the level of emotional competence, i.e., self-awareness, which helps in facing a stressful situation.
9.	a b c d e	5 0 20 5 5	Managing emotions of victims who have suffered is reflective of high EQ. Response C is most appropriate.

Contd....

10.	a b c d e	0 0 0 20 10	Emotionally intelligent parents use their children's moments of being upset as challenges and act as emotionalcoaches. Evaluating emotions with self-awareness and empathy is the key to emotional management. Response D is best.
11.	a b c d e	20 5 5 0 5	Calming down and distracting yourself from disturbing situa-tions reflect high EQ. Response A is best.
12.	a b c d e	20 0 0 5 5	Handling situations with peace of mind, care and empathy is the key to emotional intelligence. Response A is best.
13.	a b c d e	0 5 10 20 5	Normal reactions to such situa-tions are feelings of failure, remorse, anger and embarrassment. However, manager with high EQ will motivate his team, take the situation under self-control and go on. Response D seems best.
14.	a b c d e	0 0 5 20 5	Rapport, harmony and comfort are key emotional competencies while dealing with groups. Open and free expression of ideas leads to creativity and mutual respect. Response D is best.

Contd....

15.	a b c d e	20 0 0 5 5	Handling relationships effectively under awkward circumstances makes you emotionally intelligent. By delaying the gratification of reactions to the situation instantaneously, you may come out a winner. Responsc A is most suitable.

Interpretation of scores

Your Score	Percentile	Interpretation
285 and above	P-90	Extremely high
250 to 284	P-75	High
176 to 294	P-50	Average
141 to 175	P-40	Below Average
140 and below	P-15	Try some other day

Chapter
7
Reprogramming the Mind for Peak Performance Through NLP

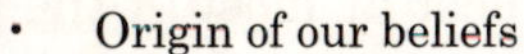

- Origin of our beliefs
- Nine useful beliefs for success
- What is neuro–linguistic programming
- NLP: principles and pre-suppositions
- This is outside my experience–perceptual maps
- Five rules in formulating the outcome you want
- Shifting beliefs exercise
- Exercise: utilizing your favourite hero/heroine (ideal)
- Six-step reforming process
- The swish pattern
- Generating a new behavior-adopting from your model/mentor
- Exercise on responding to criticism-building self-confidence
- Developing self-appreciation
- Eliminating fears and phobias
- Get rid of your compulsion/addictions
- Learning to break bad habits
- Resolving your inner conflicts/doubts
- Leveraging diversity and working with different personality traits
- Inspiring effective leadership and developing vision in others

If the instruction manual of your brain is made available to you then you may possibly like to

- Change your undesired thoughts/habits/behavior/ feelings as fast as possible in desired manner.
- Be more happy, confident and fulfilled exactly in the way you want to be.

Neuro Linguistic Programming (NLP) allows you to accomplish it and more than this. NLP is the study and practice of human excellence, upgrade your ability to be the best at most of the time. It is a powerful and practical approach to personal change and effectiveness. NLP is a unique model that can provide answers as to how people learn, motivate themselves, and change their behavior to achieve excellence in any endeavor.

By identifying areas of your performance that you need to improve, NLP focuses on changing your thoughts, assumptions, and emotions so that you can dramatically improve the results you get.

NLP has also been termed as `Science of Excellence' or 'New Technology of Achievement' in view of its impact on success. While many great achievers, gurus, faith healers and scholars have practised some form of NLP for centuries. The modern founders of NLP are the two Americans Dr. Richard Bandler and John Grinder.

Origin of Our Beliefs

Man is what he believes

When you make your mind to do something and with full assertion you do so. The act in which you believe will lead you to achieve the desired goal. With an optimistic approach, everything seems accessible and you surely get what you deserve. This belief will assure you for further achievements also.

From the earlier chapters we have learnt that our beliefs are the essential part of our success process. The beliefs can either be empowering or limiting.

Can you list your five limiting beliefs?

Realize the harmful effects these beliefs have on you. We will discuss the methods of discarding them. Sometimes just not having a limiting belief may be enough.

Now can you list your five positive beliefs?

The positive or empowering beliefs will support you in achieving your highest goals and we will discuss in this chapter how to create more empowering beliefs.

Our beliefs in life are shaped by the following factors:

1. The environment in which we have been brought up.
2. Events-small or large and our interpretations of these events.
3. Acquiring knowledge, providing new/different perspectives.
4. Our past results-either success or failure.

Since all these are related to the past, we have a limited influence now on them as many of our beliefs and our patterns in life have already been fixed.

5. There is a 5th way of forming beliefs or creating newer ones in a faster and most effective way.

Create in your mind the experience you desire in the future as if it were here and now (visualization). You can create in your mind the kind of experience that you want through artificial experiencing.

It is this device of artificial experiencing which laid the foundation for Neuro-Linguistic Programming (NLP).

Nine Useful Beliefs for Success

Successful people use to have different set of beliefs as compared to those who fail. Let us acquaint ourselves with these beliefs.

1. Everything happens for a reason and it serves us (start seeing the good even in the bad).
2. There is no such thing as failure; they are only outcomes (start learning through your mistakes).

   A successful person expects the best in life and realizes that in adversity as well as opportunity there is something to be gained.
3. Whatever happens, take responsibility.
   - Do not be at the mercy of circumstances.
   - Take responsibility for past, present and future.
   - Those who take responsibility are in power and those who avoid it are followers.

- Be more a creator of your circumstances than a victim of it.
- What we want to happen, will happen.

4. It is not necessary to be able to understand everything.
   - Find what is essential without getting bogged down by minute details.
   - Successful people are not necessarily the ones with the most information or most knowledge.
5. People are the greatest resource.
   - Sense of team, common cause and unity.
   - Win-win approach rather than manipulation.
   - Ability to motivate others and excite them.
6. Work is play.
   - Do you know anyone who has achieved success by doing what he hates? You can bring curiosity and vitality into work. This is important for enjoying your work and making a success of it.
7. There is no abiding success without commitment.
8. Everything happens twice–once in the mind and then in the physical world.
   - The ability to imagine the future and use creatively the powers of the subconscious mind.
9. Faith in abundance is needed in the self, in others, in one's organization, one's country and human-kind

Difference between faith and belief - A small story

There was a performer, who was so skilled that he could walk between two building on a tight rope with a balancing pole. Thousands of people had been watching his breathtaking performance. After crossing the building successfully through rope, having his assistant on his shoulder, he has done his task.

Everybody was amazed and gave him a thunderous applause. He asked them whether they believed that he could do it again. The crowd said, "Yes, we believe that you can!"

After a while he asked the crowd again, "Now, who wants to volunteer to get on my shoulder?" With that the crowd became silent.

We can believe in others what we see them doing. In the above story, the crowd believed in the performer because they saw his performance. But when he asked them "Who wants to get on my shoulder?" everyone was silent. The crowd had belief in him but they did not have faith in the self. The story illustrates the difference between belief and having faith. Hence faith in self is needed to accomplish what we want to achieve and NLP helps in creating that faith.

What is Neuro–Linguistic Programming

NLP focuses on the way you think about your activities, both successful and unsuccessful, and the things you need to do differently. Change what you think, feel, believe, and you will dramatically alter the results you get. With repeated practice, these skills become automatic and lead to a continuous improvement in performance.

- Neuro refers to the neurological system; the way we use our senses of sight, hearing, touch, taste and smell to translate our experience into thought processes, both conscious and unconscious. It relates to our physiology as well as our mind and the way in which our mind and body function together as one system. Much of NLP is about increasing our awareness of neurological system and learing to manage the choices we have available to us.
- Linguistic refers to the way we use language to make sense of our experience and how we communicate that experience to others and ourselves. The study of our linguistic patterns enables us to explore how we influence others and ourselves. Our language patterns are rich in clues regarding how we structure our internal world.
- Programming is the way we code our experience. Our programs are a combination of thought patterns and behaviors influenced by our beliefs, values, sense of identity and purpose. The results we achieve, the effects we create in ourselves and others are the consequence of our personal programs. By increasing our awareness of what programs we run, we can begin to learn how to reproduce these programs to achieve the results we want.

NLP: Principles and Pre-suppositions

Various ideas have been formed in the course of time as NLP got evolved and are now well accepted as principles among NLP practitioners. Unlike the law of physical science, these principles are used as philosophical guides than the hard, unbendable rules. They represent a kind of instinctive wisdom- or simple common sense.

Basic principles

1. Our map is not the territory.
   - Our mental maps do not completely reflect the territory but we always respond to the territory or reality in terms of our mental maps only. But none of our maps is the territory of reality-it cannot be. We tend to filter our experience to fit our maps and beliefs. True communication is to first understand the perceptual maps of others and then take appropriate action to fit the individual and the situation.
2. Experience has a structure/pattern in the mind.
   - When we change the patterns of our mind, and experience then its interpretations also get changed. We can thus neutralize the unpleasant memories and replace them by more positive association/ thoughts. Thus with NLP we can avoid the sufferings and remove fears/phobias when we decided to do so.
3. If one person can excel then anyone can learn to do it by knowing and following his strategy.
   - Learn the mental map of achievers. Just go out and try that by adopting too your ideal.
4. The mind and body are two parts of the same system. One affects the other.
   - Our thoughts instantly affect our muscle tensions, breathing, feelings and these in turn affect our thoughts. Learn to change either one and the other will be changed. Those practising yoga or meditation can understand this better and may have experienced it well.
5. People already have all the resources they need. The required resources are not in shortage.
   - Mental images, thoughts, inner voices etc. are our

mental/physical resources needed for achievements and are available in abundance. They can also be created if one is determined.

6. Body language.
   - We are always communicating at least non-verbally. Your posture, body movements, voice-tone, eye movements always communicate the inner state of your being. Even your silence speaks. Just be aware and start using it for effective communication.
7. The meaning of your communication is the response you get.
   - Do not blame the attitudes of others if your communication could not get the desired outcome. Notice how your communication is received and then adjust. There should be a congruency in behavior and thoughts.
8. Every action of a person has a positive intention for him.
   - Behavior has its positive purpose in its original situation. People have different perceptual maps by which they operate and if something fits our map we call it positive, otherwise it becomes negative for us. Behind a so-called unwanted action the intention lying deep rooted below our consciousness may be of gaining attention or recognition or avoiding a feared outcome. Find out your and other's intentions to understand the map of reality. Rather than condemning these actions, just separate them and replace with more positive choices to the people. This is way the habits/ behavior/ outcome can also be changed.
9. People always make their best choices. Unless people know more options they will continue to make the best choice they had.
   - Everyone has a unique personal history, which makes him learn what to do or what not to do and what to value. Had there been a better choice available to them as per their interpretations, it certainly would have been acted upon.
10. If what you are doing is not working then try something else or do it differently.
    - If you do what you have always done you will get what you have always got. If you want something new, do something new.

11. There is never failure but only feedback.
    - Analyse your experience and determine what you have missed. Failure is the way to excellence. It is all a part of the learning process and helps us to grow further.

This is Outside my Experience–Perceptual Maps

A tribe lived on a remote island and had never been beyond that. One day a large ship that had deviated from its intended course anchored on the shore of the island. The ship's crew came out to the shore on landing craft and small boats.

The crew was greeted enthusiastically by the islanders who asked them where they had come from and how they had traveled there, as they could not understand how the visitors' small boats could have weathered the rougher seas further offshore. The sailors explained that their main ship was anchored offshore and that was the boat in which they had journeyed from their country.

Since the tribals were very curious, the sailors took them to the mainland from where they could see the ship. But the tribals could not see it, no matter how often the crew pointed it out to them. The tribals had no concept of boats larger than their own fishing craft and they literally could not see the sailing ship. This boat was out of their expectations and continued to be so.

- People often act as per their mental maps; unless the map is broadened, people will continue to miss those things that lie outside their map.

What can NLP do and where can this be applied?

It enables you to achieve human excellence in any form. With NLP, you can identify what makes someone exceptionally skilled, and get that skill for yourself or teach it to others. NLP can help you become adept at whatever is important to you.

NLP is valuable to enhance results in a wide spectrum of areas including business, management, counseling, therapy and even personal relationships.

Some specific areas where NLP is highly useful

- Discovering your mission and setting goals.
- Shifting the limiting beliefs to empowering ones.

- Adopting from the strategy of your favorite role model/ideals to make you more successful.
- Enrolling others to make them a part of your goals.
- Change and enhance your personality in desired manner will change your life too.
- Re-framing your inner voice.
- Removing past fears and guilt.
- Responding to criticism more effectively and staying confident.
- Developing self-appreciation and self esteem.
- Eliminating fears and phobias.
- Getting rid of your compulsions/addictions/changing habits.
- Re-parenting. Changing your interpretations of what your parents did to you to make it more positive and empowering for yourself.
- Improving relationships and establishing better rapport.
- Improving communication.
- Creating a powerful presentation or achieving great performance in chosen areas like sports, swimming, climbing, shooting, interviews, arranging the meetings and so on.
- Achieving the sales target.
- Generating a desired new behavior.
- Handling of dilemmas and generating new/ creative solutions.

Communicating for Results Using NLP

Let us do some preliminary experiments relating to communication. Follow these instructions:

'Don't think of a white cat with stripes'.

- What really came to your imagination-a black cat.
- I had asked you not to think of a white cat, but it still appeared to your mind.
- Can you see the working of the human mind?

Once Sachin Tendulkar, the former captain team of Indian cricket sent a complimentary message to Sehwag, that time an upcoming star player who was playing the series for India against Sri lanka. Sehwag had played the last inning wonderfully well. The message was like - "congratulations-I hope you will not disappoint me in the finals."

Sachin might have done it with all good intentions and to boost up Sehwag for the finals, but one can imagine the mental pressure the last lines might have created for Sehwag. If the picture of `what if I don't play well this time' gets expanded with the related association of Sachin getting disappointed by Sehwag's not so good performance, it can induce doubts in the mind of Sehwag regarding his own capability. Although one can't generalize the impact of such message unless we know the motivation style of the receiver, but one can assess the negative result it can produce sometimes. Unfortunately the performance of Sehwag in the next match was really disappointing and India lost the final.

In this instance one can easily say that Sehwag not performing so well in the next match might have been just a coincidence. But very often the language used leaves an impact on others, which may be undesirable towards outcome or towards providing strength to the actions. If the communicator knows what generally motivates the other person i.e. an avoidance of pain or the pleasure of achievement, one can make one's communication more effective and result-oriented. The other way of sending the message could have been "Congratulations, keep it up. I am sure you will do it again."

Let us study this in more detail.

Some more examples on how the mind responds to language

It was at a time when Richard Bandler, cofounder of NLP, was trying to make his mark in the professional circle as NLP was still in its infancy. Bandler was desperately trying to get an appointment with the world-renowned medical therapist Dr Ericson over the telephone. Dr Ericson was a busy person and had been introduced to Richard by a common friend. He was keen about this new concept but simply had no time to meet Richard, a young person with no great credentials. While applying some of the principles of NLP, Richard used a different language and you can see the impact it had on Ericson:

Richard-"Some people, Dr. Ericson know how to make time".

(Emphasizing Dr Ericson and the last two words make time more strongly)

The impact was more positive and result-oriented as Ericson's answer was, "Come over any time".

Consider some more examples of how words and communication affect the outcome.

1. Your idea is good but . . . or . . . You did well but... .

   vs

   There is difficulty, . . . but your idea is really good.

   - The word used last is mostly remembered and should be positive to leave a good impact.
   - The word `but' leaves a doubt in the mind from the first example.
   - The critical factor is conveyed but the last words used are more positive in the second example.

2. Do not jump the red light.

   vs

   Relax-life is fast, just relax.

   - Delhi traffic police has used the second example to regulate traffic and the published reports suggest that the results have been positive.

3. If you get well.

   vs

   When you get well.

   - On using the first sentence, the patient gets more worried about whether he will get well or not.
   - The second sentence leaves an image of a healthy person who is already well.

4. Do not play on the street

   vs

   The street is dangerous, play in your own yard.

   - You are now suggesting an action rather than merely stopping.

- Many parents prohibit their children from doing certain things and keep preaching to them what not to do rather suggesting positive action plans.

5. This time let just just complete on schedule and under budget. So no deviations, or no change. OK.

   vs

   This time no deviation or last minute change. Let us get this done on time and under budget.

   - The first message just reminds us that we did not complete on time and within budget and need to be extra careful. It becomes restrictive in nature while the second message emphasizes action and is more positive.
   - Hence it is better to use the restrictive part first if it is needed and make the closing part of the message action suggestive and positive.

6. We have to resort to a cost reduction.

   vs

   Let us identify the waste elimination areas.

   - The first sentence merely creates a worry as to what is going to happen to one's perks or the job and the main focus may get lost.
   - While the second gives a feeling to the listener that without wasting time we need to identify and overcome hurdles for the betterment of the organization.

The learning model

This is the process of learning a new skill so that, at each stage you have a higher level of competence. You move from unconscious incompetence to the mastery of unconscious competence.

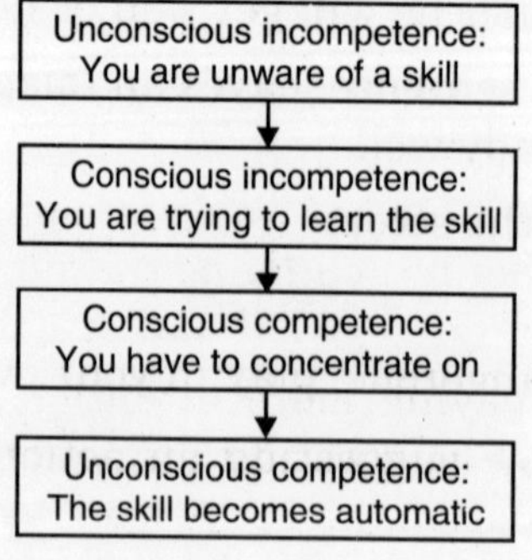

Five Rules in Formulating the Outcome You Want

As explained earlier artificial experiencing is a useful technique in NLP. To make it more effective in achieving our goal, the following rules can be helpful:

1. *Affirm your outcome in positive and visible terms*: Articulate the result you want to see in a positive statement. Too often people state what they don't want to happen while achieving their goals. So be careful in this affirmation.
2. *Be very specific*: How does your outcome look, sound, feel and smell? Engage all your senses in describing the results you want. The more sensory rich your description, the more you will empower your brain to create your desire. Also be certain to set a specific completion date for it.
3. *Visualize your outcome*: Imagine how you will look, how you will feel, and what you will see and hear in your external world after you have achieved your outcome.
4. *Be in control*: Your outcome must be initiated and maintained by you. It must not dependent on other people to change themselves for you to be happy. Make sure your outcome reflects things that you can affect directly.
5. *Verify that your outcome is socially sound and desirable*: Project into the future the consequences of your actual goal. Your outcome must be one that benefits you and other people.

An example of modeling

She had spent many holidays cycling, mostly in an area with hilly terrain. To enjoy cycling there, it is necessary to have the tenacity and commitment that the hills demand! Having done a lot of cycling on the flat surface, she found the hills more enjoyable. Her practice and skills were more suited to speed than to hills. So cycling in the hilly terrain resulted in her husband accelerating away from her, then waiting at the top of the hill while she laboriously struggled behind. She decided that for her own state of mind and enjoyment, she needed to sort out her hill-climbing technique by learning it from her husband.

She then started paying more attention to the way that her husband cycled uphill. She noticed that not only could he maintain his speed on the inclination, he could also accelerate, whereas she could only hope to maintain enough momentum to get to the top.

She observed the way he moved, in particular rhythm he adopted. As she paid attention to this, she also noticed that he constantly looked at the ground. This was in stark contrast to her style, where she constantly and longingly looked to the brow of the hill. He never did. Her rhythm faltered as she struggled to maintain her speed, whereas his pace and rhythm stayed the same no matter what the hight was.

When both of them were on the hill next time, she tried to adopt the same style. There was a definite improvement in her speed. But after a while her thighs ached and the pain became a distraction. There was something she was missing still.

She asked him about his strategy and, sure enough, he reinforced the importance of maintaining a constant rhythm. When she referred to the pain, he surprisingly said he felt the same, but for him the pain was an indication that he was pushing himself and developing his personal strength. So, far from disliking it, he actually welcomed it. Pain for him represented an improvement in personal fitness. He also said that as he was looking down while cycling, he enjoyed listening to the sound, the regular rhythm of the pedals.

This internal strategy was quite different from her own. She spent most of the time on the hills asking herself how far she had to go to reach the top. As much she measure distance, that much she became frustrated.

The next time they cycled up a hill, she stepped into his way of thinking as well as his physical style of cycling. She did what he did both as she had noticed him and as he had explained to her. She got to the top of the hill at the same time as he did and at the same speed, having accelerated on the ascent. She had made it.

We all can learn from the strategy of the role models. We need to study them in detail, their mental maps, strategies and adapt it to our style.

Shifting Beliefs Exercise

Select an area of focus where changing your belief would benefit you more. Select an area in your life where you would like to experience greater satisfaction.

- You have been surpassed in promotion this year while your colleague who is an MBA from an elite institution is promoted.

Find out your existing belief

Whether a belief is working for or against us can be evaluated by considering the results it produces in our lives. Continue posing questions to yourself until you find a belief that matches with your inner frequencies. It will let you know what is true about your beliefs. Truth is a felt experience.

- You have started carrying a belief that an MBA degree from an elite institution is essential for you to grow in your line of career.

Deeply examine this belief

Now imagine that you can step outside yourself and objectively explore this belief. Use your logic as well as your feelings to become intimately familiar with this belief and the power you have given to it. Take time to concentrate upon the effect, it has had in your life. Be as objective as possible. This step is not about making yourself wrong or right but about becoming familiar with an element that has had an impact in your life.

- While deeply examining the origin of this belief, you may find that there are many persons in your company and outside in the corporate world who were not MBAs and have reached the top at a faster rate than many MBAs. They had certain essential qualities needed for success in this career and had performed for results.

Choose consciously to relinquish the belief or to perpetuate it

Once you have become familiar with your belief, it is time to choose whether to accept it or not. Both choices are valid. The point of power comes from being consciously aware of the beliefs that determine the quality of your life. This step assists you in moving to a proactive, empowering and positive mode from a reactionary, powerless position.

- This belief has come to you, when in your first job you could not get a promotion on time, while someone else got it because he and the boss both happened to be from the same institution which is rated quite highly.
- It may have been due to the bias of one person, which need not to be generalized as it may create much more damage.

- Instead of getting upset by one incident, you should decide to work smarter and show better results in your performance.

Replace the belief with an empowered and upgraded belief

After choosing to relinquish your belief, replace it with a belief that will support you in realizing the results you want. Use affirmations like: "I deserve-I can. It is possible for me to-I will now".

- It is not the degree of an MBA, but the result you produce that leads to career growth.
- Being an MBA from a premium institution can be helpful to some extent in the initial phase of one's career but in the long term what matters is not the institution you studied in, but the results you produce.
- I need to work on the skill/competency development and value addition to the employer to get me ahead in my career.

Remind yourself regularly and be conscious of your empowered belief until it is fully integrated. Take all necessary steps to keep the newly upgrade belief in the forefront of your awareness. Some people take a few moments each day to meditate upon their newly adopted belief. To reinforce this new way of thinking you may place a written copy of the belief where you can frequently see it. Repeat the belief to yourself in order to assist in its integration.

Exercise: Utilizing Your Favourite Hero/Heroine (Ideal)

Choose your role model

Choose a man or woman whom you greatly admire. Pick someone who excites and inspires you when you recall that person's accomplishments. Some choose a great person from history like Churchill, Gandhi, Martin Luther or Roosevelt. Others choose great religious leaders like Krishna, Jesus or Mohammed. Let your feelings of inspiration guide you. You might want to choose someone you know personally, such as a family member, colleague, or friend. You can even choose from fiction or legend-Robin Hood or Wonder Woman or the live personalities like Ambani, Bill Gates, Kiran Bedi or anyone whom you admire in your chosen area.

See a particular goal

Choose a goal that your hero achieved through living their mission.

It might be Ambani creating an industry. It might be Gandhi leading the Indian freedom struggle. It might be Roosevelt negotiating in a meeting to secure the passage of the Universal Declaration of Human Rights. It might be Bill Gates creating MSDOS. Whatever you see, see a specific set of actions that represents the living of that person's mission a goal. Make a short 30-second movie of that goal. See the clear and vast images in your vision, vibrant colors, and run the movie in your mind. Then, run it back to the beginning and put it on pause. Make it meaningful and inspiring.

Step into the role of your Hero (ideal)

Become that hero/heroine in this particular role in this movie. Become aware of your values, purposes, principles, and your mission as this hero/heroine. Release the pause button of your mental VCR and run the movie, where you are playing the role of the hero/heroine. Complete this scene from the inside. Get in touch with the feeling you have while pursuing this.

Ask these questions

While staying in this role, ask yourself these questions: Why did I do this action to achieve the end result-the goal? How does this goal fit into my purpose of life?

Return back to become yourself again

Think of the resources which help you in becoming like your hero/ heroine and also examine the changes it brings out in you for achieving the goals within your mission. The main lesson of this exercise is to bring out what your mission-based goals will feel like when you are pursuing them with all sincerity.

Enrolling others to make them part of your goals

1. Choose a goal you want to achieve. You can pick some specific goal that you want to achieve. You can pick one, that you are already familiar with or take the time to think of a new goal.
2. Identify the image of your goal. Deeply observe how you represent this goal in your mind's eye. What pictures are you becoming aware of as you think of this goal? What sounds do you hear and what do you say to yourself as you think about this goal? What feelings do you have when you think of this goal?

3. Decide on all the people involved for achievement of this goal. Think of the people who will play a necessary part in achieving this goal. Have you included them as part of the pictures, sounds and feelings in your mind? If they are not included in your representation of the goal, put them there. With whom do you want and need relationships to achieve this goal? Make sure that you have appropriate images and voices of these people in your representation, illustrating the part that they will play in helping you to achieve it.
4. Define more specifically how the people will impact /relate to the goal. Now notice the impact/ relationship between these people and the goal. Are the people in the foreground of your image, or are they in the background? Are the people in color or black and white? What is their size compared to what's around them? You probably want the people to be clear and vivid in the foreground as part of your goal, because it is through your relationship with these people that you and they will be able to achieve your respective goals. Make adjustments in the way you represent your goal so that your relationship to the people is obviously indispensable in order to succeed goal.
5. Future planning. Think of a time in the future when you will be actually working on this particular goal. As you rehearse that situation, intentionally think of the goal the way you just created it, emphasizing the people and your relationships with them.

Creating the life as you want it

1. Make an inventory of your dreams, the things you want to achieve and accomplish.
2. Go over again on the list you made, imagining what you expect to reach as outcome.
3. Now try something else: Pick out your four most important goals this year.
4. As you have a list of your key goals, now review them again in the frame of five rules for formulating outcomes.
5 Make a list of the important resources you already have at your disposal to achieve the goals.

6. When you've done that, focus on those occasions when you used some of these resources most skillfully to achieve important goals.
7. Now describe the kind of person you would have to be to attain your goals.
8. In a few paragraphs, write down what prevents you from having the things that you desire right now.
9. Now consider each of your four key goals and create your first draft of a step-by-step plan on how to achieve them.
10. Come up with some models or ideas; they can be people from your life or famous people who've achieved great success and are a source of inspiration for you.
11. It's great to have all kinds of different goals. However, what's even nicer is to be able to visualize what all of them together would mean to you. Now create your ideal day when you have achieved them.
12. Finally, design your own perfect environment.

Reframing your inner voice

1. Critical voice. Think of a situation in which an inner voice criticized you. Put yourself back in that situation and listen carefully to what the voice says, and note the tone, tempo, and rhythm of the voice.
2. Positive intention. Ask this voice, "What is your positive intention" or, "What is it that you want to achieve for me by criticizing me in this way?" There should be some purpose behind the criticism, Keep asking this question until you can completely agree with the positive intention you hear from your inner voice.
3. Acknowledge and thank the inner voice. Acknowledge the positive intention, agree with it, and thank the voice for guiding you with this positive intention.
4. Ask the voice to join in a search for better alternatives. Ask, "If there were additional ways to get this positive intention that were at least as good as-and perhaps better than-what you are now doing, would you be interested in trying them out?"
5. Creative part. Get in touch with your creative part or the part that plans to assist you in generating lots and lots of possible

behaviors. The voice will choose three of the best ones, those that it likes and believes will better work than what it has been doing.

6. Future planning. Actively imagine carrying out each of these in turn, in the appropriate situation, to find out how well each works. If some don't work as well as anticipated go back to Step 5 to generate more choices. When you have three new choices that you both like, ask the voice if it will be willing to actually use one or more of these choices in the appropriate situations.

Take a moment and reframe these situations

1. My boss yells at me all the time.
2. I had to pay ₹ 80,000 more as income tax this year.
3. We have little or no extra money to buy Diwali presents this year.
4. Every time I begin to succeed in a big way, I sabotage my success.

Here are some possible reframe respectively

a. It's great that he cares enough to tell you how he really feels. He could have just fired you.

b. That's great. You must have made a lot more money this year.

c. Great! Then you can become much-more ingenious and make something people will never forget instead of buying run-of-the-mill gifts. Your gifts will be personal.

d. It's great that you're so aware of what your pattern has been in the past. Now you can figure out what triggered it and change it forever!

Six-step Reforming Process

Richard Bandler and John Grinder designed a six-step reframing process for changing any undesirable behavior you may have into desirable behavior, while maintaining the important benefits that the old behavior used to provide:

1. **Identify the pattern of behavior you wish to change.**
2. **Establish communication with that part of your unconscious mind which generates the behavior.**

Go inside and ask the following question of yourself, remaining alert to detect and report any changes in body sensations, visual images, or sounds that occur as a response to your questions. The question is, "Will the part of me that generates behavior X be willing to communicate with me in consciousness?"

Now ask that part, we'll call it part X, to intensify that signal when it wants to communicate yes, and to diminish it when it wants to communicate no. Now test the response by asking the part to communicate yes . . . and then no . . . so that you can distinguish between the two responses.

3. **Separate intention from behavior**

Thank the part for its willingness to cooperate with you. Now ask if it would be willing to let you know what it's been trying to do for you by generating behavior X. As you ask that question, once again be alert to detect a 'YES' or 'NO' response. Take note of what benefits this behavior has provided you in the past and then thank that part of yourself for maintaining these important benefits for you.

4. **Creating alternative behaviors to satisfy intention**

Now go inside and contact the most creative part of yourself and ask it to generate three alternative behaviors that are just as good or better than behavior X for satisfying the intention of the part we've been communicating with. Have your creative part indicate a yes signal when it has generated the three new behaviors. Now ask the creative part if it would be willing to reveal you what the three new behaviors are.

5. **Have part X accept the new choices and the responsibility for generating them when needed**

Now ask part X if the three new behaviors are at least as effective as behavior X. Then ask part X if it's willing to accept responsibility for generating the new behaviors in appropriate situations when its intention needs to be fulfilled.

6. **Make an ecological check**

Now go inside and ask if there are parts that object to the negotiations that have just taken place or if all parts agree to support you. Then step into the future and imagine a situation that would have triggered the old behavior, experience using one of your new choices and still achieving the benefits you desire. Step into another situation in the future that would have been a trigger to the undesirable behavior, and experience using another one of your new choices.

If you get a signal that other parts object to these new choices, you must start from the beginning, identify which part is objecting, what benefits it's been giving you in the past, and have it work with part X to generate new choices that would maintain those benefits and also provide for you a new set of choices. It may sound a bit weird to talk about speaking to your parts, but this is a basic hypnotic pattern that has been found quite useful by people like Dr. Erikson, Bandler, and Grinder.

If you found yourself consistently over eating, for example, you could do a Swish pattern (explained later) that would cause you to produce new kinds of behaviors, or you could identify this as a behavior that you would like to change. You could ask your unconscious to share with you the benefits of this pattern in the past. Maybe you'll discover that you ate food to overcome a feeling of loneliness. Or perhaps it helped you to create a sense of security and got you relax. Next you might create three new ways to give yourself the feeling of belonging and companionship or security and relaxation.

Maybe you could join a health club, where the structure of events would make it easy for you to connect with people and feel the security of relaxing with friends and simultaneously becoming thinner, thereby gaining the further security of knowing you look good. Maybe you could meditate, create a feeling of unity with the entire universe, by that connection feel more secure and relaxed than you did when you had to gulp more food.

THE SWISH PATTERN

This technique takes any unwanted behavior and transforms it into a desire to become more the person you want to be. It is useful anytime you want to change unwanted behaviors or feeling.

1. Get a large disassociated picture of yourself at your very best. This image will be of the way you want to be. Make this picture as big and colorful as possible. If you wish you may

attach related sounds and smells to this picture to make it even more realistic. Store this as your, "very best picture."

2. Establish a picture of problematic behavior you wish to remove (nail biting, cigarette smoking, etc.). This is an associated picture, through your eyes. Store this image as your cue picture.
3. Put the cue picture (the image of the unwanted behavior) in front of the "very best picture." Place a dot in the center of the cue picture and have the dot open up, similar to a camera shutter, so that all you see is the big colorful picture at your very best. Open your eyes.
4. Repeat this process 5-6 times.
5. Test it again.

Generating a New Behavior-Adopting from Your Model/Mentor

1. Choose a person you want to model, a mentor, a person who has the skills and abilities you want.
2. Watch a movie of your model doing the things you would like to do.
3. Watch the movie again. Be sure to notice all the nuances in details. (See and feel how comfortable they are.)
4. See your model's aura, his force. Notice the color, vibration and sound. Notice how it gives them that special something, and know that the more we think this for them, the more we have for us.
5. Now watch the movie while replacing your model with yourself.

   Do everything your model did while keeping the aura about you.
6. Watch yourself again, noticing the nuances and see how comfortable you are. Absorb their life force.
7. Step into the movie. See, hear, and feel everything as you replay the scene. Make it entirely under your possession.
8. Give yourself a cue to generate these talents. Talents and abilities emerge when you need them.

Exercise on Responding to Criticism-Building Self-Confidence

The technique allows you to stay resourceful when you're criticized, whether it's at home, at work, or with friends. This enables you to use criticism as feedback to improve your relationships.

1. See yourself as X in front of you. X is a copy of you and is going to learn a new approach to criticism, while you watch from the outside. Do whatever you need to do to feel detached from X. You can see X farther away, in black and white, or behind Plexiglas.
2. Watch and listen as X gets criticized and instantly dissociates. There are several ways X can dissociate. He can surround himself with a Plexiglas shield when criticized. Or, X can see the word of criticism printed within a cartoon balloon (like the comic strips), etc. X uses one of these methods to keep feeling neutral or resourceful.
3. Watch as X makes a slide or movie of what the criticizer is saying. What does that person mean? Does X have enough information to make a clear, detailed picture? If the answer is "no," gather information. If the answer is "yes," proceed to the next step.
4. Have X decide on a response. For example, X can agree with any part of the criticism that you agree with. Or, X could apologize, saying, "I'll give it some serious thought." Or, "I see things differently now," and so forth.
5. Does X want to use the information you got from this criticism to act differently next time? If so, have X select a new behavior? X will then imagine using the new behavior in detail in the future. Next, X can step into this movie for using new behavior, to feel what it will be like.
6. Having watched X go through this entire strategy, do you want this for yourself? If the answer is "no," ask inside how you can modify this strategy so that it becomes appropriate for you. If the answer is "yes," continue.
7. Thank X for being a special resource to you in recognizing this strategy. Now pull X into you, feeling her/him fill you, so that this knowledge becomes fully integrated within you.

Developing Self-appreciation

Seeing Yourself Through the Eyes of Someone Who Loves You.

It will help you to gain the appreciation for yourself that others have for you. It is useful for building self-appreciation and confidence.

1. Identify someone who loves you. Or think of someone for whom you've done something and who, as a result, sincerely appreciates you.
2. Then, imagine you are writing your autobiography. As you do so, glance up to see, on the other side of a glass door, the person who loves or appreciates you.
3. Now, resume your writing, and include the qualities and characteristics of that person.
4. Next, float your awareness outside the room and stand next to this person. Now see yourself through the glass door, making your own observations.
5. Then enter the body of the person who loves you; see yourself through this person's eyes for love or appreciation. Also, listen to this person's thoughts of love about you. Have this person's feelings.
6. When this is completed, float back into your body, write the qualities and aspects of yourself that you saw and heard when you looked through the eyes of love and appreciation.
7. Think of possible times and places, both now and in the future, when you'll want to re-experience this sense of deep self-appreciation.

Eliminating Fears and Phobias

The Fast Phobia/Trauma Relief Technique

This technique neutralizes the powerful impact of phobias and traumatic events.

Remember that most people learned to be phobic in a single situation that was actually dangerous, or seemed dangerous. The fact that individuals can do what psychologists call "one-trial learning" is proof that a person's brain can learn quite rapidly. This ability to learn rapidly makes it easy for you to learn a new way to respond to any phobia or trauma.

The part of you that has been protecting you all these years by making you phobic is an important and valuable part. We want to preserve its ability to protect you in dangerous situations. The purpose of this technique is to refine and improve your brain's ability by updating the desired information.

1. With your eyes open or closed, imagine you're sitting in the middle of a movie theater and you see a black and white snapshot of yourself on the screen.
2. Now, float out of your body and up into the projection booth. See yourself sitting in the movie theater seat, and also see the black and white photo on screen. You may even wish to imagine plexiglas over the booth's opening, protecting you.
3. Now, watch and listen, protected in the projection booth, as you see a black and white movie of a younger you going through one of those situations in which you had experienced that phobia/trauma. Watch the whole event, starting before the beginn ing of that incident. Observe until you are beyond the end of it, when everything was OK again. If you are fully detached, make the theater screen smaller and farther away, make the picture grainer and stop and start the film so that when you have finished watching it, you're completely detached. End the movie after the phobia-causing event, with a freeze frame of yourself.
4. Next leave the projection booth and slip back into the present self on the theater seat. Next step is to freeze photo of the younger you, who is feeling OK again, at the end of the movie. This is double dissociation. Now, see the colored flash back of entire movie within two seconds. Be sure to go all the way back to the beginning. See, hear, and feel everything while going backwards in those two seconds or less.
5. To test the process, attempt to return to the phobic state in any way you can. What if you were in that situation now? When will you next encounter one of these situations? If you still get-a phobic response, repeat the steps 1 to 4 exactly, but faster each time, until none of the phobic response remains.
6. Since you were phobic/traumatized, you have stayed far away from those particular situations which can trigger your phobia, so you haven't had the opportunity to learn about them. As you begin to encounter and explore these situations

in the future, we urge you to exercise a certain degree of caution until you learn to be more comfortable with them.

Get Rid of Your Compulsion/Addictions

1. Choose a compulsion you want to get rid of. Make a large, bright colored image of the compulsion and set it aside for a moment.
2. Think about what you would look like if you were already in control of your own destiny, and having all the choices you would want in your life. Make this image totally compelling and attractive. Add a compelling voice telling you how much you want to do this.
3. Take the large bright compulsion image and put a dark image of your desired state in the lower left-hand corner. Have the large bright picture suddenly get dark, as the small dark picture simultaneously springs up in size to replace it and gets very big and bright.
4. Repeat this process very quickly five times in a row and make the sound "swish" each time. Open your eyes for a second each time after you complete the process.

Learning to Break Bad Habits

Bad habits can prevent you from getting things done with ease. However, it is relatively easy to change a habit by replacing an old behavior with a more productive, new one. Remember that this is one of the easiest ways to continuously improve performance.

Understanding habits

Habits are ways of automating a bundle of thought and behavior sequences. For instance, when you think to yourself "collect e-mail"; you press the entire computer key automatically, without conscious effort. Unfortunately, your brain is as good at running bad habits as useful ones. Realize that if you continue to think the way you have always thought you will continue to get what you have always got. If a bad habit is automatic, it will keep occurring because it is outside conscious awareness.

Recognizing habits

Blind spots about your shortcomings can limit your professional development. Be willing to admit your own weaknesses so you can look objectively at your own bad habits that hinder you from achieving the highest standards. Notice yourself using these habits so that you will know what to change for the better.

Extend your concept of positive habits to include any thought or behavior that will boost your effectiveness. Remember, nearly everything you do, whether thought or behaviour, becomes habitual once you have repeated it a few times.

Points to remember

- Remember that the level of your performance is related to the effectiveness of your habits.
- People's personalities consist of the habits that they keep running over and over again.
- Generally, people change their habit when an alternative seems more appealing.
- Your habits need to be changed when you are no longer getting the results you want.

Examining *Good* and Bad Habits

Habits worth losing	***Habits worth having***
Experiencing stress	*Feeling in control*
Feeling pressurized causes stress and anxiety.	Focusing on your strengths is empowering.
Procrastinating	*Setting daily goals*
Wasting time is inefficient and saps motivation.	Working towards set goals is motivating.
Self-criticizing	*Expecting the best*
Being hard on yourself undermines confidence.	Having high standards results in good returns.
Being a victim	*Remaining persistent*
Not being assertive lowers your potential.	Being determined increases your confidence.

Using the "Swish pattern"

1. Identify and focus on a bad habit you want to change. Visualize it.
2. Imagine your ideal self in the future having broken that habit. Visualize the new, ideal habit.
3. Replace the first image with the second one by making a `Swish', and then look away. Repeat five times.
4. Recall the first picture and check whether it now starts to change itself automatically into the new one.

Changing habits

Once you have spotted a habit you want to change, such as getting frustrated with a colleague, use the NLP "Swish" pattern to change it. Re-run the experience of being frustrated. Identify what you see when you are being frustrated. Magnify this image. Now, give your mind something more useful to aim at. Imagine an ideal image of yourself in the future having handled the issue well. Expand this image over the original one. Shift your attention elsewhere. Now repeat this process five times until the second image replaces the first automatically. Do this regularly until the new habit is automatically triggered whenever the old habit tries to run.

- Remember that all top performers have spent years building the habits of success.

Resolving Your Inner Conflicts/Doubts

Resolve any doubts you have before you commit to an action. This will give you strength.

Recognizing inner conflict

There are many types of internal conflict that are relatively common and easy to spot, such as your own interests versus those of your colleagues, or professional demands on your time versus family demands. Internal conflicts often show up as mixed feelings. For example, when someone puts pressure on you to do something, you hear yourself saying "yes" while noticing a small, uncomfortable feeling. Realize that this feeling shows that you have an inner conflict. Pinpoint these feelings so that you can start to resolve any conflicting issue.

Points to remember

- Top performers know how to get the best out of themselves by using their unconscious.
- Poor performers massively use the potential of their unconscious.
- Most of our inner resources are unconscious.

Resolving issues unconsciously

You may often find that problems get resolved after a sound sleep. This is because your unconscious mind works on problems while you are asleep. Use the potential of your unconscious mind. When you cannot resolve a problem, turn it into a question for your unconscious mind to think about. For instance, an employee may be under performing and you are unsure what to do. Ask your unconscious, "Come up with some options. Let me know how to motivate him."

Resolving issues consciously

A conflict implies two aspects of your ownself fighting with each other. For example, if you want career success but feel you can only achieve this at the expense of other people, you have a conflict. Think about how these parts can work together and imagine what each part wants. Ask the "success" part what it wants – you realize it wants recognition. When you think about the "expense of others" part, you realize it wants better results. Think about how they can work together. Imagine a future "You" that can improve both results and recognition. Recognize that you can achieve both by spending time supporting others.

Example

1. You want to make more money, but you also want to have more free time.
2. Look at ways to merge these desires into one, practical aim.
3. Imagine a future "you" who is focused on the positive intent of both desires.
4. You will begin to develop ideas which would help you achieve more money and more free time.

Seeing possibilities

Visualize two seemingly contradictory possibilities you want to work towards. Imagine the future resolutions of the conflict by spending time, looking at the positive intent behind each "part". Think how each part could help the other to achieve mutual aims.

Leveraging Diversity and Working with Different Personality Traits

In most situations, there are some ways in which people will behave consistently. Recognize these consistent patterns in yourself and others, so that you increase your effectiveness and ensure you avoid the same problems repeating themselves over and over again.

Looking at differences

There are mental habits that we all use in different situations. For example, some people follow a set procedure to achieve their goals, while others prefer to have options. Evaluations can be based on people's own opinions, or on those of others. Some people initiate action, while others are reactive. Some aim to achieve positive goals, and others want to avoid negative effects. Some people think in terms of the broad picture and others focus on fine details. People may also determine how things are similar to, or different from, each other.

Adapting to difference

Two people with different personality traits may find it hard to communicate with each other and establish a rapport, and this can be damaging in business. Learn to recognize different patterns of behaviour in your team members, and work with these differences to maximize performance. For example, when you delegate a task to someone who is intuitive and favors "options" to achieve aims, as opposed to a sensing type who favours `set procedure', avoid telling them exactly what to do; rather emphasise to them the goal and let them decide on the best way of achieving it. Try to differentiate between people with different personalities in your team and you can improve their performance by ensuring that people's characteristics fit their job specifications.

Make sure people's natural personality preferences are well matched to the tasks that they perform.

Set Procedure	"This is the way it is done here"	"If you keep things going, I would like you to consider the best option".
Option (Intuitive)	"Yes, but we need fresh approaches".	
Towards Motivation	"I really want to meet this deadline".	"If you plan how to meet the deadline, you can make sure we do not repeat mistakes.
Away from Motivation	"We can't make another mistake".	
Similarity	"We have had this problem before"	"Let's see what worked last time and tailor it to what is different".
Difference	"The pace of change is different".	

Inspiring Effective Leadership and Developing Vision in Others

Inspiring others

If you want to lead others effectively, you should learn to inspire and develop vision in others by appealing to their values and interests. Compulsively seek improvements, implement new initiatives and procedures. Empower others to act by giving them the resources and responsibility to deliver results. Achieve credibility by setting a good example, and lastly, reward achievements to give encouragement.

To be a leader you must gain the respect of others. Recognize the five qualities that all great leaders embody, and work on developing these in yourself.

Solving problems with effective leadership and inspiring others

Problem	***Solution***	***Manager's Intervention***
An employee feels a lack of motivation.	Focus on vision and motivation.	Find out more about what matters most to them. Clarify positive values and find creative "win-win" ways to satisfy these.
An employee feels a problem is inevitable.	Focus on seeking improvements.	Implement new approaches to get everybody thinking about and suggesting improvements. Act on the best suggestion.
Your team talks about what they cannot do.	Focus on empowering staff.	Find out what skills and resources they would need in order to carry out what they would like to do and explore ways of making them possible.
Staff does not believe you or do as you say.	Focus on teaching by example.	Only say what you mean and always follow it. Whatever you ask from others, make sure you are willing to do yourself.
Staff feels their work is not valued.	Focus on giving encouragement.	Aim to frequently catch people doing the right things. Develop a wide range of ways to acknowledge and appreciate their work.

Leading yourself

Start to learn the skills of leading by setting yourself compelling goals and being responsible for achieving them. Welcome circumstances that stretch your skills, seek out better ways of doing things, constantly strive to recognize and work on your weakness. Do this by having mentors and by using coaching sessions to develop your skills. Aim to find ways of enjoying every work project that you have. Learn to love your work, especially if you believe this is impossible.

Leading others

Once you have developed leadership qualities in yourself, you will be able to lead others effectively. Remember that there is nothing that a small group of committed individuals cannot achieve. Learn to inspire and develop vision in others by appealing to their values and interests. Compulsively seek improvements and implement new initiatives and procedures. Empower others to act by giving them the resources and responsibility to deliver results. Achieve credibility by setting a good example, and lastly, reward achievements and give encouragement.

Chapter
8
Stress and
its
Management

- Are you leading a life of stress?
- How does stress arise in us?
- Various stress styles
- Type A personality
- Being always under the pressure of time
- Ego and stress
- Is competitiveness good or bad?
- Ambitions at what cost?
- Anxiety
- Relax and let go
- Helplessness and hopelessness
- Depression-the feeling of sadness
- Burn out
- Methods of relieving stress.
- Managing attitudes is vital for managing stress
- Alpha state of mind Relaxation stage
- Meditation
- Useful tips to reduce anger.
- Managing Job Stress

Are You Leading a Life of Stress?

Stress can have various manifestations and reasons would be explained later on in this chapter. It can also be defined in many ways. It usually relates to an imbalance between expectations, and our capabilities to meet these demands. When you expect too much and do not have enough time to do it all, you can be stressed. If we are tired or have to wait at the traffic signal we can be stressed. If the company culture is not appropriate we can be stressed. There are many more reasons for our stress, but the growth of modern civilization has certainly impacted most of us through this deadly disease. It threatens our happiness and also creates conditions for physical diseases like high BP, coronary heart disease, peptic ulcer and many others.

It is believed that a reasonable amount of stress is normal and leads to increased effort and better performance. Without it people would feel no great urge to overcome many problems and obstacles they face each day. A threshold is reached, however, when additional stress begins to effect people's ability to function effectively, with commensurate deterioration in performance. Excess stress causes unwanted distress. Everyone agrees that stress is most serious when it becomes an ongoing, chronic condition with no end in sight. A large number of people find themselves in trouble, ignored of how to fight back.

There are many misconceptions about stress, relating to its origins, effects, and cures. Psychologists say, stress results when people's perceptions of their world are in conflict with their hopes and aspirations. Since stress leads to unwanted consequences, we need to study its reasons and methods of managing it.

How Does Stress Arise in us?

Stress can be defined as the consequence of any internal or external demand forced upon the body, whether that demand is pleasant or unpleasant. When we are exposed to cold, for example, we shiver and shake to produce more heat, and our blood vessels contract to reduce heat loss. There is a certain amount of stress inherent in any adaptive response that the body deems necessary. The degree of stress that is created is directly proportional to the extent to which the body must adjust or adapt in order to re-establish the normal state of affairs.

There are basically two ways the status quo or return to normalcy can be achieved: through accommodation or learning how to live with change, or resisting change by way of a fight or flight response. Medical practitioners strongly recommend the former, which could be called adaptive coping behavior, versus the latter called aggressive coping behavior, because accommodation results in considerably less damage to the human metabolism.

We daily face, many challenges in life which force us to focus more on the problems and complexities of the world, which we may perceive as negative and life threatening. Man is forced to respond in a certain way to save his life, in the same manner as modern man is when confronted at knife-point by a psychopathic serial killer. In either case, the choice is the same-fight or flight in order not to perish! In such instances, the sympathetic branch of the autonomic nervous system is aroused into a state of red alert. That part of the brain stem known as the hypothalamus activates the pituitary gland, causing the release of the hormone ACTH into the blood stream. It travels to the adrenal glands, which are located above the kidneys, resulting in steroids such as adrenaline and cortisone being added to the blood. These hormones, though important for a survival, response are toxic and cause harmful changes to the human system. The pupil of our eyes dilate, making them more sensitive to gradations in light. Our heart rate and blood pressure increase, providing more blood to carry required energy to our muscles, our breathing and oxygen consumption increase, providing more energy for quick thinking and vigorous physical activity.

Such life-threatening situations, thankfully, are not the daily norm. However, we often assume that daily incidents require a similar fight-flight response and, in the process, the body unnecessarily pays a tremendous price.

It is an individual's attitude profile that is the key factor regarding stress management. In its simplest terms, a problem is a question, matter, or situation that we find difficult to resolve. Often, however, we take a simple fact, add to it interpretations and connotations that are unrealistic and inappropriate. It end up with something that really doesn't exist at all, except in our own mind. Then we really do have a problem. In fact, stress does not exist anywhere in the environment; it is only created in the minds of individuals by their own reactions to events and circumstances that they encounter in their daily lives.

Stress is the price the body pays for motivation. As such stress can either be productive or destructive. *Effective people possessing a high degree of positive self-motivation use stress as a positive force to facilitate higher achievement, not as a negative force that contributes to fear and failure.*

Research clearly shows that if the fight or flight response becomes the normal method of coping, long-term chemical changes will occur in the body that result in higher blood pressure, high rate of arteriosclerosis, and a decrease in the body's natural immune system. These all make the body more susceptible to infection, disease, and decay. Research also shows that a high degree of stress will most likely result in ulcer, psychiatric disturbances including sleep loss, or even more serious ailments such as heart disease and cancer.

Various Stress Styles

How people respond to their environment generally depends on prior learning experiences, including the role models they looked up to while growing up. If a father reacted aggressively to difficult situations, chances are his children will do as well. The experience becomes embedded in the child's subconscious mind as normal coping behavior and forms the basis for conditioned reactions in similar situations. Each one of us has similarly developed a particular mindset or outlook on life.

It is an individual's personal belief system pertaining to an event, which is mostly defined by his attitude profile, or his personality type that determines his level of stress.

Medical researchers have not fully determined the reason as to why some people are able to copeup stress better than others. Certainly several factors are involved, including heredity, culture, race, and-to a significant extent-a person's mental attitude.

Type 'A' personality

Type 'A' personality is also known as the `hard-driving style' or 'overdrive' personality. It means being completely achievement-oriented and being highly competitive. It means living fast, doing everything quickly, getting upset, frustrated and angry at delays, incompetence and `acts of God', wants to do even better, beating not just yourself, but others too, coming first all the time, winning and not agreed for the second place.

This can both lead to stress invite a response to stress and hence is a difficult lifestyle to comfortably sustain. It can also be a lifestyle for high achievers who however, say they are not stressed and who, by most criteria, do not appear stressed. All too many of us believe (or desperately want to believe) that stress truly does not affect us, but all the time, this lifestyle is insidiously taking its toll.

You may have read about, or seen interviews with, some of industrialists who rise in the early hours of the morning, are in the office by 8 a.m., stay there until 9 p.m., or even later and seem to thrive on it. What we do not see are those who tried this and dropped dead in their forties or fifties or who keep going, not very successfully, on an unstable combination of drink, stress relieving drugs and anxiety. Those who manage to survive rather enjoy this hard-working lifestyle and reach the top are exceptional. To take such people as role models may be a mistake. Most of us need to lead more balanced lives to be healthy and happy. It is all too easy to convince ourselves that we can think of one, or even 10 people who live like this, and have not (yet) had a coronary, but that does not mean that it is acceptable for us all to live like this.

Are you the type 'A'?

Before reading further, answer the questions as honestly as possible. The questions describe different aspects of behavior. Rate how each applies to you using the rating scale 0-6, where 6 that could not describe me better', 0 is 'completely opposite to me', and 3 is neutral.

Checklist for type 'A' behavior

- Do you always feel rushed?
- Do you walk fast?
- Are you competitive?
- Are you impatient?
- Are you an extremist?
- Do you have none, or few, interests outside work?
- Do you hide your feelings?
- Do you talk fast?
- Do you try to do more than one thing at a time?
- Are you hard-working?

- Do you anticipate others (e.g. interrupt, finish sentences)?
- Are you emphatic in speech?
- Do you want recognition from others?
- Do you eat quickly?
- Are you ambitious?
- Do you look ahead to the next task?

Your total will be in the range from 0 to 96. The higher the score you have, the more typical of Type 'A' you are; the lower you score the more typical of Type 'B'. Many people will be neither dramatically one nor the other but will fall towards the middle, with one type predominating. Rather than looking at absolute scores, see your score as falling in a particular group. Around the 48 mark you are neither one type nor the other. As you move along the scale you become one or the other. Or you become more typical of Type 'A' or Type 'B'. Thus at 60 you are pushing your way towards being Type 'A', whereas at 72 you are definitely in the Type 'A' camp.

TOTALLY TYPE 'A'. 96 84 72 60 - 48 36 24 12 0 -TOTALLY TYPE 'B'

Let us look further at the description of Type 'A' behavior.

TYPE 'A' BEHAVIOR

American cardiologists Friedman and Roseman coined the term Type 'A'. The typical picture of a Type 'A' is of a person who is hard working and demanding, both from himself and others. He or she is ambitious, particularly in the material sense, highly competitive, works at a number of different tasks at the same time, constantly looks ahead, works under pressure of time and always seems rushed. He/she is likely to be aggressive, critical, undemonstrative, more interested in work rather than the family and more likely to blame others or external circumstances when things go wrong. There can be positive aspects to Type 'A'. Such people often have a high degree of mental and/or physical alertness and can accomplish a great deal, carrying others along with their drive and enthusiasm.

Many of the young executives striving to reach the top of their career ladder believe they must behave like this if they are to get ahead and accomplish anything. It is a mistake to believe that it is only hard working, strongly competitive, aggressive person who gets things done. Type 'B' personalities can often achieve just as much-only because they go in a different way. Whether you measure success by what you have, what you do or, you are who is your choice. But whatever you want, there are more, as well as less, healthy ways of achieving it. Vedanta's philosophy of Karamyoga describes this concept of detached involvement.

Being Always Under the Pressure of Time

Why does 'Traffic move slowly in the rush hour'

Being always under time pressure means that you usually feel rushed or hurried and never have enough time for the things you must do, let the things as it is. It leads to irritation and impatient, especially with other people or things around you. You end up trying to hurry others in their behavior like interrupting a person and finishing his sentences for him, flashing the car headlights while driving or blowing your car horn frequently and needlessly.

In trying to do more and more in lesser time, you end up doing two things at once. Dictating while driving, reading and watching the television, talking on the telephone and punching figures into a computer, reading and eating, talking business and playing golf. The list is endless. At times we all think of one thing while doing another, but for the Type 'A' person it is a way of life. It also means not allowing for occurrences, which are beyond your control. It is simply not accepting the reality. Such a person would always wonder `why does the traffic move slowly in the rush hour?'

In overcoming this tendency the major hurdle is your own belief that time pressure is a positive thing. It often does spur you on, to do more but in the short term only.

Such time pressure can also show itself in general irritation and impatience with things, from others and with self. Waiting for anything is intolerable. You can even get irritated with yourself when you have to do repetitive tasks, or tasks you consider boring or unnecessary which stop you from doing what you really want to do. With some people this can go as far as resenting any time not spent on work or on achieving their main objective-including time spent in socializing or even time spent in sleep. Things are postponed as you find it difficult to `make time' from everyday chores and necessities-be it sparing time for having your hair cut or simply having lunch.

Learning what is realistic to expect, what is best, left to the Almighty, planning time better, can help to achieve more with least effort and energy. Furthermore, this attitude would enable you to feel fit and happy at the end of it.

Ego and Stress

Since Type 'A' personalities have little time for other people, particularly their problems, difficulties, have no patience if things do not go as they want, they may become egocentric and selfish . They may express superficial concern at the difficulties or problems of others but do not alter their behavior. They simply do not want to be inconvenienced. If a colleague or subordinate complains about his workload-too much, badly prepared, impossible deadlines, or whatever-the Type 'A' person can show surprise or give his own examples of overcoming the problems.

Is Competitiveness-Good or Bad?

Unless locked into competition with someone or something, typical 'A' type personalities do not feel alive, remain happy in isolation. It is as though they feel compelled to challenge one another, almost regardless of the circumstances. To win is one of the hallmarks of success, and it is frequently a powerful motivator. To this extent, the element of competition is useful.

When does competition cease to serve as a useful motivating function and become excessive? Straightforward guidelines include checking whether you spend more time acting negatively - i.e. damaging others, than you do; positively - i.e. seeking solutions to the real problems, achieving the stated goals, and positively promoting yourself.

Also, examine whether competition is taking over your life--It is your car that drive first at green traffic light?

Are you competing while relaxing?

Do you always have to win-even if you are playing fun games like snakes and ladders with your children? If you are competing, even when you are supposedly relaxing, you have problems. We have all heard of the person who drops dead whilst jogging, playing squash, or taking some other form of exercise, furthermore, which is usually undertaken to improve cardiovascular functioning and resilience.

Such people usually set themselves unrealistic targets, to be achieved in too short a time, or compete against people younger than themselves. Sometimes a fit 50-year old may run faster than unfit 30-year old, but normally he will not beat a fit 30. Choosing sensible and realistic standards is important to remain stress free.

Find time to sharpen your skills as well- don't be too busy in action

A very strong woodcutter asked for a job from a timber merchant, and he got it. The pay was really good based on the number of trees cut in a day and the woodcutter was determined to do his best.

His boss gave him an axe and showed him the area where he was supposed to work.

The first day, the woodcutter brought 18 trees.

"Congratulations," the boss said. "Go on that way!"

Very motivated by the boss' words, the woodcutter tried harder the next day, but he only could bring 15 trees. The third day he tried even harder, but he could bring only 10 trees. Day after day he was bringing less and less trees.

"I must be losing my strength", the woodcutter thought. He went to the boss and apologized, saying that he could not understand what was going on.

"When was the last time you sharpened your axe?" the boss asked.

"Sharpen! I had no time to sharpen my axe. I have been very busy trying to cut trees..."

Are you chasing impossible targets?

Let us consider the importance of irrational ideas and unrealistic expectations. If you are 40, no matter how good is your tennis, you are not suddenly going to win Wimbledon. Most of us can accept this. Applying the same realistic criteria to work-related ambitions need not stifle them; rather such criteria can be used positively to achieve what is possible, rather than chasing impossible targets and creating frustration.

Why do you need to compete, to win? Are your concepts of self-worth based on the irrational notion that if you are not first, you are nowhere? If competing and winning are ends in themselves then you probably need to review your ideas about yourself and your life. If, however, competition is only the means to a greater end-namely, success of some kind, better salary and fame-then you need to consider whether other strategies were less stress to yourself, others might not bring you closer to your goal and also promote your happiness.

Review your belief about competition

Many persons dismiss any tendency towards seeing themselves as Type 'A' saying `But I am not competitive'. They will say that they need not to measure themselves against others to see how well they are doing. They know they are doing well or even very well, and monitor present performance against their own past performance. This can certainly get you away from the notion of competing against others and need to sabotage them, but can still set up intolerable competitive pressures, be it running that bit faster or further than last time or selling that bit more. You cannot always beat yourself. It may be important to review your answer to the question about being competitive.

AMBITIONS-AT WHAT COST?

Let us examine what we mean by being ambitious. 'I am not ambitious', you may say confidently or 'I am not seeking material success' meaning that you do not want to climb a corporate, or any sort of ladder.

Because you have opted out of the rat-race, it does not mean that your ambitions are therefore dormant and will not cause you problems. Whether your ambitions center on money and material success, on acquiring more knowledge, or on social justices, these are all philosophical and ethical choices for you to make. It is how you achieve these ambitions, as much as what they are, that will be reflected in your health. Academicians are unlikely to be seeking success in financial and material terms, but may be ambitious in terms of the number of papers work they have done books they publish, the amount of research and thus the number of research assistants working under them.

To be ambitious is not a bad thing in itself and clearly we would never progress if we did not set out to achieve things. But if ambition is pursued to the exclusion of everything else, then it is likely to be harmful to the individual. Even people working for the most altruistic ends must occasionally ask themselves whether their self sacrificing endeavour and excessive zeal is not degrading them burnt out before age.

An over-ambitious person may be hard-working to the point where relaxing is considered unproductive and doing `nothing' involves guilt feelings. This is linked to feelings of being under pressure of time. Sleeping becomes unnecessary because it achieves nothing. Meals are either skipped or eaten on the move. Staying healthy includes being able to relax and to take some time out from work. Going away for the weekend is not a relaxing experience if you spend most of the day catching up on reading reports or technical journals and spend the evening with a colleague or client who just happens to live out this way'. Reading a novel instead of a report may not suit everyone but don't forget there is an incredible variety of subjects out of your course i.e. listen music, involve in art and spend quality time with family.

Enjoy the life rather than waste the essence of life in unnecessary comparisons

A group of alumni, highly established in their careers, got together to visit their old university professor.

Conversation soon turned into complaints about stress in work and life.

Offering his guests coffee, the professor went to the kitchen and returned with a large pot of coffee and an assortment of cups porcelain, plastic, glass, crystal, some plain looking, some expensive, some exquisite - telling them to help themselves to hot coffee.

When all the students had a cup of coffee in hand, the professor said: "If you noticed, all the nice looking expensive cups were taken up, leaving behind the plain and cheap ones. While it is but normal for you to want only the best for yourselves, that is the source of your problems and stress. What all of you really wanted was coffee, not the cup, but you consciously went for the best cups and were glancing at each other's cups.

Now if life is coffee, then the jobs, money and position in society are the cups. They are just tools to hold and contain Life, but the quality of Life doesn't change. Some times, by concentrating only on the cup, we fail to enjoy the coffee in it."

Don't let the cups drive you... Enjoy the coffee instead.

Enjoy Coffee [LIFE] instead of worrying about the Mugs [Other materialistic things].

ANXIETY

It is possible to be anxious and stress free instead of being, stressed and not anxious, although the latter may be less common. Many of the signs of anxiety are similar to early signs of stress. Anxiety might be a part of the reason you are stressed, or be a response to stress. Anxiety, like stress, can be a transitory state, a phase you pass through, or it can be a more chronic, pervasive way of life, and is usually seen as a personality trait.

New solutions and fresh ways of seeing a problem do not typically emerge from getting worried, especially chronic worry. A burning desire or a worry will consume your conscious mind from morning to night and your subconscious mind from night to morning! Instead of coming up with solution to problems, worries simply ruminate on the danger itself. Experts believe that stress lowers the body's defense mechanism, thus increasing susceptibility to depression and disease. It has also been linked to cancer. A stressed person can never be happy or healthy.

In the first case, you can worry or be anxious about something specific-you have, an important presentation to make, or you are going for an interview. These are the things that make everyone anxious, and are to some extent realistic but your anxiety may get out of hand, particularly if it is linked to unrealistic ideas. Where anxiety is realistic it can be useful in stopping us from progressing too soon or too far, or in showing us what we need to learn before we move on.

Anxiety should be helpful and protective, it becomes a problem only when it hinders the path of success. Sometimes anxiety may not be linked to anything in particular but just is `a mood you are in' then it may be a personality trait.

Anxiety-A great enemy of relaxation

Just as we cannot escape some kind of stress, we cannot escape some kind of anxiety. The key question is, whether your anxiety is appropriate? By this I mean are you anxious about the right things, in the right proportions, at the right time? Being phobic is an example of disproportionate anxiety.

Those who exhibit anxiety as a personality trait always experience it with any change in their life that brings anxiety, rather than feeling of challenge or excitement. Such people are usually well known as `worriers' and they are often highly talented and creative in searching things to worry about. Coupled with this is usually a general sense of pessimism because when everything that happens is worthy to worry, it is hard to be optimistic. It becomes a mind pattern.

They are the persons who worry when things are going badly (they might get worse) and who worry when things are going well (what is around the corner). If things are going really well, they worry that why or how is it all going too well? and if there is nothing to worry about, they worry about that as well. Their whole way of life is geared to look at the world in this particular way. Encouraging them to reassess their beliefs can help a lot.

An anxiety, which is persistent and not related to any particular object or experience, is termed as 'free-floating anxiety'. In a mild form it may be connected with habitual ways of thinking and behaving. It might be hard but such people have to learn how to see the jug as half-full rather than half-empty?

Actually the Type 'A' person needs to view his self worth. He believes `I am worthy enough to achieve it'. He always wants to be in control. This is a wrong concept to life. The answer to these issues lies in managing the mind as is explained next.

Relax and Let Go

Have you noticed what happens when you are trying really, really hard to remember something or to hit a tennis ball just right or to solve a problem? Invariably, you don't get the results you want.

In their search for ideas and solutions to problems, most people note that they have their greatest success while engaged in activities where they are naturally relaxed. Hence they have their brainwaves in the shower, in the bath, in bed, in the toilet, places where we relax easily.

To understand this scientifically, when we relax, our brain rhythms move into a slower mode-the alpha mode-where we are far more capable and creative. Results come easily. When you step into a warm shower, or lying down on bed, you are naturally relaxed and best ideas infused your mind. You are open to ideas in the toilet, because you have to relax in there just to get the job done!

Of course, physical relaxation is equally important for peak performance. As we relax our physical body, our whole metabolism comes into balance; our blood pressure, as well as breathing becomes normal, and the organs in our system work harmoniously.

We get the best results in our life when we are prepared to go with the flow. This means finding the delicate and elusive balance between effort and relaxation, between attachments and letting go. But it takes practice to achieve this.

Again, we can learn from nature. The birds and the animals work, but they don't work day and night. They know when they have had enough. Can you find a sparrow working in a night shift? Sparrows know when it's time to have a break. Even the soil needs a rest before yielding next crop.

Helplessness and Hopelessness-Another Reason of Stress

'Being stuck means only one way to see the situation and not liking what you see'

Hopelessness is a feeling of vacuum towards the future for the person who sees no way of changing things and most importantly, no way out in the future. They may be called as rigid or stubborn people. It is a no options stage. For some people it may also be a response to stress. You feel helpless, in the face of overwhelming odds, helpless to change yourself, to change others, to change your physical situation or the demands being made on you. You may become apathetic, doing what you have to do and no more; you give up searching for solutions. You take whatever comes at you with little or no response in a light manner. Gradually this helplessness may take the pattern of mentally opting out, fantasizing about other things altogether, or looking back to how things used to be.

Depression-The Feeling of Sadness

Depression can be confused with stress, as it may be a response to some types of stress. But it is generally a very different problem. Some of the symptoms might be the same but not all. Depression is sometimes considered as feeling sad, unhappy or `down', but clinical depression involves other symptoms, such as withdrawal, slowed thinking, problems with concentration, feelings of guilt, self-depreciation. Insomnia, disruption in eating patterns and loss of libido are also common symptoms in depression.

If one suspects that he (or someone else) is depressed rather than stressed, then he should consult a doctor. Depression can arise because of many reasons, some of them biochemical, all avenues should be explored in terms of causes and treatment.

Burn Out

Burn out is an extreme reaction to a continuing stressful situation. Symptoms of burn out include apathy, helplessness, hopelessness, overlaid with cynicism and possibly selfishness. Some of the reasons of burn out can be working in a bureaucratic organization or having low pay and/or status. Working in isolation with little social support, reaching a career plateau with little chance of advancement, face demanding clients and no clear criteria of success or feedback about the task completion can also be the other reasons for burn out.

The most common response to burn out is to leave both the job and the profession. Bitterness may pervade within the individual who then has difficulty settling into any job. Burn out is an extreme and severe response, which probably requires professional intervention or sabbatical leave.

Setting priorities - A story

A professor stood before his class and had some items in front of him. When class began, silently he picked up a large empty jar and proceeded to fill it with rocks upto the top, rocks about 2 diameter. He then asked the students if the jar was full. They agreed.

The professor then picked up a box of pebbles and poured them into the jar. He shook the jar lightly. The pebbles rolled into the open areas between the rocks. The students laughed. He asked his students again if the jar was full. They agreed that yes, it was. Professor then picked up a box of sand and poured it into the jar. Of course, the sand was also filled up.

Professor said, "I want you to recognize that this is your life"

- The rocks are the important things - your family, your partner, your health, and your children -anything that is so important to you that if it were lost, you would be nearly destroyed.

- Pebbles are the other things in life that matter, but on a smaller scale. The pebbles represent things like your job, house, or car.
- The sand is everything else, the "small stuff." "If you put the sand or the pebbles into the jar first, there is no room for the rocks.

The same goes for your life. If you spend all your energy and time on the small stuff, material things, you will never have room for the things that are truly most important.

Pay attention to the things that are important in your life. Some of the important things in life are:

- Spend quality time with your family and loved ones.
- Play with your children. Take time to get medical checkups.
- Take your partner out once a while.
- Take time to refresh yourself.
- Find time for maintenance.
- Spend time on Preventing than on Solving Problem.

Take care of the rocks first - the things that really matter. Set your priorities, the rest is just pebbles and sand. Believe in yourself, know what you want, and make it happen!

Methods of Relieving the Stress

Treat the cause, not symptoms, such that the cure is ongoing and self sustaining.

Leaving drug therapy aside, there appears to be three leading theories being practiced by psychologist to help combat moderate stress and depression. Cognitive therapy aims at inducing people to think more positively about themselves and their environment. Behavior therapy is more action-oriented, encourages people to set personal goals and get more involved in outside activities. The third, termed as rational - emotive therapy, which is based on the principle that people can live a satisfied life, emotionally balanced by disciplining and controlling their thinking in the present, using visionary techniques and more objective thinking to see their way out of neurotic behavior. All three approaches have merits, and are particularly effective when combined.

These approaches help us to see that other people and events in our life do not upset us; the interpretation really upsets us, for example, our interpretation of a traffic jam.

Temporary methods of stress release

Diversion of mind

Mind relaxation includes popular mental exercises such as games, movies, television, reading, and other pleasant distractions. It could be dinner with your spouse at your favorite restaurant. Anything that replaces the thoughts in your mind with happy, pleasing or even irrelevant thoughts will work; and all have some positive physical effect on your body and nervous system.

Body and physical relaxation

The other approach is to exercise the muscles in the body and in this way relax the mind. Recreational sports, including swimming, jogging, tennis, golf, skiing as well as hot water, steam, and mud baths, will all accomplish this. When you are in a state of complete muscle relaxation, you cannot feel stressed. Take the effect of a full body massage, for example. It will provide the necessary physical as well as emotional development because relaxed muscles improve blood circulation and naturally elevate your mood.

Biofeedback

This is a method which reveals the effects of our thoughts and teachings on our physiology. A person is connected by sensor wires to a device attached to TV screen to watch the effect of certain thoughts on various psychological factors such as BP, skin tensions, and body temperatures. Biofeedback allows skeptics, nonbelievers to be shown first-hand that specific bodily functions are the result of our feelings and can be controlled by conscious thoughts. Although we use this technique unconsciously everyday in our life, but the electromechanical device isn't present to verify the effects. Biofeedback facilitates getting in touch with ourselves-our inner thoughts. The awareness helps us to plan better our living style.

The two main drawbacks to all these mental and physical relaxation exercise are that they provide only temporary relief and some take a considerable amount of time.

Managing Our Attitudes is Vital for Managing Stress

Studies confirm that a positive mental attitude and ability to relax both contribute not only to happiness, health, efficient output in the workplace, but to longevity as well.

People are encouraged to schedule their time more carefully and to insert relaxation...exercise into their daily routine.

Persons like Mahatma Gandhi or Mother Teresa or Dalai Lama who gave no sign of being stressed out in spite of functioning under severe constraints found to have certain characteristics such as faith, pride, sense of achievement, direction and feeling of control over one's life. These help dissipate the negative effects of chronic and pervasive stress on the body. People have been conditioned for centuries to believe that they are old when-they are sixty or sixty-five, and if they accept this belief, it cannot be otherwise. Expectations once firmly rooted in our subconscious mind through our belief systems invariably are manifested in our lives. Times of India reported the interview of a centurion couple (Rathee) from Bhaproda village in Haryana who have been living happily at the age of 101 and who gave the credit for it to their healthy lifestyle.

Awareness through personality tests like Types 'A' or 'B' or the MBTI personality indicator can help in counseling to some extent. As discussed earlier, Type 'A' persons are more susceptible to stress while type 'B' are better organized, do things one at a time, are better able to cope with life's events and are less stressed. Stress-prone people must be shown and made aware that, in fact, stress does not exist anywhere in the environment; it is only created in the minds of individuals.

Transcendental meditation

Repetitive chanting of a mantra in a calm and quiet posture in a soothing environment for 20 minutes twice a day control the blood pressure and stress systems. It subdues conscious thought, clears the mind and allows subconscious mental activity to take over. Maharishi Mahesh Yogi brought TM in its modern form to the world and the technique is used in many parts of the world with beneficial results.

Yoga

Our mind and physiology are parts of the same system and are interconnected. A change in one affects the other. Through deep breathing, right posture, yogic exercise not only dissipates stress from the body but also prepares us for a more relaxed and calm mode of being. Yoga centers are functioning practically everywhere now, which can profitably be used for stress relief and relaxation.

Vipassana

The technique developed by Mr. S. N. Goenka is based on the method of enlightenment by Gautma Buddha. It starts with ana-pana, the awareness of our breathing in the first stage. Later on the meditator is guided to extend his awareness to all parts of the body in which he starts developing the ability to accept the feelings and sensations without resentment. This will lead to mastering the art of self control and mind management. During the 10 days course, the meditator also learns to apply the useful principle of equanimity which itself is beneficial for stress management and living a contented life.

Art of living

Started by Sri Ravi Shanker, the method is based on *Sudarshankriya*, an ancient Indian technique of deep breathing combined with other useful *asans* and yogic exercises. It has been reported that regular practice of the method helps in controlling BP, stress management, enhance creativity development and other positive qualities.

Prekshadhyan (using *kyotsarg*-that is inner awareness), **rajyoga** (Bharam-kumaries University), **LIFE** (living in freedom-an enquiry by Swami Sukhobodhyanand), **Sahagyoga** etc. are some other useful Indian methods of meditation which offer a holistic way of life, going much beyond the benefit of relaxation. Similarly, the Japanese Zen and many other methods from the eastern world are also very useful techniques. One can adopt any or a combination of these according to one's nature and convenience. One basic purpose of these techniques is to help the mind reach the alpha state without which real relaxation would not be possible.

Alpha State of Mind-Relaxation Stage

A totally relaxed position of the mind is called Alpha waves of mental state. The mind emits some kind of electrical waves on the basis of metabolic functioning of the body, which are categorized into four types.

- **Beta state** when the mental cycle goes beyond 14 per second. It is the wakeful, active state.
- **Alpha state** between 7-14 cycles and is a state of calmness, serenity and tranquility. This state of mind is more productive and creative.
- **Theta waves** are measured between 4 and 7 cycles per second, which is a mental state of drowsiness before sleep. The consciousness of the person is blurred.
- **Delta state**-below 4 cycles per second. It is when a person is totally unaware of his external world/stimuli like in deep sleep.

Importance of alpha waves

1. The productivity and creativity of a person will be at its peak when the mind reaches the alpha state.
2. This is the best time to take important decisions.

How to reach alpha waves of mental state?

- Everyone has to reach this state of mind everyday before going to sleep.
- When a person does not get sleep due to stress, tension, anxiety and worries, he will not reach the alpha waves of mental state. Therefore, he cannot get peaceful sleep.
- Only in the absence of stress and worries, can a person reach the alpha state then drop into slumber.
- All meditation techniques bring alpha waves. The practitioner of meditation will not find any difficulty in reading the alpha waves of mental state.

MEDITATION

The mind is mostly not in the present moment. It is constantly vacillating between the past and future. You are anxious about the future or angry about the past. All your anger is about the past, which is gone, finished and all your anxiety is about the future, which is not yet here.

Bringing the mind to the present is called meditation

1. When your mind wanders around, allow it to go. Do not try to hold it back. Do not try to force it. Where it goes, let it go. Follow it and bring it back. Do not start hating your mind. Do not create a fight with your mind (stop reacting).
2. Meditation is the practice of gently freeing yourself from the worries of the future or upsets of the past, so that you can be attentive to the needs of the moments, and experience the joy of being fully present.
3. It is becoming aware of who you really are.
4. Unless you learn to know yourself, whatever you do in the external world will be insufficient (inner balance).
5. Our essential nature is peace, happiness and bliss. It is the worrying or wandering mind that creates a barrier to this. Meditation helps in self-mastery.
6. Meditation releases the energy that has been trapped in mental discord.
7. Meditation helps the mind to be concentrated and focused.
8. Instead of reacting without experiencing or interpreting based on fears, expectations, prejudices, the meditator responds openly and creatively.
9. Meditation through introspection brings to your attention the inner complexes, immaturity and habits. You become a natural person without any mask.
10. Meditation is not withdrawing from the world. It is not avoiding one's responsibilities.

25 Useful Tips to Reduce Your Anger

1. For every 10 minutes you are angry you lose 600 seconds of happiness. A little pot soon hot!
2. The key to anger reduction is knowing yourself.
3. When you make mistakes, learn from them rather than getting angry.
4. Don't criticize, condemn and complain because it makes you angry.
5. Learn to say no.

6. Choose a job you love and you will not have a day of anger in your working life.
7. Most problems are really the absence of ideas. Think ahead... anticipate... do it or get it done, even if second best... you will be less angry.
8. Organize your mind and organize your desk for 5 minutes every hour.
9. Accept what you cannot change & change what you cannot accept.
10. Ask even stupid questions to avoid mistakes to further avoid others getting angry with you.
11. Say sorry at the right moment to reduce the anger of others.
12. A short pencil is better than a long memory. Use it to reduce your anger.
13. Nobody can make you angry without your consent. Nobody can disgrace us other than ourselves. So why get angry?
14. The most common disease of an angry person is his inability to listen.
15. Never reply to a letter when you are angry.
16. Anger is a luxury in which only men of abundant means or absolutely no means can indulge. Never get angry with a man who has nothing to lose.
17. Never go to bed with an argument unsettled.
18. Expectation breeds frustration. Frustration breeds anger. If everything else fails, lower your standards to make you less angry.
19. Men who do not know how to fight anger, die young.
20. Make common sense and humor your best friends to reduce your anger and the anger of others.
21. Indecision makes you angry. Therefore, decide this way or that way.
22. You cannot change others as easily as you can change yourself.
23. Do not just catch others including your children doing wrong things; it will make you angry. Catch them doing right things.

24. When you want to get things done, use creative ways to remind people as they tend to forget constantly; this will reduce your anger.
25. Most people remember 20 % of what they hear... understand this fact to reduce your anger.

Managing Job Stress

Job stress comes in many different forms and affects the body in various ways. Minor sources of stress may include equipment that won't work or phones that won't quit ringing. Major stress comes from having too much work, not having enough work, doing unsatisfactory work, fearing a job layoff, or not getting along with your boss.

Usually it is the major sources of stress that lead to burnout, causing people to become unhappy and less productive in their work. Job stress can affect your health and domestic life as well. Low levels of stress may not be noticeable; slightly higher levels can be positive in order to challenge you to act in creative and resourceful ways; whereas high levels can be harmful, contributing to chronic disease.

The major sources of job stress fall into seven categories:

- *Control.* This factor is the most closely related to job stress. Studies show that workers who believe that they have a great deal of responsibility but little control or decision-making power in their jobs are at higher risk for cardiovascular disease and other stress-related illnesses.
- *Competence.* Are you concerned about your ability to perform well? Are you challenged enough, but not too much? Do you feel secure in your job? Job insecurity is a major source of stress for many people.
- *Clarity.* Feeling uncertain about what your duties are, how they may be changing, or what your department's or organization's goals can lead to stress.
- *Communication.* Workplace tension often results from poor communication, which in turn can increase job stress. An inability to express your concerns, frustrations, or other emotions can also lead to increase stress.
- *Support.* Feeling unsupported by your co-workers may make it harder to resolve other problems at work that are causing you stress.

- *Significance.* If you don't find your job meaningful or take pride in it, you may find it stressful.
- *Increasedresponsibilities.*Assumingadditionalresponsibilities in your job can be stressful.

Steps for Managing Job Stress

Here are some options for lowering stress on the job:

1. *Meet with your supervisor at least once a year* (every 3 or 6 months is better) to talk about your performance and your job. If a performance review is already part of your job, treat it as a chance to clear up issues that may be causing stress for you. Discuss the following:
   - What is expected of me in this position?
   - Where this company heading towards, and how do I fit into that plan?
   - How am I doing? What are my strengths and areas for improvement?
   - What can I expect from you if a problem with my work or my job would occur?
   - If I continue my current high-quality performance, how and when can I expect to be rewarded?
2. *Manage your time well.* It's important to leave your job at the office, even if your office is a room in your home. If you give up free time to get more work done, you may pay for it with stress-related symptoms. If your employer offers a flexible work schedule, take advantage of it to fit your own work style. For instance, come early to have a longer midday break or to make time for a yoga class or workout.
3. *Unplug.* Technologies such as cellular phones and the Internet have made it possible to be available to everyone, including clients and coworkers, at all times. Do not allow technology to eliminate the boundaries between your time and your employer's time. While at leisure or family holiday, leave your cell phones and other irritating things at home so as to avoid stress and enjoy the quality time. Avoid checking work *e-mail at home.*
4. *Know when to quit.* If you are truly miserable because of a stressful job and the suggestions have not worked, it may

be time to think about changing job. Make sure you know whether it is 'you' or the 'job' that's the problem. Before quitting, spend time searching other job options. Being unemployed will probably also lead to stress. Getting another job before quitting is ideal, but sometimes that isn't possible. Decide what is less stressful for you: unemployment or being miserable in your current job.

Chapter

9

Beyond Success – Happiness

- Story of 1000 marbles
- Happiness is in the present and not in the future
- Paradox of happiness
- Meaning and purpose of life
- Pleasure may be illusory
- Where is real happiness?
- Handling the problems and limitations in life with equanimity
- Managing your desires
- Happiness formula-the essence of vedanta
- Detached involvement-mantra for sustaining at peak performance
- Karam yoga-an art of relaxed and efficient working
- What work should we do?
- 'Purushartha' (self-effort) and 'prarabdha' (destiny)
- Fulfillment and inner bliss

Most people are happy as they make up their mind to be.

----- Abraham Lincoln

'Success without happiness has no meaning'

"Success is not defined by obtaining everything you want, but by enjoying and appreciating everything you have!!!"

'Even if all our "if only's" come true there is no guarantee of happiness'

'Selfishness turns life into burden. Unselfishness turns burdens into life!'

Happiness is a state of mind, a decision to adopt a mental strategy that leads to a more effective and satisfying life.

Story of 1000 Marbles

I am sharing with you one of the most important lesson of life that was narrated by a Management Guru.

He was talking about "a thousand marbles" to someone named "Roshan". I was intrigued and sat down to listen to what he had to say. "Well, Roshan, it sounds like you're busy with your job. I'm sure they pay you well but it's a shame that you have to be away from home and your family so much. Hard to believe a young fellow have to work seventy hours a week to make ends meet. Too bad you missed your daughter's dance rehearsal. "He continued, "Let me tell you something Roshan, something that has helped me keep a good perspective on my own priorities." And that's when he began to explain his theory of a "thousand marbles."

"You see, I sat down one day and did a little arithmetic. The average person lives is about seventy-five years. I know, some live more and some live less, but on an average, folks live about seventy-five years." "Then, I multiplied 75 times 52 and I came up with 3900 which is the number of Sundays that the average person has in their entire lifetime.

"Now stick with me Roshan, I'm getting to the important part. It took me until I was fifty-five years old to think about all this in detail", he went on, "and by that time I had lived through over twenty-eight hundred Sundays. "I kept thinking that if I lived to be seventy-five, I only had about a thousand of them left to enjoy. "So I went to a toy store and bought every single marble they had. I ended up having to visit three toy stores to round-up 1000 marbles." I took them home and put them inside a large, clear plastic container right here in my living room. Every Sunday since then, I have taken one marble out and thrown it away.

"I found that by watching the marbles diminish, I focused more on the really important things in life. There is nothing like watching your time here on this earth run out to know your priorities straight." Now let me tell you one last thing before I sign-off and take my family out for lunch. This morning, I took the very last marble out of the container. I figure if I make it until next Sunday then God will blessed me with a little extra time to be with my loved ones...... "It was nice to talk to you Roshan, I hope you spend more time with your loved ones, and I hope to meet you again someday. Have a good time!"

The story has given us all, a lot to think about. I had planned to do some work that morning. Instead, I went upstairs and talked to my wife and planned a dinner with close family members. "What made you think so?" she asked with a smile. "Oh, nothing special," I said. "It has just been a long time since we spent a Sunday together with the kids. Hey, can we stop at a toy store while we're out? I need to buy some marbles."

How many marbles do you have?

Incidents are bound to happen

It is not what happens to us in life that determines our happiness so much as the way we react to what happens. One person might, just having lost his job, decide that he now has the opportunity to initiate a new work experience, develop himself, explore new possibilities and to exercise his independence in the workplace. His other colleague might, under the same circumstances, decide to jump off a ten-storey building and end it all. Given the same situation, one man plans ahead while the other man commits suicide! One man sees opportunity and the other man sees disaster. We decide how we react in life. Happiness lies not in the events but in our interpretation of events.

Happiness cannot be purchased by money

Materials gains will not bring happiness to you. People who search for happiness in terms of money, real estate, possessions, or investment portfolios always ends up in a rude awakening. All the money in the world will not buy happiness. I have known some very wealthy people, they have just as many problems as you and I do. They are not happier than you or I. In fact, money frequently brings with it more problems and less happiness. Wealthy people are often lonely and suspicious of people's motives.

I have also know famous people and many of them live a life of despair. You might be aware of several movie stars and performers whose names were so familiar, who had achieved the highest level of fame, but who were so unhappy that they end up all in suicide.

Happiness is also not the absence of problems

Happiness neither dependent on whether or not we have problems, nor on material wealth. There are people who are happy even though they have very little. There are also people who are unhappy, even though they have the wealth of kings.

> *Look at what you have in your life; never look at what you have lost.*
>
> *What happens to good people when bad things happen to them? They become .... better people.*
>
> *Add up your joys; never count your sorrows.*

At a time of sorrow you are so overwhelmed and swamped by the shock, the pain, and the grief that you are not even conscious of the joys that still are alive deep under that blanket of grief.

- Count your garden by the flowers, not fallen leaves.
- Count your days by golden hours.
- Don't remember clouds at all.
- Count your nights by stars, not shadows.
- Count your life with smiles, not tears.
- And with joy on every birthday.
- Count your age by friends, not years.

Happiness is not just in always winning or through fame, success or power.

Many great achievers say that after the excitement of winning or being successful, there was always emptiness and a restlessness that stayed afterwards. Satisfaction, happiness, and fulfillment – all are as elusive and fleeting as shadows, when we search for them through fame, success, power, or sexual gratification.

Do you count compliments or carry trash

Being happy is not always easy, though it can be one of the greatest challenge that we face, can sometimes take all the determination, persistence and self-discipline that we can muster. You should take responsibility for your own happiness and choose to concentrate on what you have got, rather than on what you haven't. We decide our thoughts. No one else puts thoughts in our mind. To be happy, we need to concentrate on happy thoughts. How often, though, do we do the opposite? How often do we ignore the compliments that are paid to us yet dwell on unkind words for weeks afterwards? If you allow a bad experience or nasty remark to occupy your mind, you will suffer the consequences. Remember you are in control of your own mind. Most people remember compliments for a few minutes and insults for years. They become garbage collectors, carrying around trash that was thrown at them a year back or even ten years ago. And they suffer by becoming pessimist.

The moment you decide to be happy, you are happy.

Happiness is in the Present and not in the Future

We say, "I'll be happy when…." Well, life is NOT perfect. Life is about being exhilarated sometimes and missing out sometimes. As long as we say "I'll be happy when ...." we're deluding ourselves. If we're unhappy, it's because life is not as we want it. Life is not matching our expectations of how it `ought' to be and so we're unhappy.

Happiness is a decision. Many people live life as if some day they'll arrive at `happiness' like one arrives at a bus stop. They figure that some day everything will fall into place, they will take a deep breath and say, "Here I am at last ... happy!" Hence their life story is one of "I'll be happy when ..."

Ask an old man who is closer to death and he may spell out his wisdom about life and happiness.

- "If I had my life to live over again, I'd try to make more mistakes next time. Make more fun out of life and wouldn't be so perfect. I would relax more. I'd be sillier than I've been on this trip."
- "If it would be possible, I'd have gone to countryside, visits more beautiful places, seen more sunrises, would have also played more with children."
- "I will quickly forgive more people and stop blaming them and just accept them as they are, if I had my life to live over again."
- "But you' see? I don't!"

The message is a beautiful reminder to all of us. Let's make the most out of life so long we are on this planet. The old man realized that, in order to be happier, in order to get more out of life he didn't have to go and change the world. The world is already beautiful. He had to change himself. *Happiness lies inside.*

You cannot be happy if you look for perfection in everything

The world is not 'perfect'. The degree of our unhappiness is the gap between the way things are and the way they `ought' to be. If we cease to demand things to be perfect, the business of being happy becomes easier. We then choose to have preferences for the way things might be, and decide that if our preferences are not met, we will be happy anyway.

As an Indian guru once told a pupil who was in a desperate search for contentment, "I will give you the secret. If you want to be happy, BE HAPPY!"

Happiness can only be found within

Your happiness can only be found within. Your happiness depends on three things, all of which are within your power: your will, your ideas concerning the events in which you are involved, and make use of your ideas.

Real happiness is always independent of external conditions. How easily dazzled and deceived we are by eloquence, title, status, degrees, high honors, fancy possession, expensive clothing etc. Don't make the mistake of assuming that the celebrities, public figure, political leaders, the wealthy, or people with great intellectual or artistic gifts are necessarily happy. To do so means to be bewildered by appearances and this will only make you doubt yourself.

Remember: The real essence of good is found only within things under your own control.

Story of an old lady

An old lady looked in the mirror one morning. She had three hairs on her head, and being a positive soul, she said, "I think I'll braid my hair today." So she braided her three hairs, and she had a great day. Some days later, looking in the mirror one morning, preparing for her day, she saw that she had only two hairs remaining. "Hmm, two hairs... I fancy a centre parting today." She duly parted her two hairs, and as ever, she had a great day. A week or so later, she saw that she had just one hair left on her head. "One hair huh...," she mused, "I know a pony-tail will be perfect." And again she had a great day. The next morning she looked in the mirror. She was completely bald. "Finally bald huh," she said to herself, "How wonderful! I won't have to waste time doing my hair any more."

Think Positive ...be optimistic always.... and you will be happy ever.

Paradox of Happiness

Getting what you want is success. Loving what you get is happiness.'

To remain happy you should:

- Align your expectations (of results) in a manner such that your basic experience, at any given point of time, is one of satisfaction.

  In other words;
- "Satisfaction or happiness consists of striving to get what you want but at the same time experiencing the desire of whatever you get."
- You experience satisfaction while functioning in your daily activities because you are drawing your basic satisfaction from an inner source of joy and not from the results or rewards for which you strive in your external environment.

Essence of Excellence

We can find this in:

1. Being involved but not imprisoned.
2. Being interested but not addicted.
3. Managing by detached involvement.
   - The confusion starts when you think that you would get better results from another way, when you have already chosen one way.
   - You cannot live without performing actions. And whatever action you undertake, they always have consequences- depending on your motive. It is your interpretation of these outcomes that will decide your happiness.
   - Start enjoying your actions as these are guided by your inner voice.

Once you have set the purpose of your life, your goals, directions and actions will become very clear. While we will discuss more about detached involvement later on, let us first discuss the purpose of life.

Meaning and Purpose of Life

Many people spend their life by indulging in whatever work comes their way. They just run here and there without understanding the larger aim of life. They take up something and after becoming tired in a while, they take up another thing. They wander aimlessly in one direction or other, seeking as many adventures as possible. But after traveling through the uncountable variety of lands, homes, jobs, encounters, relationships and projects that life has to offer, they remain puzzled as to what it was all about? Wondering as to what was the purpose of all their running to and fro?

Expansion of consciousness: Self realization

They believe that by accumulating a lot of such experiences, they gain awareness and consciousness but in reality the process is just the opposite. It is only by giving up and letting go that the consciousness expands. The expansion of consciousness doesn't lie in the quantitative accumulation of experiences but in a qualitative change in one's consciousness which is self-realization. The reason for this aimless approach to life is that the consciousness of most human beings is not fully developed.

One important goal of our life is to attain the highest state of consciousness where consciousness is fully expanded and developed. In this state our identity is not confined but embraces all. Everything can now be known and understood properly in its true and unbiased state. In the process of growth, this underlying purpose of our lives should remain stable despite all the changes we undergo. This is what provides meaning and purpose to our life.

From self-centeredness to selflessness

When consciousness expands, one of the major changes that occur is a movement from self-centeredness to selflessness. Thus an individual whose consciousness is not well developed will be unable to appreciate the concerns and viewpoints of others. There will be considerable conflict in this person's life, in relation to his environment. But as consciousness expands we become less preoccupied with trivial individual concerns and less self-centered.

We can see things from a larger perspective as our consciousness gradually expands. This allows us to be less concerned, anxious and enables us to see things as they really are, not as we imagined them to be from a narrow perspective. One's thinking, feeling, attitudes and self-concept are systematically transformed as consciousness is broadend. Circumstances remain the same but our point of view towards them changes totally, which is a paradigm shift. When consciousness remains at a low level, one's identity remains totally confined and narrow. One's life is always occupied with `I', `me', and `mine'. This creates for us a sense of separation from others. And this separation creates discomfort, disharmony, at times a feeling of loneliness and isolation.

The narrower one's concept of identity is, the more insecure one will be, feeling small in the world. He looks at himself as an isolated being struggling against the rest of the world. His chief concern becomes self-protection and security.

Spirituality and self-realization helps us transcend constricting identities to achieve a more encompassing awareness of who and what we are and finally establish ourselves in our true nature which is full of peace, happiness and bliss. Expanded identity involves less self-preoccupation and more concern for others. When this happens, even in a minor way, there is a feeling of openness and lightness. Rather than for me and mine, we organize our lives to work for the common benefit.

The aim of all Yoga and spirituality is a movement from alienation to unity. If we wish to grow, all the identifications in terms of `me' and `mine' must slowly be abandoned and replaced.

Pleasure May be Illusory

Pleasure and pains-two sides of the same coin

A normal person spends most of his life in constantly pushing pains and attracting pleasures. He attempts to repeat pleasurable experiences and becomes addicted to those objects, people and situations that have given him pleasure. He rapidly tries to hold on to them; simultaneously avoiding all that is unpleasant and goes through all the stress that is involved in the process. He either ignores the needs and concerns of others or acts against his conscience, which creates an internal conflict. He realizes at the end of his life that it is all a futile race that he has been running and wasted his whole life in this struggle.

Characteristics of pleasures and pain

From the context of Vedanta we are referring to 'pleasure' in this text to *Rajasik* as well as *Tamsik* pleasures and not the *Satwik* pleasures. For example, when you enjoy natural scenery, it is also a pleasure but it is *satwik* pleasure and is not harmful for you. It is pleasure without the element of desire. Similarly, when you relish a melodious song or 'bhajan', it gives you *satwik* pleasures which is beneficial for you.

Pleasure and pain are inseparable

Pleasure and pain are two faces of the same coin. They both represent each other. This is inbuilt in the nature of worldly things that pleasures obtained by them are mixed with pain.

Pleasure and pain are transitory

Neither pleasure nor pain is permanent. They are always changing. This is because of the ever-changing nature of the world where nothing remains static. They provide only momentary thrill.

Pleasure ceases to be pleasurable after sometimes

Every experience of pleasure has a peak beyond which it won't give pleasure. We know very well that the same thing cannot give us pleasure for a long time. For example suppose you are very anxious to eat some sweets. For sometime you will relish this experience very much. But a stage will come when you wouldn't want it any more and if it is given forcefully, you will rather feel repulsion. To quote another example, suppose you are very excited and keen to visit some place. Initially, you will enjoy the experience and obtain great pleasure but a stage will come when you start feeling bored by frequently going at that place.

The more pleasure you get, the more addicted you become for it

The temporary enjoyment you get from these pleasures makes you more restless and desperate to repeat those pleasurable experiences again and again. Pleasure never satisfies a person, it only leads to a more desperate search for further pleasure. It is like an itch that increases when scratched, like a fire that increases as more fuel is poured on it. In fact attachment to pleasure is like an addiction where we constantly seek higher levels of pleasure for satisfaction.

It is an endless race in running after objects of pleasure

Once you get bored from an object of pleasure after some time, the matter does not end there. You do not remain silent after that. Then you start searching for another object of pleasure. The mind constantly wants to be tickled by a variety of pleasing sensations.

Actually the pleasure is in the mind, not in the objects

Suppose while enjoying a pleasure you hear some sad news, or some horrible thought of fear arises in your mind suddenly, then the same pleasure immediately lose all its charm. Similarly if your mood is not good, then you can't enjoy the pleasure in a similar manner. It is in the mind where we feel pleasure. Objects play a secondary role.

Time spent in pursuing pleasures is more than in actually enjoying them

A person, who constantly run after pleasures, spends most of his time in pursuing them and hardly has any time to enjoy them later. He lives in a state of uneasiness, restlessness and loses so much energy in the pursuit of pleasures that even when he gets the objects of pleasure, he is not able to enjoy them fully.

The actual time spent in pleasure is less than the imagined one

Imagination always projects things in an exaggerated and magnified form, different from the reality.

Pain coupled with pleasure is usually more than the pleasure initially enjoyed

While every pleasure is mixed with pain, yet if you examine carefully, you will realize that the quantum of pain associated with them is much more than the pleasure. Quoting an example, suppose you are attached to a person and want to live with him. Now even after you manage to live with that person, you also come across many other facets of his behavior, which trouble you and you have to bear with them. Further, when such a person leaves your company after some time due to any unavoidable circumstances or even leaves you for the time being, you suffer further mental agony of his/her separation.

Where is Real Happiness?

No permanent satisfaction can be gained in pleasures of the world. They can only increase the restlessness and agitation of one's mind. Then how to attain peace of mind and real happiness?

Our real happiness does not reside in the external objects but in our state of mind, which is independent of these objects. It is an intrinsic property of our inner self and can be tapped if we learn to turn our attention from the external world, to the inner world like in meditation. Most people feel that without objects to strive after, we would be in a state of emptiness or boredom. This misconception is based upon viewing objects as the source of gratification in the world. Joy can be experienced without objects. Real source of joy, peace and happiness is within us. However, it does not mean that we should abandon the world or hate material objects. Material objects, themselves, are not the problem; it is our attachment towards them, which creates problems. Yoga encourages a healthy attitude towards material objects. We should use them as our servants and not allow them to dominate us and become our masters.

When we develop detachment and dispassion towards worldly objects and events, then pleasure and pain automatically loose their hold on us. We are released from the tight rein of pleasure and pain. We develop a deep attitude of equanimity towards all pleasures and pains, thus remain equipoised in most adverse circumstances, neither elated by gains, nor depressed by losses. No worldly situation can disturb our inner peace and balance. Instead of becoming attached to the sensation of pleasure and trying to hold on to it while pushing pain away, we can simply witness them like, a detached observer and take note of their coming and passing with a complete control on the mind. This is the stage of self-mastery.

Handling the Problems and Limitations in Life with Equanimity

Problems are an essential part of life

There will always be ups and downs along with unexpected things in life. You have to be prepared for anything. Such is the natural law of life. In fact if a person's life is devoid of any problems or challenges, he may be bored.

Problems teach us certain lessons for our good

Don't view these problems as burdens coming to us suddenly out of nowhere. They have come to us as per certain law. There is nothing in this world that happens by chance or accident. There is a reason for everything, which happens to you. For every effect there is a cause and for every cause there is an effect. You are bound by this great relationship.

Instead of getting puzzled by problems, we should stop for a while, do some self-evaluation, introspection and learn the needed lessons from them. We can derive some benefit and learn lessons from every problem/difficulty and exploit it to our advantage. You should consider all problems as projects and new opportunities, instead of hindrances.

Problems in your life will also be proportionately reduced and your life will be comparatively smoother as you learn many lessons. One can see it happening with yogic personalities.

There always lies a solution in any problem

When problems come along with solutions. If you look back upon your life you will surely find that although you encountered many problems, still you could always find some solution or the other. It was rare that you got stuck to a problem forever and couldn't go beyond it.

It is never a permanent problem

Nothing remains static in this world. Everything is in a state of constant flux and motion. Such is the law. No problem or difficulty confronting us is permanent. They all will pass. Darkness is always followed by light. There can never remain the same condition always. Even the darkest days of your life will surely pass. This is an in-built phenomenon created by nature. Hence don't run away from problems. Face them boldly.

The problem is never greater than you

There is no problem in the world that is greater than your strength and which can't be solved. There is nothing, which can be called a catastrophe. Hence you should treat the problems, control them and never allow them to become your master. All forces of nature and circumstances must bow down before a serene and calm mind.

If problems are useful to us, should we not thank God for the difficulties?

Do we realize that as compared to the comforts given to us by God, these problems are nothing? While enjoying comforts and luxuries of life, we neither thank God nor question why these luxuries have been given to us. But in pain and problem, we are so much perturbed. Is this not a fallacy?

Don't surrender before the limitations of life and difficulties.

All these limitations are with you according to the law of karma or the law of destiny. No one is to blame for this except you yourself because of your past actions. So there is no point in cursing yourself or God or others. It is also true that you can't remove many of these limitations overnight, i.e. you will have to live with them. But remember in whatever conditions you live or whatever limitations you have faced, you can always make some changes in your life.

If you have a strong desire and will, and are working for a right cause, there is no power on earth or heaven which can prevent you from success. All the forces of the universe must support your mission and right cause.

Continue your development and progress even during problems. It is an opportunity

Are you awaiting the problems to be over before starting your own development? Let problems not interfere in the process of your development. In whatever miserable state you may be, go on developing yourself on whatever fronts you can because whatever be your problems, some avenues always remain open for further growth. It never happens that you can't do anything. If fate closes one door for you, it opens another door also. Life is full of opportunities.

Just face the problem as they come rather than imagining them now

Focus on the present task rather than getting worried about the future. Many people waste a lot of their time in imagining future problems, i.e. lest this or that should happen to them. In this connection do remember that problems and adverse happenings in life should be just faced as and when they come. Don't think of what will happen if I get tumor,, what will happen if my children leave me alone in old age or what will happen if I lose my job and so on. In fact you will find that ninety-nine per cent of things you imagine never take place. They are just creations of your wild imagination and doubtful mind.

Don't dwell on and brood over the problems. Just face them.

Cope with problems-one at a time. Prioritize them

If we start thinking to tackle all the problems at the same time, we will surely become mad and won't be able to solve even one problem in the right manner. Hence the correct approach is that you make a list of all your problems and then first pick up one problem on priority basis and concentrate on solving that problem only for the time.

Managing desires

Man is a bundle of desires and it is these unlimited desires which keep him constantly agitated and active. Unfulfilled desires keep the mind troubled and restless. A man with desires in his mind has never died peacefully. For achieving true happiness and contentment, detachment from desires is a must. However detachment from desires doesn't mean sitting idle. The term desire is used for becoming too desperate and mad for obtaining something, feeling terrible if you don't get it.

Types of desires

Desires can be broadly classified as follows:

- Sensuous desire
- Materialistic desire i.e. accumulating more and more wealth, property, money, relatives, friends, connections with high people etc. make tip for the feeling of insecurity and inadequacy.
- Greed for lust and materialistic desire.
- Ego-centric desire e.g. attainment of name, fame, status, power, children, family etc.

Managing Your Desires

Nobody can satisfy all his desires, as the list becomes endless. Desires multiply faster than you can satisfy them. According to Swami Vivekananda, if your power to satisfy desires increases in arithmetic progression, the power of desires increases in geometric progression. When you have started your first job, you wanted a scooter to commute as going by bus consume more time and it has been a sincere need. Later on when you became a manager you wanted a car. When you became General Manager you wanted a bigger car. But one day you came to know that another company where your class fellow is working have a luxury car at this level and suddenly you wanted an expensive luxury car and your existing big car no more gave you any pleasure. Isn't it a vicious cycle and where is the end? The possession of the desired object only feeds or ignites the desire further instead of quenching it.

Our needs can be fulfilled but not the desires because the basis of desires is greed that can never be satisfied. Furthermore, happiness obtained by fulfillment of desires is momentary and illusory. Desires are preceded and succeeded by anxieties. Desires create stress and strain us to grab the objects at any cost. When the object is obtained it creates an anxiety and fear of losing it. The fear is now how to keep or maintain it. People purchase a flat for material security. They are worried as it is unoccupied and hence they rent it. Once rented, they worried about its maintenance and the nature of occupants or become anxious whether the flat will be vacated on time. Our mind cannot stick to one thing for a long time. It gets bored with one thing after sometime and then seeks another thing for its satisfaction. It wants variety. It is a trap. If left to its own, it will wander after countless desires. To prevent this aimless wandering one should always channelize one's mind towards some constructive activities because an undirected mind without a goal can turn negative.

True and lasting happiness can neither be achieved by the fulfillment of, nor a repression of desires, but by detached involvement.

Happiness Formula-The Essence of Vedanta

The formula of happiness can be expressed by the following manner:

$$\text{H (Happiness)} = \frac{\text{A (Achievement)}}{\text{E (Expectations)}}$$

This means that happiness is a factor of two things; one is your achievement in which case it is directly proportionate, and the other is your expectation of an outcome of your efforts in which case the happiness is disproportionate. The more you achieve more you will be happy; but if your expectations are unrealistic, it will create more unhappiness.

Meaning of expectation

- Our intention to achieve something is always different from expecting the results or an outcome. On the surface it may appear to be same but there is a great difference and only a person of an expanded level of consciousness can understand it.
- It is important to have an intention to achieve, and make the necessary effort, without being worried about the fact that results may not be achieved or may be different from the goal set.
- Results depend on several factors, both internal and external, over which you cannot expect to have full control. There is an inherent uncertainty involved in the actual achievements of results despite your best effort. Therefore fixation with results causes an unnecessary degree of anxiety and tension while making the effort which affects the performance adversely.
- Once a goal is established, it is better to pay full attention towards efforts or the process which leads to results.
- By remaining detached from expectations and yet being in touch with your intentions/commitments, you give greater attention to efforts and avoid incurring negative emotions, frustrations, tensions and resentments.

In fact, with detached involvement you experience full joy and satisfaction all the time then efforts become a natural flow which helps in attaining better performance.

Detached Involvement-Mantra for Sustaining at Peak Performance

Our happiness and our free self-expression are much more assured if we let go of end results; work towards goals and not be imprisoned by them.

People, who make a lot of money, only start to MAKE it when they stop WORKING for it! In other words, they find something they love to do and the wealth flows automatically. They have money because they go after it. An outsider might say of someone who is financially successful, "The greedy man. He is worth crores of rupees and he is still working!"

The man is working because he LOVES THE CHALLENGE more than the money. That is why he is rich! If you go out and plant your tomato crop, and then keep digging up the seeds after every twenty minutes to see if they are evolving, it won't help! You need to relax a while. Let nature take its course.

Detachment doesn't mean aimless work

While non-expectation of fruits is emphasized in Karma Yoga, it doesn't mean that one shouldn't have any goals or aims while doing work. It basically means that after you have decided the goals and done necessary planning to achieve these goals, put your whole mind in the process of work and not on the results or fruits. It is going to take some time before your effort starts resulting into fruits. In fact aimless work is discouraged in scriptures or Vedanta. Leading life aimlessly is like kicking a football in the field here and there without aiming it towards the goal of the other team. You must make some short-term and long-term goals in your life, be it professional or personal sphere, and then systematically work towards them step by step. All these short-term and long- term goals will finally become the basis to attain the highest aim of life which is 'Self-Realization'. An aimless mind normally succumbs to its lower nature and becomes the victim of all type of vices.

Will the non-expectation of rewards not lead to lethargy?

Too frequently many people question that without any expectation of fruits what will be the motivation to do a work. Little do they realize that it is not the fruits or the results which give you the joy; it is the consciousness or attitude associated with work which gives you the joy. In fact no matter how insignificant or trivial a work is it can always be made interesting to a supreme degree by paying attention to every detail and by trying to do it in the most systematic and committed manner. Hence the work done in the above spirit itself becomes a source of enjoyment. So you don't have to depend upon the fruits for getting enjoyment. You enjoy the entire process of work and that action itself becomes your reward or fruit.

Example of detached involvement in a marathon race.

Let us consider the case of marathon race runners-A and B.

Mental dialogue of participant A.

I am here to win this race. The only way I can win this race is to reach the winning line first before anyone else does. The only way I can do so is to remain ahead of others all the time and that will be my unremitting focus (Expectation).

Mental dialogue of participant B

I am here to win this race. The only way I can win is to reach the winning line first, before anyone else does. The only way I can do so is to do my best, run fastest, and that will be the focus of my attention all the time.

A's focus is on result while B's focus is on effort

- Assuming *A* and *B* have equal running abilities, *A* will give his attention to observe others and will have an anxiety about others getting close.
- In fact in almost all long races, the ultimate winner is not always in front. When someone is neck to neck, he may feel demoralized and there is energy leakage.

However fear of losing may sometimes generate more adrenaline in *A*, which can trigger a faster running in the short run. *A* may overtake others once again. But such a thrust may be temporary, since due to release of adrenaline he will be exhausted and not be able to run at his normal pace in the long run.

- Because of fear of losing, many managers in the corporate world today run far beyond even their peak level but only for a short time since they are not able to sustain it.
- In your job or life you are not interested only in short-term performance or gain but in *Sustainable Peak Performance.*

In the case of the marathon race, suppose *B* or *C* wins and *A* loses. In such a case what is the reaction of *A* likely to be? Mostly it would be that of frustration or even depression. Most importantly the mental state of *A* during the race would be tense.

Position of B

- Focus on doing best.
- Attention and energy totally absorbed in achieving full potential.
- Although he knows he is in a race and his only purpose is to win, but he does not allow his attention to be disturbed by the performance of others.
- Even if A wins, B's reaction would be: I did my best and that is all I could do anyway. But my best was not good enough. Now let me find about how better I can do my best-a positive, constructive approach.
- He identifies or merges himself with running without tension and thus enjoys the process. It becomes an effortless flow like a musician at his best or a dancer totally involved in a performance.

Peak Performance becomes peak experience operating on the joy of doing

- If you operate out of fear, with adrenaline generated energy; you may get peak performance but not the peak experience, and very soon you may get exhausted.
- This type of temporary success is the cause of growing psychosomatic problems in today's world.

As per Vedanta philosophy, once a goal has been set, the performer simply should focus and enjoy the process of doing rather than worrying about the outcome.

> *Your life is a journey not a destination. Enjoy your journey first.*

KARAM YOGA-AN ART OF RELAXED AND EFFICIENT WORKING

In yogic parlance there is an art of performing actions called Karma Yoga by which you can do your work most skillfully, efficiently while remaining cheerful and stress free. In fact, work becomes a means for the upliftment and happiness of such a person.

Work can be a source of joy

No matter how trivial, routine or mechanical your work may be, but your awareness shouldn't drift from that activity. For example, suppose you are teaching, then you should be completely absorbed in that task, oblivious of anything else in the world. This should be the most important activity for you in the world at that time. You should be fully aware of each and every step involved in teaching. This is the meaning of sincere attention and awareness. This attitude is also called present centeredness or remaining in the present moment. Normally it is seen that when a person does any habitual activity like driving a car, taking a bath, eating food, his mind easily drifts from the activity of the present moment. His mind will drift either to the past or the future or some other activities going on in the vicinity. But this is exactly what is to be avoided. By an exercise of your will power and the practice of meditation, you can bring your mind to focus on the current activity. This eventually increases the strength and control over your mind. A weak mind drifts too frequently from the task in hand.

Focus on one work at a time by giving it full attention

We are usually faced with many tasks to do, many problems to handle, many new plans to implement. People very often worry about and try to do all the work at one time. The proper way to handle work is to first make a list of all the tasks in order of priority. Now take out one work at a time from that list and at this stage forget all other tasks and get completely absorbed in this work as if this is the only task with you. Once the task done, forget it completely like a closed file and take up the next task in queue. This is the way you can handle maximum workload with the least confusion and stress.

The moment you learn to pay attention to each and every small activity you are engaged in, you will not only be able to do that activity in the best manner, but you will also feel a sense of inner joy in your mind. Day-to-day mundane and routine activities will become quite interesting and a source of great satisfaction. With this attitude you can enjoy each and every moment of your life. Happiness doesn't come from the work we are doing but by our attitude associated with the work and our ability to remain fully immersed in it.

Benefit of detached involvement

You should also be able to forget an activity completely after the job is over, without any thoughts about it, lingering in your mind, if you have done it with one-pointed awareness and sincere attention. You should now be fresh and wide awake for the next activity or work in hand and while taking it up, there shouldn't be any thought of the tasks completed or yet to be done.

In other words, one shouldn't get attached to any work in terms of its outcome or its fruit but should be involved with all sincerity and dedication. With the power of concentration, you can develop the ability to detach yourself from a task and attend to another task at a moment's notice. This is what all great yogis have always said and practiced.

You have to eliminate the feeling of selfishness, me, and mine while doing work, e.g. I am doing, or I have done, or only I can do, etc. The harsh truth is that in reality you can't do anything on your own. Controller of the world is a much superior power than you and me. If you reflect deeply, you will readily understand as to why it is true that you are not the doer. There are so many uncertainties and other factors (natural as well as man-made) involved in the execution of a thing that it is impossible to associate your proprietorship in doing a thing. Many of such factors are beyond your control. The truth is that you can achieve a thing only if supported or cooperated by God. You simply act as a physical instrument and in the final analysis it is God who does everything and not you.

Yoga in action

This blessed and fundamental shift of your attitude from doer to divine will bring about a considerable change in the quality of your mind and quality of your work. Your ego will be completely erased leading to purity of mind. Ego is the greatest hindrance in the spiritual progress of a man and the above shift in attitude gradually puts an end to this great barrier, clearing your way for your onward journey towards the ultimate truth and reality. This shift in, attitude converts all your ordinary work into spiritual activities. You in fact then practice 'Yoga in Action'. Quality of your work will automatically improved because there is no particular desire or expectation to distract your mind as results are totally left to God.

Non-expectation of fruits also gains weight from the fact that result of any work whatsoever is not in our hand. This is the domain, which is totally under God. Freedom is given to us only in the performance of action and not in the achievement of results. God, depending upon so many factors and merits of individual cases, bestows the fruits of our efforts or actions. There is no point in wasting time or breaking head over this aspect when it is none of our business. Since God is perfect, so we must be satisfied with whatever results are awarded to us for our actions.

What Work Should We Do?

The yogic attitude to work is of absolute detachment, not to have any choice, but to accept and do whatever is given to you or whatever comes to you in your normal course of life or as a duty. If you consider the work pattern of various achievers you may find one common thing in them. They either did what they loved to do (of course they got it weighted by their conscience) or they simply started loving what was available to them and both ways did an excellent job.

What is a Selfless Action?

A `karma yogi' is a man of selfless action.

Any selfless work or service with the feeling of giving and helping others expands your consciousness, fills you with inner contentment and bliss. Bliss is never attained by living a life of limited self interest. Any work done selfishly contracts your consciousness and leads to bondage creating discomfort, disharmony and restlessness of mind.

This inner joy and deepest sense of fulfillment obtained through selfless service, which is the highest satisfaction achieved by a '*karma yogi*'. Swami Vivekananda has said, `The end of all work is to bring out the essential divinity in man by selfless service.' All work whether management, leadership, administration are manifestation of the essential divinity in man by working for good of others, good of millions, good of all beings.

Work, regarded in this way, is not something which you have to do just for earning your livelihood or as an obligation on others. When done in the right spirit, work becomes the instrument of growth, a way to self-realization. Swami Vivekananda has beautifully explained in his book *Karma Yoga* that paradoxically we don't need to do work in order to help the world or any person for that matter. The world is self-sufficient and will continue to operate forever even without us. We require to do good work basically for helping ourselves because every good work done by us purifies us, it helps to bring out the hidden divinity and elevates us.

Work is *God's* wish bestowed on us

Consider all work as orders from the Divine, no matter through whose medium they have come to you. No work is personal work in karma yoga. They are all God's work. Since a karma yogi considers himself as servant of God, he does the work with sincere, dedication and as best as he can to fulfill his role as a servant of God then after completion, hands over the work to God in all humility.

We are simply given the opportunities by God to help others to thereby, improve ourselves. Otherwise God basically does what all is needed. We simply become the instruments of help because of our willingness to do so. Hence any egocentric feeling of helping others should totally be eliminated. In fact any help rendered by you should be forgotten the moment you complete it with full devotion.

'PURUSHARTHA' (SELF-EFFORT) AND 'PRARABDHA' (DESTINY)

Mankind has remained puzzled on the subject of Destiny and Freewill. Some people think that their entire life is predetermined according to some destiny allotted to them by a whimsical God and they can't do anything about this and they are just puppets in the hands of fate. However, there is an another group which feels that everything in life depends upon one's efforts and destiny is nothing. However, the truth is that neither of these two views is absolutely correct. Both are projecting only a partial truth of the matter. The fact is that both destiny and freewill play their part in determining what happens in our life. The relative proportion of these two forces determines the ultimate result.

Our fate or destiny is our rough life map and boundary conditions imposed by the Almighty. Freewill, on the other hand, is the limited freedom given to us for the performance of actions. Nobody's hands are totally chained in this world. Some freedom, either to a lesser degree or greater degree, has been given to everybody with the help of which he can make some changes and improvements in his life. These little changes pave the way for bigger changes leading to greater freedom. Everybody is given a chance to improve and based on the proper utilization of these opportunities, we are given more freedom by nature as a part of our success system.

Balancing the 'purushartha' and 'prarabdha'

We can better understand the concept of Freewill vis-a-vis Fate; by the following analogy. Suppose a cow is chained to a peg by a rope. Now the cow can't cross the circle formed by the rope (acting as a radius of the circle). This can be similar to `Fate' or limitation. But' the cow has full freedom to walk inside the circle, which is the 'Freewill.' By observing the discipline and behavior of the cow in her movement in the smaller circle, the farmer permits the cow to move in a larger circle, gradually enhancing her freedom. A time may come when he can leave the cow totally free if he has faith in her. He may release the cow after observing her performance from time to time.

As a parallel example, man is neither totally chained nor completely free. Looking back at the past, he is a slave of his destiny but looking at the future, he is a producer according to his freewill. But seen with the totality of the vision, he has a limited freedom and limited bondage. The relative strength of these two states varies depending upon how he has lived his life in the past and how he is living it presently.

If we take real life incidents also, the self-effort when exercised mixes with the destiny to bring about a resultant effect of their combination. So your past (or destiny) can be modified in the present. The freedom to modify the present and to create a future either for the better or worse is 'purushartha' or 'self-effort'. 'Destiny' is subject to constant correction and modification depending upon the exercise of your limited freedom or freewill. So one can see that `destiny' is not something rigid.

One needn't to revolve helplessly like a slave in the wheel of destiny. Destiny can never be greater than `freewill' because it itself is the product of freewill exercised by one in the past. All the forces of destiny must bow down before a determined will. If you haven't been successful by applying some self effort, you should increase your self-effort with redoubled vigor till you become victorious, overpowering the forces of 'prarabdha' (destiny). Hence the individual freewill has the power to alter destiny.

Man always has the power to increase his freewill to such an extent that destiny can be neutralized to a great extent.

Simply stated, luck is what you got but success is what you made. History does not remember the lucky people but it does remember the successful persons. The luck and efforts influence each other to a great extent in as much as sustained effort can create better unit.

FULFILLMENT AND INNER BLISS

Everything we do in this world is for happiness. There is nothing wrong in it as it is in our nature. We cannot be fulfilled unless we achieve complete happiness. An absolute fulfillment should contain perfect peace, love, wisdom and joy. The further we go into the inner self, the more happiness we experience. We have been searching for this happiness in possessions, in external world, in relationships. We search at wrong places and become a prey to despair, anger and resentment. Happiness always lies inside and to achieve it we need to travel inside. Yoga and meditation are excellent tools for this inner journey.

Changeable and perishable things can't give lasting happiness

Everything in this creation is changeable, perishable, it is only logical to understand that impermanent and temporary things or situations can't give you lasting and permanent happiness. They can only give temporary and illusory pleasure and thrills. Another major reason why anything in the world can't give us true happiness is that creation is built on the principle of duality.

Duality of the world

Everything in the world is made of two opposite aspects, e.g. day/night, life/death, summer/winter, male/female, young/old, pleasure/pain, joy/sorrow, association/disassociation, etc. These two aspects can't be separated from each other. They are two faces of the same coin as explained earlier. Anything that gives you pleasure also gives you pain. Any person or thing that is associated with you must also dissociate or leave you at some time. If you have certain advantages from something, you will have certain disadvantages also. For example, when you marry you have certain pleasures and advantages but you have certain disadvantages too in the form of extra responsibilities and adjustments.

People see only one aspect of a thing and conclude that it is good or bad. But actually they forget to see the opposite aspect. This is why it is said that what appears is not always the reality. According to this law of nature, if you want to avoid pains and discomforts in your life, you will have to avoid pleasures and comforts also. If you don't want insults you will have to give up the desire for praise also. But the problem is that each of us would like to have just the good things, the pleasant and the beautiful, but not the unpleasant and bad things. People believe that they can separate out all the suffering, pains and unpleasantness from the so-called joys and pleasures of life. But this is impossible. In this dualistic world, there can't be pleasure without pain, light without darkness, and good without evil. You can't have just one side of the coin without the other.

Real happiness and bliss requires us to transcend this duality of the world. The best way to remain unaffected by this dual nature of the world is to deal with worldly things and incidents with a detached outlook as if you are merely a spectator, i.e. neither gets elated by success nor grieved by failure. Remain balanced in gain/loss, success/failure, and praise/insult. Once you reach to this mental level, you become free from the clutches of sufferings and are enlightened.

Inner bliss-the peace within

Bliss or everlasting happiness comes from inside. As you become more aware of your inner self through yoga and meditation, you will automatically withdraw from dependence on objects and people as sources of gratification. This doesn't imply that you will no longer enjoy outside experiences. In fact you will enjoy this world more, being more free and without any expectations from it. External events are never as important in giving us true joy as compared to our reactions towards them. However hard the external realities and facts may be, it is our attitude towards them which matters more. Without support from our mind, no condition or circumstance can act as a stressor for us. Your contentment and satisfaction is never dependent on the outside world but lies inside.

If our mind runs with a tremendous velocity with one thought after another, it cannot remain calm even for a moment. In such a condition of mind, one is always planning, worrying, moving and becoming tense. Gradually it becomes a deep-rooted habit and a type of mindset. Even when there is nothing to worry about, such a person searches for some cause for worry and remains under free floating anxiety. When there is nothing to do, he becomes tense as to what to do now, instead of utilizing this opportunity to relax his mind. So you need to calm down your mind or restore the power of silence. Calm down your mind essentially means reducing the number of thoughts in your mind or quieting the thoughts when you want. That is the reason why meditation is so useful to us.

During emotions of hurry, impatience and desperation, the mind velocity is particularly high. High velocity of mind or the tremendous rush of thoughts in the mind is essentially a sign of weak and uncontrolled mind. A controlled mind can continue to keep only one thought for as long as it desires without allowing other thoughts to come in. It may even remain thoughtless for a period of time if it desires, which is the true power of silence and the benefit of meditation. The way to reduce the velocity of mind is to slow down it to attend present activity. Don't remain in the memory of past and anticipations and apprehensions of the future otherwise, the speed of your mind increases and it leads to poor performance of the present task. Normally while doing anything, we think ahead of the time when this work will be finished and we can enjoy our leisure. In this process we neglect the present and spend our time in unhappiness. There is always a search for better happiness by an agitated mind while the real happiness lies in the present mind.

Your past is history
Your future is mystery
Present is the only gift-enjoy it

It is our rushing mind which blocks our happiness of the present moment and keeps our mind constantly agitated. Once you learn to slow down your mind to the activity in hand, you will find that the most ordinary and mundane work, which used to be quite boring earlier, becomes quite interesting along with a source of great joy and satisfaction.

It is only by slowing down and paying attention to each moment that many of the things happening around us, that are normally taken for granted, seem dull and uninteresting, become enjoyable. If we want to experience joy and happiness in our work, we should banish the attitude of rushing through our activities and to somehow finish them as early as possible. This should be replaced by an attitude of care and awareness in each activity however trivial it may be.

A contented person will never feel bored and lonely

A lonely person is he who can't face himself, only such a person runs after other objects and people to keep his mind occupied. When he doesn't have any object or person to engage his mind, he feels bored. Boredom comes from expecting something but unable to have it. He doesn't realize that joy can also be experienced without objects by turning the attention within. Depending on other persons and objects for your gratification is highly illusory because nothing is going to remain forever with you in this world. Everything will leave you one day, and then either by choice or by force, you will have to live only with yourself. Even in our normal day-to-day busy life, moments come when we are alone and are only with ourselves. If you can't live alone, it means you are not at peace with yourself.

There are many conflicts and disturbances within you, which come to the surface as soon as you sit alone. So to avoid them you always want some external props in the form of objects and persons so that your mind may get directed. These stop-gap arrangements won't give you the eternal peace and satisfaction which you are craving for at the core of your heart.

Sooner or later you will have to come to terms with yourself in order to achieve peace. Running away from yourself is never the way to attain peace. It only delays the attainment of peace. So the crux of the matter is that you have to learn to like yourself, to live with yourself. If there are any disturbing factors in your personality, try to resolve them rather than running away from them. Remember that finally it is only your own self, which will live with you and not anything else in the world. So for a few moments in each day, start living as if you are alone. This has been explained earlier in the power of silence.

Don't hold-Let it go and share with others

Many persons operate on a myth that the way to one's development and happiness is to accumulate as many things as possible, encounter as many people and relationships in life as possible, change as many jobs as possible, travel to as many places as possible. The truth is just opposite of this.

If you follow this track, then you will remain most dissatisfied. When one is exhausted with life and looks back, he wonders what it was all about. Why had he done all such running about? The truth is that happiness consists not in accumulating things but rather in giving up, letting go and sharing. The more you let go and share, the more relieved and relaxed you become. When you let go of everything, you become totally free. When you get attached or stuck to certain things, freedom of thought and action is lost. You are likely to think and act in the world in terms of those attachments. Thereby you won't be able to see the reality as it is. This ignorance of reality creates discomfort, disharmony and stops your further growth.

Managing 'Ahamkara'–the Ego

Our ego inflates our vanity in thoughts like

- I am the first person to do so
- I am the chairperson of that committee
- I am the only person who can do this

Further, we experience resentment when we are not invited to important parties or are not involved in important issues. These are some of the manifestations of our ego. From the point of view of yoga psychology, the word ego means 'separate I' i.e. your feeling of separation from others, from God, from the whole creation. '*Ahamkara*' is one of the offshoots of this wider aspect of ego where you want to feel important, superior compared to others, where you want to prove to others that `I am something'. '*Ahamkara*' in other words is associated with feelings of superiority, importance and pride. Ego is associated with our feeling of separateness which is manifested in our day to day life in our feelings of I and mine.

As long as one is caught in this I and mine business, his state will be a sorry state. There will be laughing for one moment and weeping the other moment; now up, now down; now very loving, now very distant - all conflicting and difficult situations. As long as a person is caught in the vice-like grip of the I and mine, this will be his fate. `Not I' and `not mine' constitutes liberation and freedom. These two terms give ultimate peace, joy and all problems come to an end thereafter. The purpose of all yoga and spiritual practices is the demolition of the false I and emergence of the pure or real I.

The moment the I undergoes expansion, our identity expands or we feel oneness with everybody and with the whole creation and this leads to the emergence of all positive qualities in us. There can't be any conflict or friction with anything in this state. Scriptures say 'as long as you are there, God can't be. Only when you are not there, God can be.' Both can't live together. So for attaining God and peace, you will have to lose yourself. People don't attain God because they don't want to lose themselves. They are not ready to become `nobody'. And this feeling of `nobody' spontaneously makes you everybody without any effort on your part. Then everything comes from nothingness.

Loss of this ego or becoming of `nobody' is not a state of emptiness or boredom as people misinterpret. It is rather a state of bliss, joy and peace. It is this awareness of pure I which is proclaimed in the Indian scriptures as 'aham brahmasmi', i.e. 'I am God'.

The practice of Yoga and meditation helps us to know this pure I or pure consciousness. As we see it more and more, we become transformed. It is this awareness which removes all our suffering and delusion. It can also be called our true and original nature or our innermost consciousness. Our ego or false I is simply a superimposition over our original nature, is not a permanent part of us and can be discarded as soon as we wake up from our sleep of ignorance. This state of happiness and bliss is the real self transformation and goes well beyond success.